Henry Ward Beecher

Royal Truths

Henry Ward Beecher

Royal Truths

ISBN/EAN: 9783337039035

Printed in Europe, USA, Canada, Australia, Japan

Cover: Foto ©ninafisch / pixelio.de

More available books at **www.hansebooks.com**

BY

HENRY WARD BEECHER,

AUTHOR OF "LIFE THOUGHTS," "EYES AND EARS," ETC.

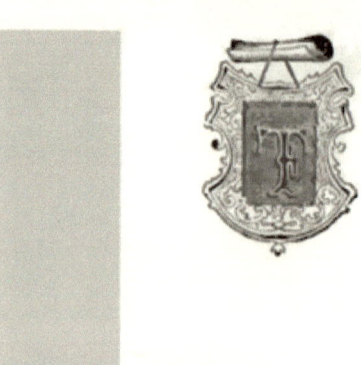

BOSTON:
TICKNOR AND FIELDS.
1866.

PREFATORY.

MY DEAR MR. FIELDS, — I comply with your request and send you a copy of "Royal Truths." Its history is this: When, in the summer of 1863, I landed in England, my first trip was to Northern Wales. I arrived late on Saturday at *Bedgellert*, and spent Sunday there. An estimable young Welsh clergyman called to request me to preach, which, yet drenched with the ocean, I declined to do. In the course of conversation he spoke of having read my works, and mentioned " Royal Truths " among the number. Supposing him to have mistaken the title of " Life Thoughts," I corrected him. "Yes, I have read 'Life Thoughts,' too; but 'Royal Truths,' I mean." " But, my dear sir, there *is* no such work of mine. I never issued such a work, nor heard of it. If it exist, it must be by some other person." — No; he was firm, and declared that I should find it at Strahan's in London! Sure enough, on reaching the capital, I found a book by myself, of which I had never heard. It seems that some one had taken from my sermons, published every week, such extracts as were fitted for standing alone, and framed them into a book, baptizing it " Royal Truths," of which, as you will see by the copy which I send you, six editions had been published in 1862, and I know not how many since. The book is, therefore, mine, and not mine. I furnished the contents, but neither selected them, nor gave them a name.

My surprise at this unconscious authorship would have been greater, if I had not already had a not dissimilar experience, which, perhaps, it may be amusing to narrate.

In 1861 or 1862, a gentleman in New York happened into a friend's store, a publisher, who handed him a little book, called " Aids to Prayer," saying that it was an English work, just sent over to him, and that he liked it so much that he immediately determined to republish it for American reading. The gentleman took home the work, and the next day returned to the store, saying, "I like your little book very much, *and always have.*" — " Why; what do you mean? "

" The book is made up wholly, except some texts and hymns, of Mr. Beecher's writings, and may be found in ' Views and Experiences.' " Thereupon, the mortified but innocent publisher posted the book to me, with apologies for violating copyrights, etc. The work had, with a single exception, been taken bodily from the English " Summer in the Soul," which was the new name, given without my knowledge, by London publishers, to my book called " Views and Experiences in Religion." Nor was there a hint of its Transatlantic origin or authorship, — for fear, said the publisher, that others would " print it upon him," (I think that is the phrase,) unless they supposed it to be an original English book!

" Royal Truths " has been useful abroad, and may do good at home, — in part, because the selections are short, and can be read in moments, when a book demanding hours would be rejected.

HENRY WARD BEECHER.

BROOKLYN, N. Y., November, 1865.

ROYAL TRUTHS.

LL along the way of life we have premonitions of a coming future. Our very struggles, our sorrows and yearnings, are so many indications of that coming state. The tears that men shed, if they be of ungodly sorrow, are of no moral moment; but jewels every one, if they are symbols of unrest which the inward life experiences by reason of the imperfection of the outward life. In this state we groan being burdened, the apostle said, not that we would be unclothed, but clothed upon. We groan not so much because we are discontented with the allotments of God's providence here, but because He has given us a conception of things hereafter so much better, that our aspirations rise above the present, with longing for the future. It is not so much discontent as aspiration. There is high meaning in these yearnings of the soul. The summer is passing; the autumn is coming; birds are gathering; they meditate a far-distant flight. And shall the soul have no sense of migration? There come to God's children hours of transfiguration in which the heavens are opened, the ground is suffused with glory, and Christ, our Head and Saviour, shines out royally before us.

And these momentary glances into the invisible world are the most precious part of a man's life.

THE crucifixion of Christ was that, on the scale and in the spheres of Infinity, which we see every day on the scale of the cradle and the nursery. And the brightest thing which we see in this world is not the most conspicuous thing; it is the most hidden and obscure, — it is the accepting of life, as the mother does, for the sake of another life, — it is the accepting that love as the centre of attraction, and the point around which it revolves, and making night and day glad and songful and cheerful, only because it gives permission to yield everything a tribute to another nature, — to the service of another and an unrequiting being, — for the least helpful and least requiting thing is an overgrown child. And there is a love brighter than the morning sun, fairer than the evening star, and more constant than either, — there is a love sweeter than all the blossoms in the fields to-day, clearer than the whole air that fills the earth to-day, — the love most unselfish, and therefore most divine, that makes suffering itself most sweet, and sorrow pleasure, — that love which the mother bears to the child, — the mother that is in parentage. It is the only one that glows with any considerable resemblance to that great central fire from which it flows, for it is a revelation of the love of God, it is a suffering love, it is the whole self-hood, the whole being, used simply as a universal instrument for others' welfare; and it is that which, it seems to me, above all other things, our Lord and Master, Christ, came into the world to express, — to express first, by coming, then by the way in which he lived, to express, as we understand life, character, and conduct, by the way in which He died.

The Apostle Paul, with extraordinary courage and fidelity, set forth, against the whole reigning intellectual forces of the world, his faith in Christ.* He insisted on presenting that side of Christ's life and history which was the least acceptable to the world, which was most repulsive to educated men. To us, now, there can be no full sympathy with that hatred of Christ crucified which then existed. Now it is nothing to preach Christ crucified, or the cross of Christ, in the ordinary methods, for that symbol has reigned for fifteen hundred years supreme in art, in literature, in religion. The cross has twined around it, every association of dignity and beauty in the world. Not one other thing has received from the fertile minds and the all-fashioning hands of men of genius so many extrinsic beauties as the cross of Christ. Millions never hear of it without a throb, nor see it without a genuflection. It dawns upon the child in the cradle next to its own mother's face, and it is the last thing from which the light disappears when this child, in old age, is dying. The cross is now as universal and as beautiful to the associations and the memories of men, as then it was rare, peculiar, and odious; it is that which now to us is not only suggestive of a fact in Christ's history, but it is also a memorial of two thousand years of history. Around that simple cross-wood the heart of the world has gathered for twenty centuries its stores of admiration, of love, of devotion. But none of this was then known when the apostle entered upon his solitary way. It was then the very sign and symbol of ignominy. It was as far toward the bottom of disgrace as now it is toward the top of honor. It was the convict's mark then; it was the slave's, the criminal's sign; it was a hundred times more odious then than

* See 1 Cor. i. 17, 18.

to our ears is the word "gallows" now; but that word is softening, and may yet become agreeable too, when it bears a little more of right fruit. There is no word among us that is significant of the deep and acknowledged and universal detestation that belonged to the cross.

WHEN a musician is called to perform music which he has composed, before a great congregation, he knows that many will call for melodies, for ballads, for simple airs, and he may be disposed to gratify their taste; but if he knows that in the congregation there is one Mozart, or one Beethoven, who is able to follow him through all the intricacies of harmony, as he rises up to the majesties of sound that expresses thought, and feeling, and imagination, that one single musician will inspire him and reward him more than the thousands of those who know only how to take in the lowest forms of his exhibition.

Now, we not only live among men, but there are airy hosts, blessed spectators, sympathetic lookers-on, that see and know and appreciate our thoughts and feelings and acts. And if we can bring ourselves to realize this, it will lift us above the necessity of vulgar praise, and above any depression that we may feel for the want of appreciation and praise from men. It is the great tribunal, airy and invisible, before whom we live more really than before visible and fleshly men. We perceive, then, that by and by, if men live with patient continuance in well-doing, they shall have honor and glory. You only sow the seed here. You do not reap the remuneration here; but you live with, and toward, and among, an invisible host that understands the law of excellence; that understands how much more valuable are the higher traits and magnanimities than the lower; that understands how much more noble and admirable are the things which the soul does than the things that the mind does, and how much more noble and admirable are the things which the mind does than the things which the body does. All, therefore, which is hidden in obscurity in this world, is reserved for disclosure in the world to come.

The gravest events dawn with no more noise than the morning star makes in rising. All great developments complete themselves in the world, and modestly wait in silence, praising themselves never, and announcing themselves not at all. We must be sensitive, and sensible, if we would see the beginnings and endings of great things. That is our part.

When Christ was teaching men what was the highest conception of human character, what did He say? The serene, large-browed intellect, — the deep, calm, untroubled oceanic enthusiasm, — the exquisite sensitiveness of taste and purity combined, — that large, flexible nature which revolves in orbits of beauty, and stands the point of admiration to all round about, beautiful and harmless! Was that the conception of character? Such is the notion we have of beauty and genius. These are the men that we love to paint to ourselves, — men that do no harm, to be sure, but that are self-cultured, and work off every part of themselves with elaborate workings, and make themselves, according to some preconceived model of human development, symmetrical, and large, and manly, and perfect, and stand simply in that self-poised strength and power! Does Christ say that is the idea of character? Not at all. Self-seeking and self-building, as an end,

were simply hateful to God, as they should be hateful to
men, but are not. What, then, was Christ's ideal of
manhood? Weakness, subtleness, insignificance of character? . No, no! but power in the head, and power in the
heart, and art in the hand, — the sovereignty of man in
every single one of his faculties; but the whole of it
taken with sweetest humiliation of love, and carried down
into the lowest place and meanest, to that which is weak.
It is strength glorified with purity and beautified with
taste, making itself a servant, as Christ is said to have
made Himself a servant. The Divine ideal of character
is that it is a power, no matter how resplendent, how
high, so that it is devoted to the welfare of those who are
about us; first to those who are the lowest and furthest removed from our taste and sympathy. The man you hate
is the man you ought to love most, that is, with beneficence; the man that shocks every taste and sentiment is
the man who should receive the contribution of your
being, — that is the man into whom and around whom
you are to pour yourself, that by all the influences in
which you are superior to him, he may find the ocean
tide of your life buoying him up and taking him from out
the mud and sand in which he swelters, and giving him
at last launching and sea room. That is the conception
of the highest character.

———

It is narrated of a Moravian. I know not if in any
other name of Christians could be found an instance that
can parallel this : — A Moravian Christian heard of the
sufferings of the West India slaves, and desired to be a
missionary to them; but when he reached them, he found
they were driven to the field so early, and came home so
late, that there was no life or strength in them to listen

to his instructions; neither did they believe that any man whose face was white had a heart that was other than black, and they would not listen to him; and he found, at last, that there was no way to preach to them unless he preached to them in their sufferings while he suffered with them himself. He sold himself, and was driven afield with them himself, that while he suffered and toiled as they did, he might have opportunity to preach to them the unsearchable riches of Christ. Now, I ask if there reigns a king upon his throne that was so lordly, so large a man as that poor, sweating Moravian, who, for the sake of serving these poor, miserable, dying slaves in the field, had sold himself into like estate to preach the riches of Christ. The largest conception of manhood is that which knows how to take itself, as though of no consequence to itself, but of all possible consequence to those to whom it may make itself an offering, a power, and an instruction.

It is said that no one can at first take in the scope and magnitude of St. Peter's at Rome, and that the first impression is one of disappointment. Our senses are so unused to large measurements, that they do not take the meaning of such a gigantic cathedral until they have been practised to do it. It is only when, by a patient waiting and growing familiarity, our senses have opened and grown to a nobler use, that the full meaning of such a massive structure begins to come to them. Then the immensity of the space, the richness of the parts, the universality resulting from a well ordering of innumerable details, begin to impress the mind; and every day swells the dome, and carries forth the length and width of the interior, and harmonizes the multitudinous details until they lose their separateness, and become only the means and instruments of a wonderful whole.

As you recede from it, miles and miles across the Campagna, there rises high into the air that sublime circle; and when, by distance, all the subjacent parts are sunken and lost, that magnificent globe hangs upon the sky, **as if,** like heavenly spheres, it needed no foundation, but hung suspended in the ether, buoyed up as ships **are** floated in the seas.

It is even so with the Epistle to the Romans. The close of the eighth chapter is the dome of the cathedral. It is only one's own whole life that can interpret it. At the first reading it seems confused. A certain wonder and wealth of meaning is apparent, but neither order nor **harmony. But** gradually the parts seem to unite; the exceeding richness of single **words** or thoughts goes to compose a harmonious whole. **And the** closing verses, rising like a vast dome, **lift** themselves above the earth, above the stars, and into that **sacred space where heaven** is and the glory of God. No human **hand hath** builded this. These glorious thoughts that hang above the world, glowing with radiant colors, came from no mortal genius. Not he who filled the dome of St. John at Parma with the wonderful uprising of the apostolic and angelic host, accompanying the Virgin to her coronation — Correggio, — **nor that greater** priest **and** king of art that filled the **air of the Sistine Chapel with the** sublime congress of prophets and sibyls — **M.** Angelo, — reared this tower of grandeur, nor filled its heavenly summit with undying colors. A greater Artist — the Artist of artists, — **the** Father **of** beauty, — the God of all glory — hath given these immortal scenes to the world. And they shall never lose their color. Age shall not dim, and vapors and smoke shall not blacken them. They shall be fresh forever. The child shall see them. The ignorant shall behold them. Yea, and most wonderful, the blind shall see them by an inward vision, and rejoice in their celestial glory.

It is quite in vain for any of us to have a hope in God which is valid only in the fair hour of prosperity and of health. When an anchor is thrown overboard, if it floats in the stream it is useless. No anchor is of any use whatsoever to a ship that cannot by its cable go down to take hold of the firm bottom, and that, taking hold of it, is not able to keep the ship. If when the storm beats, if when the whole concentrated fury of the storm beats on the ship, the anchor holds it, that is an anchor worth having. Woe to the mariner whose anchor breaks in the time of testing!. If you have a hope that is good when you are young, when you are prosperous, and when you are happy, but does not hold you when you are sick, when you are cast out, when you are bereaved and discouraged, when life is taken away from you — if you have no hope that holds you then, you have got nothing at all. An anchor that not only deceives men with the appearance of safety, but that gives way in the hour of danger, is worse than none at all — a hope that holds a man when he does not need holding, but breaks when he does.

What must be the value of anything desired, when the price you are willing to pay for it is one of your children? What personal pain in watching, in care, in patience, are not parents willing to undergo for the sake of their children, rather than that those children shall be given up to any trouble? What abundant trouble does the eager parent take upon himself to shield the child? What ease, what prospects in life, has the parent gladly given up for the sake of the well-being of his child? How easily would one sacrifice his property — the whole of it, if need be — rather than that his beloved child should suffer! Nay, how easy it is for love to die that never dies! And how easy would it be for many and many a one to say, as David said, "Would to God I had died for thee, O Absalom, my son, my son!" The tenderness of the record may be rare, but the experience is common. When, then, an emergency comes in which a parent consents to give up even a child, what an unspeakable testimony is that to the strength of his feeling. There is no other thing in human life that can measure feeling like such an instance as this.

Now, that is the image which God sends to kindle in our heart and imagination some faint conception of what was the power, the depth, the omnipotence of His feeling of love toward the whole race of men. Consider what that ocean must be in God, where such a feeling exists of desire and love that it puts into a subordinate place His love for His own darling Son! What must be that emotion which rises higher than our love for our own offspring! And transferring that idea to God, considering what is the might and majesty of every feeling in God over the slender experience of the human heart, considering what is the wonder of increase in every emotion and every function in God when compared with the corresponding emotions and functions in us, what must have been the length, and breadth, and height, and depth of the love of God to human souls! This is that which the apostle holds up before us in the passage, "He that spared not his own Son, but delivered him up for us all, how shall he not with him also freely give us all things?"

———

I THINK that men look upon repentance and humilia-. tion before God very much as they do upon a voyage from the tropics to the North Pole. Every single league, as they advance toward the Arctic region, they leave more and more behind them greenness, and fruit, and warmth, and civilization, and find themselves more and more in the midst of sterility, barrenness, ice, and barba- rism. I think that men repent toward the frigid zones. They think that to go to God is dreary and desolate in the extreme. It is not! The sinner is an Esquimaux! He lives in ice, and burrows underground, and is but little better than a beast! But if by any means he be- comes fired with a conception of a better clime, and leav- ing his hibernating quarters, he takes the ship Repentance, and sails toward the torrid zone, at every league he is sur- prised by the new forms of vegetation by which he is surrounded. He has seen oak-trees only about as high as his knee. Not long after he sets out on his voy- age, he is astonished to see them as high as his head. By and by, as he draws near the tropics, he is lost in wonder and ecstasy to see them lifting themselves far above him in the air. And with what satisfaction does he compare the delightful home that he has found, with the miserable one that he has left behind!

———

MEN move and march, and we must keep step, and for- ever move and march! We are strangers and pilgrims. We are not settled. We never shall be in this world. Nothing is finished here. Every step is a preparation for the next. That is a preparation for the next; and that for the next. The whole of this life is one grand march toward life indeed, and life in earnest!

CONSIDER what is the thought of Divine parentage; consider what are all the ways by which God has sought to impress upon the human race the fulness of His love. What figure is there that bears the conception of a power, an honor, an ease, a glory, an achievement, a victory, which God has not taken and set in the sanctuary, to light up in man's mind the divinity of that love which He manifested by the gift of His own beloved Son, — a love which is more than motherhood, or fatherhood, or brotherhood, or sisterhood, or friendship, or love of lovers? Sitting central in the immensity of that love, He says, "Come unto me, all ye that labor and are heavy laden, and I will give you rest." It is the invitation of infinite power to infinite weakness, of infinite purity to infinite sinfulness, of infinite riches to utter and abject poverty. "O Israel, thou hast destroyed thyself; but in me is thine help."

WHEN trees grow so that their branches are mostly on one side, we never restore branches to the deficient side by cutting the opposite side. We cut the most barren side, and there nature, in seeking to restore what we cut, drives out new buds and branches. So the gardener knows that where he puts the knife there will follow the fruit of the tree. And blessed are they whom the heavenly Husbandman prunes, that they may bring forth more fruit, if, when He cuts, there is a bud behind the knife. But woe to them who, being cut, have no bud to grow, and are more disbranched and barren from being pruned.

It is not that the force of our love to God is so great that nothing can ever root it up, — it is that the love of God to us is so great that none of these things will ever move that procuring cause of good in Him. God loves us so that neither law, nor power, nor earthly experience, nor heavenly adjudications, nor any human witnesses, nor any accusing spirits, nor anything, shall quench, or cause to glow with one diminished ray, the intensity of His love. None of these things shall take away that love which led Him to give His Son to die for us, and to raise Him up to be our everlasting intercessor. It shall be to us like the sun, that carries never-ending summer from age to age.

———

Sometimes men, with slippery logic, say that God employs wicked men for the furtherance of His purposes, and that they must carry on the great ends of life, — that they must be hewers of wood and drawers of water, — while good men, though more or less dependent upon such things, are not themselves to be concerned in them. Now, no man ever will be a better man by seclusion, or a worse man by engaging actively and enthusiastically in the right things of human life. As strangers and pilgrims would pass through a plague-district, not stopping, if they could avoid it, but hastening on, and taking care to touch no infected thing; so some would pass through this life. But no man is appointed to pass through this life as if it were plague-stricken and infectious. And any man that undertakes to go through the world acting on the principle that it is a sin, on the whole, to have much to do with the secular avocations and duties of life, not only will have infinite troubles and inconsistencies in his own conduct, but will not understand the first letter of the spirit of enlightened Christianity.

WHEN young men are beginning life, the most important period is that, it is said, in which their habits **are** formed. This is very important; but I take it that the period in which a young man's ideas are formed and adopted is more important still. For the ideal which you go forth to measure things by determines the nature, so far as you are concerned, of everything that you meet. If a man goes into life saying, " I am determined that I will make everything bend to the one supreme end of getting rich," he has the golden rule by which to measure everything. One man says, " I am determined to be heard from. I will live to make myself glorious." Approbativeness, **or self-esteem,** measures all things in his **case.** Another man says, " Beauty shall be the chief **element of my** earthly enjoyment." Taste is the ideal by which he measures everything.

No man who regards this life **as an end can ever be** happy in it. Men were made to be happy. Never was a musical-box so exquisitely arranged for **the** playing of sweet tunes, as the human organism is for the production of the music of happiness. The trouble is, we wind it up the wrong way. The instrument slides out of measure, and we play three or four tunes wrong, and mixed together. A most discordant thing, therefore, is man, **although exquisitely** organized for happiness. We are established **in the** wrong way. **We have been** learning how to use many things. We know how to use the stars better; we know how to use wood and iron better; we know how to use wind and steam better; we know **how to use** ten thousand things better; but, alas! **our chief** ignorance is in that which concerns ourselves.

Auspicious is the day in which a child is made to accept the truth that the measures of character and conduct are supernal; that justice, love, purity, truth, hope, and all the other elements belonging to the higher sphere of truths, are the tests by which he is to go through life measuring what is right and wrong, high and low, good and bad, desirable and undesirable. For if a child is accustomed to measure these things by his senses, he is all his life long vulgarizing himself. But if he is accustomed to measure them on the spiritual scale, he is all his life long tending to free himself from the body, and to become more and more spiritual.

A man may be outwardly successful all his life long, and die hollow and worthless as a puff-ball; and a man may be externally defeated all his life long, and die in the royalty of a kingdom established within him. That man is a pauper who has only outward success; and that man may be a prince who dies in rags, untended, and unknown in his physical relations to this world. And we ought to take the ideal in the beginning that a man's true estate of power and riches is to be in himself: not in his dwelling; not in his position; not in his external relations, but in his own essential character. That is the realm in which a man must live, if he is to live as a Christian man.

The pit that is deepest, the pit that is most unexplored and most unfathomable, is that which is the wonder and glory of God's thought and hand, — our own soul.

I can prepare ten sermons easier than I can make one visit to a person in distress. Such a visit of one hour is more exhaustive than the uninterrupted study of ten hours.

IT requires a great deal of the spirit of the cross for a man to suffer for himself; but the evidence of the extent to which the nature of Christ has penetrated into your heart is to be measured by the affluence of that spirit in you which makes it sweet to you to make any man **better** by diminishing yourself in doing it.

I do not know where to look for such a man. I see him in Paul. If there ever was a man who almost **for-got** his own personality, and thought only of those whom **he** might serve, it seems to me to have been Paul; but beside him I can scarcely find another, and the nearer home **I get** the more rarely I find them. I have a bright **ideal** of what it is to use the whole of my life and powers for other men, **or a** shaking of myself out of myself; but that cursed individuality still brings my thoughts **and** feelings back to myself, checks my enthusiasm, and I cannot pour out my life like a libation for God. That I feel in myself, and I therefore interpret it in you.

How different a thing it is to be a Christian **as men be-come** Christians, and to be one according to the example of Christ and the spirit of the apostle Paul! If you are **to become** such a one as Christ, if you are to be emptied **of yourself,** if you are to live for others, I ask you, will **not that change be like a resurrection from** the dead? O, look how selfish, **how hard, how** unfeeling, life is! See how men hate one another! **See what prejudices** separate them! See what ten thousand **things are** thrown in the way, even by good men, making the wheels turn slowly and hard! See what attrition there is! See how every part of the machinery of life draws hard!

Now, tell me, if there should come on such natures the royalty of love, — if there should be a change that should make men love as easily as violets smell sweet, — if there should be a change that should make a man's heart come out as odors do, furnishing that which men delight in, but not diminishing the supply, — would it not be a change just as great as to make a man all over again? And if that is so, what objection have you to saying so that they are born again? I think it would not hurt some men to be born twenty times more! I think we all need to be born again; that there is a continual re-creation and re-creation and re-creation, with higher conceptions and purer spiritual realizations. No man who looks at men as they are, and holds up before them the bright ideal of Christ's character, — no such man can say, if they receive such a symbol as that, that it is not a new creation.

I HAVE, in my house, a little sheet of paper on which there is a faint, pale, and not particularly skilful representation of a hyacinth. It is not half as beautiful as many other pictures I have, but I regard it as the most exquisite of them all. My mother painted it; and I never see it that I do not think that her hand rested on it, and that her thought was concerned in its execution.

Now, suppose you had such a conception of God that you never saw a flower, a tree, a cloud, or any natural object, that you did not instantly think, "My Father made it," what a natural world would this become to you! How beautiful would the earth seem to you! And how would you find that nature was a revelation of God, speaking as plainly as His written Word! And if you are alone, in solitude, without company, desolate

in your circumstances, it is because you have not that
inner sense of the Divine love and care which it is your
privilege to have, and which you ought to **have.**

———

This is an age in which we are all run mad for philanthropy. Everybody wants to be a philanthropist; and
men go out to be philanthropists. So when a man goes
down, his first inquiry is, " What shall I do?"

A man rises and is vexed that he was not called earlier, that he was not called to a better breakfast; that his
commands are not obeyed by his servant, — who is forever forgetting, — and starts out on philanthropy! He
goes to teach, perhaps, as one of the readiest things we
know of in our time, — he goes to teach the poor, and
supposes there will be a suitable conception of what a
condescension it is in him. He goes, as much as to say,
" Here, boys, am I; and I have come clear down from
that altitude in which I live ; take great care of me, and
respect and revere me, for I have come to teach you."
But when these boys cuff each other, and pull each other's hair, and kick him, are there one Sunday and away
the next, and swear, and lie, and steal, and pick his pock-
ets while he is instructing them, the man says, " This
philanthropy has been greatly cried up, but I have had
enough of it. The human race is 'totally depraved,' and
I will let them go." Here was a man who went down to
find worshippers; here was a man who went down to do
good, and save himself. It is as if a miser should go out
to distribute charity, thinking all the while how he could
do it without losing money! And here are men who go
out to do good, all the time counting how much they get,
and what it costs them. There is no bounty of feeling,
no outpouring of nature, no regality of thought, saying,

"How can I give my being to make other beings richer?"
No feeling that it is glorious to bear, and endure, and
suffer ; and when you come to bear, and endure, and suffer out of church, that is a very different thing from doing
it in church.

I never know how to worship until I know how to
love ; and to love I must have something that I can put
my arms around, — something that, touching my heart,
shall leave not the chill of ice, but the warmth of summer.
There must be something that will come near my heart,
— something that I can love, — or I cannot worship ;
and this idea of a central, inflexible, serene, passionless
God, unmoved and unmoving, that sometimes thunders,
and then, under certain conditions, loves in a proper manner, — this conception of the Divine nature is utterly
freezing ; it sets me upon the Poles, and all the revolutions of the year leave me but ice and icebergs.

You never know how much one loves until you know
how much he is willing to endure and suffer ; and it is
the suffering element that measures love. And all characters that are high must, of necessity, be characters that
shall be willing, patient, and strong to endure for others.
It is not so much the pleasure we have in affection. To
be able to have bright affections playing upon you and
giving great joy to your nature, is one thing, and to hold
your nature in the willing service of others, is another ;
and that is the Divine idea of manhood, of the human
character.

A great many men are addicted to much lugubrious
soliloquizing and complaining about this unsatisfying

world; but whether it is satisfying or not depends upon what men try to satisfy themselves with. If a man were to take a watch, and try to use it as a compass, to steer a ship by, he would say, " How unsatisfying this watch is!" Yes, to steer a ship by, but not to tell the time by. And when a man uses this world for things that it was not meant to be used for, it is an unsatisfying world; but when a man uses it for the things that it was meant to be used for, it is a satisfying world, — it is a glorious world. It is a very good world for the purposes for which it was built; and that is all anything is good for. A watch for time; a compass for direction; a plough for turning up the soil; a ship for the sea; a house for a habitation; an ox or a horse for labor; sheep for wool and food; a loom for one thing; an anvil for another; silks for persons; carpets for floors.

When you look at the globe, society, men's occupations, and the like, in this large view, the world is admirable. Its very rudeness, its hardness, its sufferings, are also a part of the primitive design, and are beneficial instrumentally. Men that love leisure never can understand what God means, who loves occupation. Men who put their supreme idea of life in self-indulgence, cannot understand what God means, who makes self-exertion, in Himself, in angelic powers, in all His creatures, the test of real being. If men are seeking to be supine, to have infinite enjoyment without earning it, and God is determined they shall be stirred up by storms of hope and fear, pain and ease, in order that they may grow and develop, of course they cannot understand Him or His administration. The prizes in this world are placed where those men shall get them who, by development, by opening and educating their powers, seek them.

A MAN may go as straight from the shop, or deck, to heaven, as if he kept weary watch in a cloister, or had shivered himself to death in a cave. It is a man dying with his harness on that angels love to take. I hope those old water-logged saints that died soaking in damp stone cells were taken to heaven. They had hell enough on earth, and it would be a pity for them to have a continuation of it in the other world; but I think they were the poorest of all human commodities ever taken in!

When God wanted sponges and oysters, He made them, and put one on a rock, and the other in the mud. When He made man, He did not make him to be a sponge or an oyster; He made him with feet, and hands, and head, and heart, and vital blood, and a place to use them, and said to him, " Go, work !" And the man that does not go and work is not a man in the end; while the man that puts the vigor and enthusiasm which God inspires into the life that now is, becomes a man indeed.

THE Apostle is setting up a peerage in the eleventh chapter of the Epistle to the Hebrews. He collects from the past the memorable names of Jewish worthies, and gives them the glory of the great title, *Faith.* The highest Order that was ever instituted on the earth, is the Order of Faith. This chapter is the portrait-gallery of the Book ; and from it look down upon us the memorable names of remote antiquity.

IT is not the first part of the voyage, but the last part, that tells whether it is a successful voyage or not. The ship *De Witt Clinton* lies on the coast just below here, disabled. The prosperity of twenty-six days she lost on the twenty-seventh, when coming into the harbor.

However prosperous your life may be here, if you stick
on the shore, and do not come in on the other life, you
are a wreck! You must take care of the last part of the
voyage, or you take care of nothing at all!

EVERY man is born with aspiration. It does not develop in every man. Neither do half the buds in trees
blossom. But they are there. And there is aspiration
in every man, whether you suspect it or not, and though
it may not blossom. Aspiration means tendril, twining,
or anything else by which one vines upward, holding on
by the way to whatever will support him. Some plants
take hold by winding around, some by little roots, some
by tendrils, some by hooks, and some by leaves that catch
like anchors. But these things take hold not for the sake
of staying where they take hold, but only that they may
climb higher. And so it is with men. We clasp things
above us by every part of our nature, one after another,
not for the sake of remaining where we take hold, but
that we may go higher. In other words, when in the
ordinary experience of life we gain satisfaction, we do it
almost only by feeding on each other. When we attain
development, we do that in the same way. The soul
feeds on soul, whether for satisfaction or development.

WHEN I ask men to come and talk with me on the
subject of religion, and tell them that whether they do or
not may decide their destiny, they sometimes wag their
head, and say, "Do you suppose God governs the world
upon such a mean and narrow plan that a man's destiny
depends upon whether he does or does not go and talk
with another man?" I know that when a train is going
at the rate of sixty miles an hour, it depends upon wheth-

er the switch is one tenth-part of an inch one way or another, whether the passengers are swept into destruction, or run along smoothly, without knowing that they are in danger. It is at these critical points that small things become omnipotent. When you have put on one side of a scale one hundred pounds, and on the other ninety-nine pounds and ninety-nine hundredths of a pound, one hundredth of a pound is of as much importance as all the rest of the weight. It is when you come to these points, where but the least things are required to turn the scale, that such things become momentous.

I THINK that when Christ said, "The last shall be first," He thought of those persons, of whom there are many, that are never known outside of their own neighborhood, or their own home ; who bear sickness in solitude ; who are weary with care from one year's end to another ; whose life is one continued series of disappointments ; who have not one single external exponent of what is called success ; but who have wrought mightily within their children, and made them witnesses before God with such faith, and hope, and purity, and exhilarating patience, that as He looks on them, He sees that their hearts are more bright than the stars themselves. And at the resurrection they shall be first, inasmuch as they are last here. They shall be kings and priests. When we get to heaven we shall not know those that are first. They will be persons that here were hidden ones, but that carried themselves with supreme fidelity toward God.

THE moment a man has the vast sweep of the eternal world for his depository, how will his troubles be alleviated or destroyed, by his looking at every part of his life as relative to that!

Suppose I *am* **disappointed!** My first feeling is one of annoyance, perhaps; but my second feeling is, "Why, He **that makes** the ground fertile by frosts, is making my life **fertile by** disappointments. He sends them upon me that I may be broken up, disintegrated, comminuted, rendered pulverulent, and thus be **in a** state to promote better growths." When a man finds that he is tasked enormously with the cares of life, God sends some angel to whisper to him, "This is the way you are to be made strong and noble." Even the beggar finds comfort in this voice of encouragement, and says, "I thought it was a **beggar's pack that I** was struggling under, but God tells me it is armor; and I am strong enough to carry it." **Let us apply this interpretation to our burdens, that it** may change **their** nature, and make them easy **for us to** bear.

———

Do you remember what, in His last interview with His disciples, in that prolonged love-feast which preceded His crucifixion,—do you remember what, when the cloud was on Him, when that time which had been deferred, **and** of which He said again and again, "It is not yet," at last came, and the great eclipse began to show itself, **and the shadow was** falling, and He was uttering His last words to **them, and preparing them with** all zeal to be scattered like sheep without a shepherd, — do you remember what in that hour was the state of **the mind of** Christ? He says, "My peace I give unto you." In that hour of tempest, and darkness, **and coming anguish, while there** was agitation everywhere else, in the heart of Christ there was peace, — peace enough not only for His own wants, but for the wants of His dear disciples. And when you think of Christ as a man of sorrows and acquainted with grief, think also that He gave an exemplification of the power of the soul to overcome these things. When you forget to eat or drink because you are so busy; when your child is sick, and you forget to take your accustomed food; when public affairs are at a high key, and you are enthusiastically devoted to the interests of the commonwealth, and you forget to give the body its proper nourishment, and wonder what ails you, and think, "Why, for twenty-four hours I have scarcely tasted food," remember that our Saviour was so absorbed in the following out of the great cause of God in this world, that He forgot to be hungry, that He forgot to be tired, and that He forgot to sleep.

THE family, — the school, — the church, — regulated and virtuous civil society, — wholesome and normal occupation, which increases physical comforts, — all these make the number of children reared to high moral character greater, and the training of such children easier. Therefore, the very way to train our children for heaven is to surround them by such conditions of human society as will have a powerful, though indirect, influence upon their moral amelioration and upbuilding. I would rather undertake to bring up my child to virtue and morality and piety in the city, bad as it is, than on the desert of Sahara, or on a flat rock where there was nothing but him, me, and the rock. You could bring up a toadstool there, but not a man. A man must have something to feed on, something to think about, something to wake him up, something to inspire him. What kind of a battle could a man fight alone? A man to fight, and to be a victorious, courageous man, must have something to fight.

I WOULD not, for all the world, be made so of stone that I could not weep with those that weep, and that I could not sympathize with those who feel that war is a dreadful calamity, and that war among brethren is an awful thing. I know it is. I have probed it for years in imagination. It has been like a cloud of darkness before my mind. For twenty years God's messengers have been telling us that this thing would come * if evils that were tending toward it were not put down. And when we have been disposed to hold back our hand from duty, and to compromise with wrong, they have said that the mischief must inevitably roll on and over, collecting strength as it rolled, till it should end in gulfs of distress and abysses of misery. We would not heed their warning; we chose to take the way of present peace, rather than listen to and act upon their prophecies. And now that the results which they predicted have come, let us not make the mistake again of measuring by the way we *feel.* If we love our children more than the cause of God, we are not worthy to follow Christ. If we love an ignoble living more than a glorious living, we are not worthy to follow Christ. If we look upon the face of war and see nothing but its physical terrors, if we do not look through that and see what is the moral reason, and what are the moral triumph and the moral glory of the whole cause, we are not worthy to follow the Lord Jesus Christ.

It is how much of the invisible we can bring into this

* The rebellion in the Southern States.

life that makes this life rich and valuable. I will tell you a secret of gardening. Turnips, and other crops that have long roots, and depend mostly for their nourishment on the soil, exhaust the soil; while those crops that have broad leaves, and take the greater portion of their nourishment from the air, organizing it, and turning it into the soil, enrich the soil. Now, let me tell you that that which makes this life rich is that broad-leaved experience which derives its support from the air of the future world. And the man that is most impalpable and invisible in this life has most of this life itself.

THERE is a sense in which a man, looking on the present in the light of the future, and taking his whole being into the account, may be contented with his lot; that is Christian contentment. What philosophers want is that a man shall be contented in just the state he is in. But I tell you, if a man has come to that point where he is content, he ought to be put into his coffin; for a contented live man is a sham! If a man has come to that state in which he says, " I do not want to know any more, or do any more, or be any more," he is in a state in which he ought to be changed into a mummy! Of all hideous things mummies are the most hideous; and of mummies, those are the most hideous that are running about the streets and talking! I would rather see the old Egyptian cerements than those men that are content with what they are, and do not want to be any more.

THE world is a grindstone, and races are axes which are to get their cutting edges by being ground on it! The very object for which God thinks it worth while to turn and roll this round globe is that, by its very attrition and working, men may be **made men** in every sense of the term.

GOD puts the oak in the forest, and the pine on its sand **or** rock, and says to men, "There are your houses : go hew, saw, frame, build, make." God builds trees : men must build the house. God supplies timber : men must construct the ship. **God buries iron** : men must dig for it, and smelt it, and fashion it. What **is useful for the** body, and, still more, what is useful for the mind, is **to be** had **only by** exertion, — exertion that will work man more than iron is wrought, that will shape man more than timber is shaped. Clay and rock are given us : not brick **and squared stone**. **God gives us** no raiment : he gives us **flax and sheep.** If **we would have** coats on our backs, we must take them off our flocks, and spin them and weave them. If **we would have** anything of benefit, we must earn it, and, earning it, must become shrewd, inventive, ingenious, active, enterprising.

THE doubts and fears which prevail in Christian minds — whether their sins, their infirmities, and their **foibles** do not exhaust God's patience — are utterly unreasonable the moment we look at God.

A child **has** his little box that he keeps his money in. He has kept it unbroken — marvel of a child that he is — for a whole year! From time to time he drops in rattling **pennies and halfpennies,** — contribution coin, — until by **and** by he has a conception that he must have a great treasure ; and, unsealing it and counting it, **he finds** that he has really a whole pound! And **now he** begins **to have** some thought of what he shall do with this **treas-** ure. He at first thinks he will buy a library with it ;

but before he knows it he has run over in his mind enough books to come to ten pounds. Then he thinks he will lay it out for playthings; but, oh, at every step he finds that the thing he would buy greatly outmeasures his means; until at last he feels, "I can buy nothing; I have only a pound, and that will pay for none of the things that I desire." But the child's father is a million-naire, and owns houses, and lands, and ships, and banks; he is wretchedly rich! and the child knows it. Instead, then, of saying, "What can I do with my pound?" he might well say, "What need I that I may not have in my father's wealth? What need I, of food, or raiment, or books, or proper pleasure, that it is not over and over again in the power of my father to give me?"

Now, that poor little child's pound and his want bear about the same relation to his father's wealth, that our power and our want bear to the glory and richness of God's power. What is a man's power? He has power to resolve. And what is the power of resolution? It is the power of a bubble which reflects for one instant the glory of heaven, and then is broken and gone. Our resolutions are good for a second, and then they are forgotten. What are men's throes and struggles against inward passions and outward temptations? They are as nothing. We are swept before the evil influences which come upon us in this world, as chaff before the summer's storm. We are routed and driven as miserable, cowardly militia before courageous soldiers.

THE prouder a man is, the more he thinks he deserves; and the more he thinks he deserves, the less he really does deserve. A proud man, — the whole world is not big enough to serve him. The little he gets he looks upon with contempt because it is little. The much that he does not get he regards as evidence of the marvellous inequality of things in human life. He walks a perpetual self-adulator, expecting until experience has taught him not to expect; and then he goes forever murmuring at what he looks upon as partiality in God's dealings with men. Such men are like old hulks that make no voyages, and leak at every seam. They are diseased with pride. They have the craving appetite of dyspepsia in their disposition.

THERE are emergencies of religious experience in which the soul can do nothing but simply abandon itself, and lay hold on God. I suppose that every person who has a work of grace that is deeply rooted in him, remembers days and hours at some periods of life (they are more marked than at others) in which there is nothing that it can rest upon. There is just this one thing, — helplessness the most utter hanging upon the neck of strength the most august, — a sense of the most profound unworthiness standing before the most profound worth and purity and excellence. As the stars that rise in the morning over against the light, never rise so brightly nor last so long as the stars of the evening that rise from darkness, and that grow bright by darkness, so out of our spiritual experiences, though there rise up bright conceptions of God, there are none that compare for one single moment with those thoughts of God when the soul feels prostrate in the dust with its own sinfulness. There is majesty in the thought of mercy, and wonder in the graciousness of God, when we feel that we are sinful. In these wonderful hours, when, touched of the Divine finger, we are pervaded with a sense of our unworthiness, there is but one thing for us to do, to hope in Jesus Christ, and hope simply, or else despair. Not that you understand how He atones and pardons; not that you can see what is the relation of Christ to you. There is no philosophy about it; there is nothing but this simple instinct of hope; we clasp, we hold on to Christ, and say, " Thou art my anchor; Thou art my safeguard and my surety." It is a feeling, and not a thought.

MEN conclude that one universal and absolute will must, of course, bar the freedom of all others. That depends not so much upon the fact of the supremacy, as upon the mind. What God's will is, has much to do with what is the freedom or the servitude of man's will. For if our freedom is a part of our nature and heritage; if it is that for which God thought it worth while to make man; if it is that that gives value to man, being made; if it is that through which God means to illustrate His own glory in ages yet to come; if it is that that separates between man and the lower creations of God in this world; then it is that part of us which is immutable, and the Divine will will insure, and not subvert, the liberty of ours. God made us to be free, that in a lower sphere we might be like Himself.

AFTER that hoary old despot, Ahab, had revelled in iniquity knee-deep, — yes, from his loins to his neck; after he had slain the prophets and ramped up and down like the devil, and walked about like a lion, one poor starveling prophet came to him, when he says to him, "Ah! art thou he that troubleth Israel?" This man had carried devastation and revolution through the land, and destroyed its faithful prophets, and the moment he comes in sight of a surviving one he says, " Ah ! you are troubling Israel ! " It is the same game over and over. For the nature of despotism is the same every-where, in every age, and under all circumstances ; and what you read in the Book you can read on the planta-tion, in the halls of Congress, and in the speeches and conduct of men in your own day.

THE public sentiment of a community, instead of being adverse to truth and right, is mighty in helping men to do difficult things. There are periods of the world when heroic traits are almost drugs. There are times when the whole public mind is inspired in certain directions. There are periods when men die easy, and hundreds and thousands cast away their lives almost at the beck of one man, who is leading them on to great deeds. There are times when generosity and disinterested benevolence are abundant, and it seems as though there were a mania among men to do noble things. Such periods show the power of public sentiment ; and it also shows how impor-tant it is to bring as many great truths and principles as possible within the approval of public sentiment, in order that they may be easily adopted and acted upon by men. If you create a moral public sentiment, then you have a power by which to enforce moral lessons. There is a despotic element in public sentiment, which consists in the overaction of power. Everywhere power is prima-rily despotic, and therefore it is so in public sentiment.

HERE is a man that stands very high, and is much praised. He knows, that if he makes his mark in the community men will praise him ; and he takes care to do it, and he is praised accordingly. He builds him a fine dwelling, and he is praised for that; he lays him out magnificent grounds, and he is praised for that; he exerts a great power, and though it be an unregulated and immoral power, he is praised for that; he surrounds himself with wealth, and all the various other things that are most esteemed in this world, and men point him out, and nudge each other, and say, "There is the most prosperous man in the whole town." He is a walking poorhouse; he is a walking hospital; he is a walking lazar-house; he is rotten in conscience, and foul in passion; he lives for brick and mortar, and that which they contain; he lives for the lowest forms of power, and all of them run centrewise, for his heart is like a tunnel, flaring out toward this world, and growing small toward the other, and ingurgitating, ingurgitating, all his life long. Men say that he is prosperous; but bones, flesh, and skin are all there is of him. His conscience is dead; his taste has never been developed; all his sweeter affections are overlaid and cast down. As statues and pictures in overwhelmed cities of the Orient have for a thousand years lain covered with the soil, so the aspirations that early manifested themselves in many a man have long been covered by the soil of business and pleasure. Men say he is prosperous, and they pass by his grounds with a certain sense of awe. To them there is a kind of mysterious grandeur about his house; and they know not but he is wellnigh omnipotent. He is called the first.

By and by, when he goes to judgment, he will carry up everything that belongs to his spiritual excellence, and leave here everything that belongs to his temporal excellence. He will leave here his grounds; his house, its furniture, and pictures, and books; his stable and horses; his body, its passions, and tastes; all earthly

2 *

lore, everything tnat belongs to the flesh. He will carry with him nothing but his generosity, — and you could take that on the point of a needle; his faith, — and there is but a speck of that; and all the heroic elements of his nature, — and there is not so much as a pinch of them.

A MAN that puts himself on the ground of moral principle, if the whole world be against him, is mightier than all of them; for the orb of time becomes such a man's shield, and every step, every year, brings him nearer to the hand of Omnipotence. If a man takes ground for truth, and justice, and rectitude, and piety, and fights well, there can be no question as to the result. I would that I could inspire any man to do right with courage, therefore, by making him feel that right is itself a host. Never be afraid of being in minorities, so that minorities are based upon principles.

WE are far down in the years of time, when God works revolutions against appetite, and lust, and avarice, against power without love, against every mere material interest of men, without the employment of physical force. And when such a revolution as this takes place, and that by mere mind-power, it is time to begin to look, not for the star, but for sunrise. We are near to it.

IT is defeat that turns bone to flint; it is defeat that turns gristle to muscle; it is defeat that makes men invincible; it is defeat that has made those heroic natures that are now in the ascendency, and that has given the sweet law of liberty for the bitter law of oppression. Do not, therefore, be afraid of defeat. You are never so near victory as when you are defeated in a good cause. For

then they had Christ when they kissed Him; but that
kiss, so foul on Judas's lips, on the face of Christ shone
like a jewel. Yes, then they had Him, when they hauled
Him before the Sanhedrim   midnight; but it was like
a triumphal march. Then, when they led Him toward
Calvary, they had Him. And then, when to the music
of hammers they lifted Him up, and He hung suspended
and groaning, and with implorations of unutterable agony
died, and the heavens were dark, their victory was accomplished, and so was their everlasting defeat; for not till
He died could He live, or we in Him. It was slaying
Him that gave Him power. And so of everything that
has the nature of Christ in it,—every truth, every cause,
every sanctity, every noble thing. Slay it if you can,
and, like the gashes of Milton's angels, its wounds will
close by the healing, heavenly virtues of its own nature,
and it will stand forth with even greater power than
before.

THERE are many patriarchs of the pool. Have you
never seen these patriarchal croakers, of a summer evening, on the borders of some inland lake? Have you
never heard their croakings all through the night?
There is many and many a man who sits squat on the
edge of his party pool, croaking — croaking — croaking;
and you would think, if you did not know what the sound
was, that all the spirits of the lower regions, weird and
mischievous, were in the air. And yet, when you go and
explore, what is the noise? It is a frog!—nothing
more!

WHEN you are in a cause, see if, when you sound it, it
touches the bottom, — God Almighty; and if you find a

truth as everlasting as God, stand by it, talk of it; and if men would muzzle you, talk on. Talk living, and die talking; **and** make other men talk. There is no harm that can come from talking of things that ought not to be harmed. The only risk is in reticence, — in guilty silence.

COULD you not point out some in your church that are forever under a cloud because they are not appreciated, — because their worth is not understood, — because their value has never been justly estimated, — because, being weighed in the great scale of society, they are always too light? You may be sure that nature, and society, and **universal** experience, do not lie about these men. Where is their labor? **Where is** the exponent of their industry? **Where is** their bountiful beneficence? What tears have they wiped **away?** What houses have they builded for the poor? What **contribution have** they made **to the** public **weal?** What noble example have they set before the world? What explorations have they made upon the sea or upon the land? What useful thing have they invented? Where are the evidences of their **desert?** They are barren and granited from head to foot, so that even moss will not grow on them.

A MAN should be lenient with everybody but himself. A man should be **rigid with** himself, and nobody else. Let a man say **in the beginning** of his life, "My life depends upon me." There **is a divine,** overruling Providence, but it is **a Providence which favors those that favor** themselves by taxation, **responsibility, care, wise exertion.**

THE relation of health to a man's disposition, and so to his capacity of conferring and receiving happiness, is worthy of serious study. The happiness of our life does not consist in a few great sources. It springs from innumerable minute and constantly-recurring causes; and, more than from all other things together, it springs from the disposition of men among themselves, and toward each other. The morbid states of health, the irritableness of disposition arising from unstrung nerves, the impatience, the crossness, the fault-finding of men, who, full of morbid influences, are unhappy themselves, and throw the cloud of their troubles like a dark shadow upon others, teach us what eminent duty there is in health.

GOD made the human body, and it is by far the most exquisite and wonderful organization which has come to us from the Divine hand. It is a study for one's whole life. If an undevout astronomer is mad, an undevout physiologist is yet madder. The stomach, that prepares the body's support; the vessels, that distribute the supply; the arteries, that take up the food, and send it round; the lungs, that aerate the all-nourishing blood; that muscle-engine which, without fireman or engineer, stands night and day pumping and driving a wholesome stream with vital irrigation through all the system; the nervous system, that unites and harmonizes the whole band of organs; the brain, that dwells in the dome high above all, like a true royalty; — these, with their various and wonderful functions, are not to be lightly spoken of, or irreverently held.

LET me say to every one that is beginning life, Do not begin with exaggerated ideas of your own worth. Do not feel that you without battle ought to be a victor, and walk from the beginning with those laurels about your head which are to be twined there, if at all, only at the end of the campaign.   Do not mistake your own turbulent pride.   Do not mistake your own false-interpreting, lying vanity.   Do not begin your life feeling that such a fine fellow as you are, — one so spruce, so handsome, so well-descended, so accomplished in various ways, — deserves a high place.   Do not flatter yourself that life owes you any more than it owes anybody else.   It owes you, in common with all others, just as much as, climbing, you can bring down.   It owes you a chance to be something. It will give you that, and nothing more.   It is better for every man to begin with this understanding : — I have a chance to carve out my own way.   That is all I want. Having that I will take the consequences.

EXTERNALLY it might be difficult to judge between two men equally prosperous, and living surrounded by refinements and wealth, one of whom held this world first and predominant, and the other of whom held it second and subordinate.   There is such a thing as a man's using the things of this world consciously, as in the sight of God, for moral instrumentalities : there is such a thing, though nineteen out of twenty may not do it that pretend to. There is such a thing as a man's being a monarch, and yet being a democrat, — not in a base sense of that term, but in a high, Christian sense of it.   There is such a thing as a man's being an emperor, and sitting sole judge among men, and yet wishing to be the lowest and least among them, so far as selfish aggrandizement is concerned.   And though ninety-nine out of every hundred monarchs are self-seeking, where there are examples like David, like

Alfred, and like the reigning sovereign of England, the fact that so many counterfeits have existed is no ground for the presumption that they are not what they seem to be. And where you see professors of religion that gather their wealth from all quarters of the globe, that pile up the pyramid of their joys mountain high, that crown their days with ten thousand luxuries, though you show that ninety-nine out of every hundred of them are miserable self-seekers, and gild these things with the pretence of holding them for good, that is not ground for the presumption that the other hundredth, being called **to be rich, and learned, and refined, and** lovers and accumulators of art, have not taken their possessions and consecrated them to the service of their fellow-men. How many men have consecrated their learning, their power, their outward prosperity, all redolent and perfumed with the spirit of pure love, to the good of their fellow-men. And what if there are multitudes that pretend to do the same thing who are selfish, grasping, worldly men, that does not alter the fact that there are these men who, having a great deal of this world, hold it subject to God's requisitions, and administer it according to the highest intents of Christianity.

Do not suppose that your life is to be in external good alone. When God pays you, he pays you not altogether in bills, or silver, or gold; but partly in bills, partly in silver, partly in gold; that is, He pays you in external good; He pays you in joys and comforts; He pays you in social virtues, and sweet content therein; He pays you in the solace of noble thoughts; He pays you in the remuneration of a manly conscience; He pays you in hope and good cheer; He pays you in promises that all your orders shall be cashed when they are presented in the exchequer above. The life that now is, is but little compared with the life that is to come. The things that are in a man are better than all the robes that can be put upon him. The paying of the future world will far transcend the paying of this world. Eternity will be the end of the paying, **and with it will come a full fruition.**

THERE is many and many a man that, **by the** help of the Bible and the saddle, has gone to heaven **with** comparative ease, who would not have gone there very easily by the help of either alone.

I DREAD nothing more than to hear young men saying, "I am going to the city." If they ask me, as they often do when I am travelling about the country, what chances there are for a lawyer in the city, I say, "Just the chance that a fly has on a spider's web; go down and be eaten up!" If they ask me what chances there **are for a** mechanic in the city, I say, "Good! good! there Death carries on a wholesale and retail business! The mechanic art flourishes finely! Coffin-making **is** admirable! Men are dying ten **times as** fast **as** anywhere else!" If a man's bones are made of flint, if his muscles **are made** of leather; if he can work sixteen or eighteen **hours a day** and not wink, and then sleep scarcely winking, — if, in other words, **he is** built for mere toughness, then he can **go into** the **city,** and **go** through the ordeal which business men and professional men **are** obliged to go through who succeed. The conditions **of city life may be** made healthy, so far as the physical constitution **is** concerned; but there is connected with the business **of** the city so much competition, so much rivalry, so much necessity for industry, that I think it is a perpetual, chronic, wholesale violation of natural law. There are ten men that can succeed in the country, where there is one that can succeed in the city.

In my own experience, the cases that I have most despaired of among those who have come to me for spiritual help, have been persons that were nervinely sick. I could do them no good, because I could not reach the conditions of their body. If a person will drink green tea, which is like the quintessence of a thousand needle-points in its effects on a man's nerves, what is the use of his coming to me with complaints about blue devils? They are not blue devils; they are *green* devils! If a man gorges and oppresses his stomach, and so overlays the keys of life, — for the keys of life are located in the stomach, as the keys of the piano and the organ are located in their appropriate places in those instruments, — and he comes to me for deliverance from temptations, or for the removal of obscurities that stand between his soul and God, unless I can have control of that man's habits of eating, what can I do for him?

Merchants, business men, lawyers, ministers, all sorts of toiling and laboring men, have, in the first place, too little relaxation. We are like a violin, going from one concert to another, all day long, without once being unstrung. We are forever at concert pitch. It is a fact growing out of city life, that the intensity of our business takes away our relaxation and enjoyment. It takes the health out of the little relaxation and enjoyment which we have. Our very amusements are grim. Men go to amusements on purpose; and it is only another way of seeking business. They mechanically and consciously amuse themselves, instead of falling into amusement naturally and without thought. Laughing, singing, cheer, buoyancy,—these, and the various other means by which men rest themselves without volition, are almost unknown to us. We are a world too sober. **We are a** world too unlaughing. We do not romp enough with our children. We are not children enough ourselves.

I THINK you might dispense with half your doctors, if you would only consult Doctor Sun more, and be more under the treatment of these great hydropathic doctors, the clouds!

THERE are a great many men that do not count that worth anything in this world which has not its representative in some physical good. They go through the rooms of a library, and say, "What value is there in all these books? You cannot eat them, nor drink them, nor wear them, nor sleep on them, and therefore they are of no use." There are persons that look upon the forms of civilization, and say to themselves, "Of what conceivable benefit can these fantastic and expensive things be?" There are men who, if you take them into your flower-garden, will say, "Eh! auriculas, you call them? Cinerarias, are they? What do you do with them? Are they good for greens? Do you buy them and eat them?" "No." "Do you sell them for flowers and get money for them?" "No." "Then what *do* you do with them?" "I look at them." "Look at them! And is that all they are good for,—to be looked at? I think if I was in your place I would spend my time in something besides raising flowers just to look at!" If they would feed the mouth or fill the pocket, they would tempt such men. If, together with their elements of taste and beauty, they were of some practical benefit, they would value them as worth something. But since they do not minister to the gross senses in any way, they look upon them as value-less. External **good** is the only rule that they measure by. The fact that these things give comfort to the affections, feed the imagination, inspire the better feelings, and fill the higher ranges of a man's life, is nothing to them, for they are accustomed to measure everything by how it tastes, or how it feels in the pocket.

There are two ways in which religion **works**; the vertical **way**, and the horizontal **way**. First, we are to carry out religion as tidings of good to all the world. Then, in all the world, we are to intensify it, and carry its control more and more into every living relation of society. And our work is not done until the world is Christ's. It is not enough for us that we take care of our own children : our neighbor's children, also, are ours, in some sense. It is not enough that we take care of our own neighborhood : all that are confederated in church connection with us have a claim upon our interest, and we have reciprocal duties toward them. Nor is it enough that our own church are objects of interest and duty to us : the town or city, the county that holds the town or city, the nation that encloses the county, — all these, also, belong to us. There is a brotherhood that carries us out to every human being. Nor are they alone ours that belong to our nation : all that belong to every nation on the globe, — they are ours. Though they may not know us, and though we may not be able even to pronounce the name by which they are known, to them belongs the influence of Christianity, and they are to receive it at our hands. We are bound to take care of the world. We are bound to include in our desires, plans, aims, and Christian ambitions, all that God thinks of when He looks down upon the face of the earth.

I PUT you on your guard against the scepticism of our time. And do you think that I am about to enlarge upon the scepticism of Rousseau, of Diderot, of Voltaire, of Bolingbroke, of Hobbes, and of Hume, — that was swept away with their ashes, and is buried? The great scepticisms of our time are, — market scepticism, political scepticism, and religious scepticism. Men who feel that it would be wicked to sacrifice great pecuniary interests for the sake of principle; men who think it would be a tempting of Providence to refuse profitable business speculations, to leave profitable situations, or to refuse dividends of evil; men whose consciences will not permit them, as the members of a corporation, to expose its wickedness; men who stand in the market and feel that they have a right to do anything that wins, — these men are infidels. You need not tell me that they believe in the Bible; they believe in the Bible just as I believe in birds' nests in winter, — nests that have no birds in them. They believe in an empty Bible, — a Bible of the letter, and not a Bible of the spirit, which says to a man, " Sacrifice your right hand before you do your integrity."

WHEN even the old colored woman Katy, who earned her own livelihood; who sold cakes from day to day; who in her lifetime took forty children out of the poorhouse, and taught them trades, and bound them out in places of prosperity; who took no airs upon herself; who lived on the abundance of her poverty, — when she died out of her sphere nobody thought to ask, "What has become of her?" She was buried, perhaps, so obscurely, that no person could say, "I am sure here is where her old rattle-bones lie." But there went up heavenward a radiant procession, amidst an outburst of song, heralding the approach of some bold conqueror, crownless and sceptreless. It was the resurrected spirit of this servant of God. She lived at the bottom here, but there she lives in eternal fame. At last she broke into her crown of light, and ascended her throne, and took her sceptre.

Thou that art doing noble things and asking no praise; thou that art living to do good because it is sweet to do good, and be like Christ, and bear His cross, and walk with Him in sorrow, go up, thy Christ waits for thee. And come down, thou hoary-head of power that on earth art despoiling God's fair creation as food for thy lowest appetites, and living in selfishness for thyself alone; there is no road between thee and God that does not break short on the gulf between earth and heaven. The last shall be first, and the first shall be last.

Seek for glory, but be careful what kind of glory you seek. Work for fame, but look out that you work for the fame that addresses itself to the top of the brain, instead of that which addresses itself to the bottom.

Suppose I should urge a man to live an honest life, and he should say, "I am going to set apart from my daily duties an hour in which to be honest." Many persons think of piety in the same way that we might suppose such a man would think of honesty. They regard it as something separated from ordinary life, and to be attended to at intervals. They have an idea that it is something which is lived particularly in the closet. Now it is proper that there should be special hours set apart for devotion; but, after all, a life of piety, like a life of patriotism, or a life of honesty, is connected with, and a part of, common life.

I NEVER pass a man that is unshapen, I never pass a man that is infirm, I never pass a man to whom the body is literally a burden, that I do not think within myself, "How sweet dying must be to such a one! How gladly must a man lay aside such a bondage of trouble!" Meanwhile, if it answers the end that God meant it should, if by its pain and circumspection, by its very hindrances, it works in us patience, and relinquishment of vain things, and a seeking of noble ones, the most dwarfed body serves a better purpose than the most comely one.

I BELIEVE in the Father, the Son, and the Holy Ghost, as three distinct Persons; but I believe that above our knowledge there is a point of coincidence and unity between them. What it is I do not know. That is the unrevealed part. The revealed part is that the Divine nature stands forth to us as separate, individual Father, — separate, individual Son, — and separate, individual Spirit; and that in the vast recess of the being of God, which transcends our knowledge, there is a coming together of the three.

YE are the light of the world. We are the examples, the leaders, the models, the ideals of the world. In other words, those things that men have been accustomed to say do not belong to the church, are the very things that do belong to it. I hold that the stigma which is thrown upon churches and Christians of advocating isms, of being ismatical, although it is meant to pierce, is a part of that crown of thorns which it is their glory to wear. And that church which is never stigmatized as having an ism, is by the mind of God stigmatized as coming short of its duty, and failing to be, as it was meant to be, the light of the world. For the business of the church is not to represent the average advancement of the community, but to discern clearer light, and higher ideals, and nobler things, and to insist upon lifting up human conduct in the individual, and in carrying the community up along the line of admirableness, and toward more glorious achievements. And a church that is alive, a church that has a teaching communicancy, a church whose members are aspiring to nobler conduct, will be a disturbing church; it will be continually espousing unpopular causes; it will be all the time going aside from the preaching of the Gospel; it will be forever agitating the elements of society; it will be always unsettling men, and will never give them any rest. We are to have no rest till we take it in heaven. God meant that there should be no rest in this world, except so far as contentment, as against envy, and jealousy, and fretting, and dissension, may be called rest. Aspiration is to be the trait of every Christian body; and the function of every church of Christ is to stimulate those in the community in which they dwell, so that there shall be a holy ambition burning for higher things, nobler developments, and a purer life. Everywhere it is the business of the Christian Church to search the Word of God; and, by prayer and the interpretations of Divine truth, find out things admirable and glorious; and then bear witness, by precept and example, in respect to those things, that life may be augmenting, and that the world may be growing toward the measure of the stature of the fulness of perfect things in Christ Jesus.

———

OBEDIENCE never brings a man nearer to a law. Obedience will bring a man nearer to a rule, but obedience will not bring a man nearer to his ideal law. That goes on. It never is so small as when he touches it with perfect obedience. It opens; it effulges; it hangs higher and higher, brighter and brighter, in the heavens, and the further he travels toward it, the further he is from it. The indispensable condition of our growth and development, therefore, is that by advancing toward our ideals in attempting to fulfil them, we thrust them further from us.

———

THE imagination — the divinest of mental faculties — is God's self in the soul. All our other faculties seem to me to have the brown touch of earth on them; but this one carries the very livery of heaven. It is God's most supernal faculty, interpreting to us the difference between the material and the immaterial, and the difference between the visible and the invisible; teaching us how to take material and visible things and carry them up into the realm of the invisible and the immaterial, and how to bring down immaterial and invisible things, and embody them in visible and material symbols; — and so, being God's messenger and prophet, standing between our soul and God's.

———

"LET us, therefore," — on account of these two things; first, God's sympathy; and second, God's perfect knowledge of all our wickedness, — "come boldly to the throne of grace," — and why? — "that we may obtain mercy, and find grace to help in time of need." We go not to exonerate ourselves, not to plead our righteousness; we go boldly, saying, "Thou knowest that I am sinful; but Thou sentest Thy Son to atone for sins; I am sick, but Thou hast the medicine for souls that are sick; I am wicked, but Thou art He that delightest to forgive wickedness." We are to go boldly to God's throne, because He is so full of mercies for our want; so full of goodness for our wickedness; so full of forgiveness for our sins. And God's knowledge of what we are, and all we do, instead of being an argument for fear, is an argument for confidence.

WHEN a child has been away all day long, playing truant, and the afternoon comes, and with it hunger and the necessity of shelter, he must go home; and he goes towards his father's house, thinking to himself what plausible lie to tell, — how he can make tattered truth seem like an unrent garment. And so, with an ill-feigned appearance of innocence, and perhaps with a forced smile on his face, he enters the door, trying to look as if he were not a guilty child. He runs with alacrity to perform every errand imposed upon him. His conduct, however, is suspicious; for he is too good for an innocent child. He thinks nothing is known of his disobedience. But while he sits with the family at tea, the burden on his mind grows heavier and heavier; and he says to himself, "They are very kind to me, and if I thought that they knew it all, and they were so kind, how happy I should be!" He expects that they will find it out, and that then there will be a time of it. Now his father and mother are pleasant toward him, but he thinks that by and by it will come out, and that then will follow chastisement and trouble. And that great undisclosed guilt in the soul, that account yet to be settled, takes away all the joys of his home, and makes the evening a torment. But if, when he came in, his mother had stolen behind him, and said to him, in a gentle tone, "We know it all, my child; we are sorry; but we shall say nothing about it; we shall let it pass," the child, as soon as he found that it was all known and forgiven, and that he was the recipient of so much love, not because they did not know it, but because knowing it they saw sufficient reasons why it should be passed by, and not laid to his account, how sweet to him would have been his father's and mother's kindness! It would have brought tears to his eyes as it had never done before. And when he went to his couch at night, how sweet would their unscolding forgiveness have been to him! It would have been all the sweeter because all the time they knew his guilt.

Now, the apostle says, "With your guilt, with your trouble, go before God." He knows all. What nobody else knows, He knows. He knows what even the wife of your bosom does not know. He knows what has never been divulged to any living soul. Wicked thoughts and intentions in connection with your business, which perhaps no man knows except yourself, He knows. And when you feel an impulse to go before God, do not say, "I would go; but that crime." He knew of that crime before He invited you to go to Him. Do not say, "I would go; but that unwashed lust." He has known that lust from the beginning. "All things are naked and opened unto the eyes of Him with whom we have to do." "Let us, therefore," says the apostle, "come boldly to the throne of grace, that we may obtain mercy, and find grace to help." *Grace to help,* — that is it: grace to help you out of your sin. Let no one, then, who has a sense of his sinfulness, who is truly repentant, and who is striving to do better, hesitate to go to God, saying, " Have mercy upon me, and help me."

THERE is no boldness permitted toward God which is from our lower instincts and failings. The boldness with which a warrior meets his enemy ; the boldness of mere physical courage ; the boldness of unrestrained, irreverent zeal, — these kinds of boldness are wicked before God. But, on the other hand, there is no one of our religious feelings, in its own estate pure and zealous, and inflamed, that does not permit us to come near to God. Not only has every Christian man a key to the kingdom of heaven, but every one of our moral sentiments or feelings has its own special key with which it has a right to open the door of God's privy chamber, and go in unto Him. What is the feeling that animates you? Is it conscience ? Is this feeling carried in accordance with God's truth and spirit ? Then by it you may go boldly before God. Is it faith that irradiates the soul, — that brings light from the heart clear up to heaven ? Then as angels went up and down the sacred ladder, so by faith may you ascend into the very presence of God. Is it hope that fills the soul ? To hope is given also the watchword, and it may go to God without hesitation. Is it love? Love is a universal commoner. There is no thicket, or river, or obstacle, that love may not go through. It may go everywhere, carrying bounty, immense and universal, and only bounty. Is it want, that knows not how to speak a word ? In heaven and before God the tears of want are louder than on earth are the loudest thunders. Is it sadness of heart or remorse ? Whatever it is in the soul, that would fain draw near to God for relief, it may go to him boldly, and with confidence. There were telegraphs before Morse invented batteries or lines of wires. The longest telegraph ever made was that between the heart of God and suffering humanity. And every man that has a want is a battery: every want is a wire; every groan or tear sends a message quick to the central deposit of all petition, — God's heart; and from thence come back mercies quicker than return messages are ever received by earthly telegraphs.

Is there anything more beautiful in a lower sphere than the dressing of a bride for her wedding? The tender hands of kind nurse, of loving sisters, and fond mother, — how they all wait upon her! How the hours are consecrated to her glory! How her hair is parted and braided with sweet simplicity! How the veil is thrown over her with exquisite grace! What bracelets, what rings, what jewels, contribute to decorate her person! It is a great thing to go to the toilet-table of a bride in a wealthy family, and see what the jewel-box contains.

Now, God has opened the jewel-box with the contents of which He dresses His bride, the Church: — "Blessed are the poor in spirit." "Blessed are they that mourn." "Blessed are the meek." "Blessed are they which do hunger and thirst after righteousness." "Blessed are the merciful." "Blessed are the pure in heart." "Blessed are the peacemakers." "Blessed are they which are persecuted for righteousness' sake." "Blessed are ye when men shall revile you, and persecute you, and shall say all manner of evil against you falsely, for my sake. Rejoice and be exceeding glad: for great is your reward in heaven: for so persecuted they the prophets which were before you."

Who wants to wear jewels? There they are. Put them on!

THEOLOGY is but a science of mind applied to God. As schools change, theology must necessarily change. Truth is everlasting, but our ideas of truth are not. Theology is but our ideas of truth classified and arranged.

How tenderly God speaks when He describes the way in which He deals with those who come to Him! "The bruised reed I will not break."

What is that? Did you ever see reeds, or canes, growing, that shoot up twenty or thirty feet, and are not thicker than your finger in the whole growth? If they are strong and whole, they cannot stand unless they are in some way supported by their fellows. But suppose the field is cut through, and as the man goes along, he strikes with his axe or hatchet one that is left upon the edge, and its stem is shivered. There it stands, so tall and tremulous, but now wounded so that a breath will cause it to fall to the ground. God says, I will deal so gently with you that the bruised reed shall not break, that tremulous weakness shall not fall.

"The smoking flax I will not quench." Did you ever watch the flame when it was first applied to the wick, and you could scarcely tell whether you were deceived by your eye or there was really a light there, and the slightest stirring, the breath that you breathed, would blow it out? It is very hard to make a lamp begin to burn. Now, says God, I will deal with those who come to me for help with such gentleness that the smoking flax shall not be quenched. If your soul to-day has one aspiration, if there is one spark of that glorious flame leaping up toward God, there is the promise of that blessed Spirit that shall take that heart of **yours**, like a lamp just lit, and God **will** carry it **so** carefully and **gently** that it shall **not** go out until the whole is enkindled with light.

———

GOD'S love does not depend upon our character, but upon His own. I do not mean to affirm that it makes no difference whether **a man** has **a good** or **a bad** character. I do not mean to affirm that there do not spring up between the Divine nature and ourselves, by reason of our relations to that nature, certain deeper and more wonderful affections. But I do mean to affirm this: that there is a great overshadowing love **of** God to us, **that** stands, not **on** account of our character, but on account of His. God's love **for us** is not affirmed to exist because God perceived a **spark** kindled in us gradually flaming forth, and reaching up toward Him. It is not affirmed to **exist because our hearts**, feebly beating, seemed to knock at the door of His heart, rousing, **by** their very spent and weak sounds, **the** compassion **of** the hospitable Divinity.

Do the roots and grass and early flowers break forth from winter, and send messengers for the sun to come **back?** or does the sun, come from its far voyaging, long to overhang the sleeping places of flowers until they feel **his** presence, and, **drawn** by his warm hands, wake and come forth into a warmth **and a** light that waited above them while they were **dead, and that would have** bathed them yet, and all summer long, though they had still lain torpid?

———

You are perpetual recipients of God's mercies. **In the round year** there is not one moment in which He does not brood over you with His thoughts. His love and tenderness are to you what the sun and the dew are to the plant.

————

IF you take a microscopic instrument, and examine the sting of a bee, magnifying it a million times, you will find that still it is so smooth that the eye can detect no variations upon its surface. But if you take the finest needle that is manufactured, and look at it through a powerful microscope, you will find that it will appear rough in the proportion in which it is magnified. This figure illustrates the difference between the Divine nature and the nature of man. The more you magnify your true conceptions of God's nature, the more beautiful does He appear; whereas the more you magnify the nature of man the more ugly does he appear. And it is evident that if God loves man, it is because He has something in Himself that compels Him to love, and not because there is anything in man that calls forth His love.

————

MEN mount up into flashes of glorious realization, when it seems as if God then began to love them, because they then first become sensitive to His love. When a man has passed through religious changes from darkness to light, — when he has put off his worldly character, and taken on the character of Christ, — when, coming out of despondency, the compassionate Saviour rises before him, — then he stands up and says, " Christ has begun to love me. I have come to a state in which I know that God loves me." His impression is that the Divine love for him began when the burden which had weighed down his soul was rolled off.

Just as if a blind man, who had never seen the heavens,

nor the earth, nor the sweet faces of those that loved him, should have a surgical operation performed upon his eyes, so that he could **see objects around him,** and should think to himself, **on** going out of doors, "O, how things **are** blossoming! The earth is beginning **to** be beautiful! Mountains and hills are springing up in every direction! **The** forms of loving friends are being raised up to greet my gaze! And the sun has just begun to shine forth from the heavens!"' But have not these things existed since the flood, and since the creation, although the man's eyes have not before been in a condition to enable him to see them?

When we are brought **into the** consciousness of what God's love is to our poor **sinful natures, we** oftentimes **have the** feeling that God **is** beginning **to** be reconciled **to us. We take it for** granted that as we were at enmity with **Him,** so **He** was at enmity with us. We have **an** idea that he was just as hard toward us as we were obstinate **in** violating His will; and that it was when we **began** to love Him that He began to love us. **It was then** that we began to realize His love, but His love for us had **existed** from the time we came into being, and had ever continued with us. All the experiences of our inward and outward lives have been baptized, although unconsciously **to us,** in His tender thoughts. Those thoughts run after **us more** than a mother's for her child that has gone away from home.

O MAN, thou who art God's courier through **time and** eternity, nothing that concerns **you** in the slightest **degree** can be considered as little.

GOD stands and looks down; and all things are naked

and opened unto Him. To Him there are no locked-up covers; no concealed crypts; no dark caves; no secret places. There is nothing that is not disclosed before Him. There is no man that is so encased or enrobed as to be hidden from Him. He sees through the thoughts and feelings of men. He beholds the fountains of their feeling, and the sources of their thoughts. The intents of the heart, — those psychological tremblings which indicate that the wires will show some thought or feeling, — even these are known to Him. The very beginnings of the life of the soul are plain unto Him.

WHEN a man looks at his own state and asks whether he shall be able to prevail, and stand in Zion and before God, it is not at all wonderful that his courage fails him. But why should he think of himself? Why should he measure his chances of everlasting life merely by the slender forces that he can address to the work of salvation? Have you no God? Have you no Saviour? Was it not for you that Calvary became memorable? Was one thought thought, was one feeling felt, did one drop of blood fall to the ground, on that blessed mount, in which you had no right nor part nor lot? The treasure of Calvary is the birthright of every child that has come into life since the death of Christ; and all that was then manifested by God, in word or thought or act, was but a feeble expression of the unspeakable love that was behind it all. All that He did then was for you.

A DOCTOR, ignorant of disease, is called in to cure a man that is sick. Before he came he expected to find the patient weak, and pale, and lying on a couch; but he finds him disfigured, blotched, cramped, distorted, nervous,

3 *

fitful, pettish, and he will not touch him. He thought he was only sick, but he finds him ugly! As if ugliness was not a part of sickness!

Now, men have a romantic idea of being sinful. They think that to be sinful is something less than to be bad. They regard sinfulness as something akin to weakness, rather than wickedness. And they say, " If I were only good, God would forgive me my sins; but now I make promises and break them, I say what I do not mean in prayer, I indulge in things which I pray God to enable me to avoid, I continually exhibit passions which I know are evil; and how can I hope for salvation?" As if being filled with such things was not what we mean, and what God means, by sin! As if it was not on account of these very things that we need the Divine recuperative power!

It requires no engineering to make a road that has been made already; but to cut through the mountain, and fill up the morass, and make a road, does require some engineering. And if men were to make themselves complete before presenting themselves to God, there would be no marvel in God's supplying love. It is because men are imperfect and wicked perpetually, that there is a marvel in this love.

A GREAT many persons have almost no confirmation of hope, partly from a fault of teaching. There are a great many persons whose conscience is educated to watch over them, so that it becomes the torment of their life. They are always afraid they will make a mistake. They are forever on the doubtful edge of fear and hope. They are never able to say, " I know that my Redeemer liveth." And even if they have moments of triumph, they are like flowers that are exposed to an uneven temperature. If they have plants of righteousness, they are like early vegetables that have no settled summer. They lose all the seed sown in early periods.

WHEN I stand and look at my congregation, I am like a man in a picture-gallery. Here is a bright, radiant landscape. Right next to it is a landscape that is storm-clad and dark. There is the picture of a calm, tranquil sea. Right next to it is the picture of a sea that is rough and boisterous. Here is a scene of love. Right next to it is a tragic scene. There is a representation of wealth. Right next to it is a representation of poverty. Thus throughout the picture-gallery the most striking contrasts are seen.

Now, I see just such contrasts when I stand and look from my pulpit. Here is a man whose face betokens consolation. Right next to him is a man whose heart by affliction has been left empty and desolate. There is a man triumphing in prosperity and enjoyment. Right next to him is a man who is stricken down by misfortune and sorrow. I see all these various conditions of life portrayed before me when I look. I see light and dark shades commingled all through the congregation. Sometimes I feel inclined to preach to those who are hopeful. At other times I cannot help preaching to those who are in darkness and great trouble.

Now, you of this latter class, this is a comfort for you. God says that neither tribulation, nor distress, nor persecution, nor famine, nor nakedness, nor peril, nor sword, nor anything, shall take you out of His hands.

Let us imagine a case. An heir is so dissolute that he is outcast from his home. He determines to become an emigrant. He comes to this country, and changes his name, thinking to live here in obscurity. His prospects are anything but flattering, as is apt to be the case with children who are educated to nothing. He finds no employment. **He is at** last driven to a mine, **and he becomes** a collier. Acquiring some degree of **love for** work, he makes up his mind that he will build up a little property for himself. After toiling day and night for a long period in the mine, he feels that he has a foothold on life once more. Meantime, his father dies, leaving **his** whole estate to him. The agent, ascertaining his whereabouts, comes to bring him news of his good fortune. He does not at first disclose himself to him, thinking that he will put him to proof, and see what there is in him. Instead of saying, **"I have come to tell you** that your father's whole estate **has** fallen to you, and that you are exalted to a position of influence," he lies back, and takes means to thwart the man's schemes. The **man only** knows that his plans are overturned by somebody. He measures his distress from his own stand-point. The agent gets hold of his little property, takes a note against him to collect, and in various ways harasses and terrifies him, till he is overwhelmed with distress, and it seems to him that the end of all things has come, and he is ready to leave all his hard earnings, and run away, for the sake of escaping from his trouble. Then the agent says to him, **"I was** only tantalizing you. I came to bring you tidings that you are the sole heir **of your** father's immense estate. I have been doing these **things** just to see how you would act. I bear the testimonies of your heirship. Here is the evidence that you are the possessor **of** uncounted wealth." How different now do these **little** tantalizations seem from what they did but just before!

Then they seemed like thunderbolts; now they have no noise in them. Then they seemed dark as midnight; now they seem as bright as noonday. He laughs now to think that he cried then. He rejoices now, where then he was drowned in sorrow.

But the eternal kingdom of God is yours, God himself is yours. Sustained by Him, upheld by Him, cared for by Him, we are held out for a little while in blessed tantalization, soon to be caught up as His children, His heirs, and joint-heirs with Christ. What blessedness is there in this thought! How should it inspire us with patience as we journey through life!

IMAGINE a dove saying, "I dislike this glossy green on my neck," and trying to remove it. It may rub the feathers off, but they will speedily come green again. It cannot eradicate the color from its feathers. The sunflower will be yellow, however much it may prefer to be violet. Everything will have its own peculiar form, its own peculiar color, its own peculiar juices, its own peculiar odors, and its own peculiar constitution. God meant that it should be so; He watches to see that it is so; He holds things down in their places, and you among them, and your faculties in you. He gives you liberty to control one faculty by another, but He never gives you liberty to rub out one figure. The problem you are to work out in life requires that you should use everything put into you. You think you are not doing it, but you are. God laughs to see how deceived you are, — to see you think you are not doing what you are, and to see you doing what you think you are not.

THE vague and sad forebodings of Christians as to

their final safety are very unreasonable, in the light of
God's revelation. There are men that hope sometimes,
but doubt much more. This arises from an almost exclusive regard to one's own sickness, and an almost utter
neglect to look at the fulness, richness, freeness, and inexhaustible bounty of God's love for men. No man can
find any reasonable comfort, I think, so long as he is
more conscious of his own state than of the amazing
grace and power of God. I do not know the man who,
if he should look merely at his own disposition, at his
past life, at his Christian experience, could find argument
for anything but sadness and dissatisfaction in regard to
the past, and fear in regard to the future. It is not in
that direction that hope springs up. As long as a man
looks in upon himself he is like one that opens a trap-
door and looks down to see the stars. The stars are not
to be seen by looking that way. You do not want to
look down into a well to see the light, but into the
heavens above.

To you that are not troubled it may seem an inconse-
quential thing, but to you that are troubled it is a source
of inexpressible peace and gladness, that there is a God
who knows how to take care of men when they do not
know how to take care of themselves.

THERE is but one single view, it seems to me, on which
a man can lie down and die without fear, and that is this:
" God loves me, because it is His nature to love; God
will save me, because it is by saving me that He will
best please His own self." And if I go home to heaven,
I shall go, not on the step-stone of my own virtue and
goodness, but because I am attracted by the drawings of

that Heart that suffered for me on Calvary, and that ever lives to intercede for me in heaven. We are to die in Christ. We are to die so that we shall not die. The egg is destroyed that it may give forth the life of the bird; and death to us is emergence; it is going forth to a clime of everlasting joy and singing.

WHEN two notes are brought to the same tone they accord with each other, and each note knows that the other is right because they accord; so when two hearts are right, they will fall into such unison and concord that it will not be difficult for one to see that the other is right.

THERE can be nothing on earth half so important to a man as his own self. It is right to feel a lively interest in nature, in human society, and in the events of that great world-history which is always going on around us, and in our day. But what kingdom on earth is so wide or so important as the kingdom of God in a man's own soul? The Russian empire constitutes the largest earthly dominion; and yet the sun need not employ half its hours in going from side to side of it. And the kingdom of the soul shall not have been traversed when the sun itself is burned to the socket, and its light has gone out. It is infinite; it is endless.

WE are like men who go by their watches, but never set their watches by any regulator. We are continually regulating our lives by standards so false that they amount to no regulators at all.

THE reflection of other men's good-will toward us we

use more than anything else to estimate our characters by. Those who do this are like buoys that are always on the surface of the water, but that move with it as it rises and falls with the ocean-tides. We lie like floats on the world-tide, which goes in and out, and up and down; and we have no gauge on the shore to show what is our absolute condition. It is merely relative to the fluctuations of the ever-shifting, ever-changing tide of human feeling.

———

DID you ever think what a volume your talk would make if it were printed? If everything that some persons say in a single day were printed, what a volume it would make! and if all they say in a year were printed, what a library it would make! I pity the man that should have to read the one or the other. And yet, all their sayings, from day to day, and from year to year, are flying in every direction, producing their effects upon those on whom they fall. The exaggerations, the over-colorings, the misrepresentations, the lies (for we all lie continually) which escape us when we are speaking about ourselves, about our children, about our families, about our property, about our neighbors, about everything that we have to do with, — what must be their influence upon the world? Still, how few there are that know anything about the use of their tongue, which is forever on the move!

———

As warmth makes even glaciers trickle, and opens streams in the ribs of frozen mountains, so the heart knows the full flow and life of its grief only when it begins to melt and pass away.

———

I THINK that one of the master incantations, one of the most signal deceits, which we practise upon ourselves, comes from the use of language. There are the words that we learn in childhood which we abandon when we come to manhood. Generally speaking, our fireside words are old Saxon words, — short, knotty, tough, and imbued with moral and affectional meanings; but as we grow older these words are too rude and plain for our use, and so we get Latin terms and periphrases by which to express many of our thoughts. When we talk about ourselves we almost invariably use Latin words, and when we talk about our neighbors we use Saxon words. And one of the best things a man can do, I think, is to examine himself in the Saxon tongue. If a man tells that which is contrary to the truth, let him not say, "I equivocate": let him say, "I lie." *Lie!* why, it brings the judgment-day right home to a man's thought. Men do not like it, but it is exactly the thing that will most effectually touch the moral sense; and the more the moral sense is touched the better. If a man has departed from rectitude in his dealings with another, let him not say, "I took advantage," which is a roundabout, long sentence: let him say, "I *cheated.*" That is a very direct word. It springs straight to the conscience, as the arrow flies whizzing from the bow to the centre of the mark. Does it grate harshly on your ear? Nevertheless, it is better that you should employ it; and you should come to this determination: "I will call things that I detect in my conduct by those clear-faced, rough-tongued words that my enemies would use if they wanted to sting me to the quick."

WE imagine with wonder the passage of a comet

through space, flaming and sparkling along strange paths, and glowing upon stars innumerable as it goes; but that is not half as wonderful as the passage of the human heart, flaming and sparkling and glowing with ten thousand effects shot out upon every man we meet, as we move through life. Planets are cold and dead, and all their radiance falls without effect; but the human soul, as it passes up and down the ways of its experience, is producing ten thousand effects at every single moment, many of which we know nothing about.

EVEN in our religious feelings, we are prone to follow our sympathies rather than our judgments or consciences, and to measure ourselves by the general condition of the church or sect to which we belong. We are as if we were in a ship, and we called its voyage our voyage, and its passage our passage. And if our church or sect is flourishing, we have a feeling that we are flourishing; and so we lose our personal identity.

IN a great affliction there is no light either in the stars or in the sun; for when the inward light is fed with fragrant oil, there can be no darkness though the sun should go out. But when, like a sacred lamp in the temple, the inward light is quenched, there is no light outwardly, though a thousand suns should preside in the heavens.

DID you ever sit down and make an inventory of what you do, in order to come to a distinct understanding with reference to your use of time? You probably know all about your possessions. You know every bond, if you have bonds; you know every mortgage, if you have mortgages; you know every pound that is deposited, if you have deposits of money; you know every piece of property, if you own real estate; you know all your debts and credits. These things you look at both in detail and in the sum. But God has given our chief treasure to us in the use of time; and how many of us understand that matter? How many of us know what we do with our time? How many of us have ever taken even a cursory view of one single year, saying, "I am anxious to know, on the whole, how I carried myself with reference to a faithful use of the element of time through January, through February, through March, through April, through May, through June, through July, through August, from month to month? What is the habit of my life in this respect? Of the time that is given me, how much of it do I use well; how much do I use indifferently; and how much do I squander?" There is not one man in a hundred that ever thought of these things. We hear the general declaration that we ought to employ our time; men are exhorted to be diligent in business, and fervent in spirit; but I suspect that there is not a single person that ever sits down to make a deliberate inventory in regard to the element of time, so as to form a correct judgment of his habit of using it. Ought that so to be?

––––––––––

AT this time, all over the trees, and throughout the grass, is deposited the condensed moisture of the air; and silent dew-drops are on every flower and every leaf. If you go and look at them in the darkness of to-night, there is no form or comeliness in them; but by and by God will have wheeled the sun in its circuit so that it shall look over the horizon: and the moment its light strikes these hidden drops, small and scattered, every one

shall glow as if it were a diamond, and all nature shall
be lighted up with myriad fires, each reflecting something of the Divine glory. God has His own plans.
He never told us in full what they are. We know this,
however; that we are fragmentary in our lives; that it
takes many to make the one idea of God; that the work
of past generations is hinged upon this, and that the work
of this generation is hinged upon that of generations to
come; and that God sits in sublimity of counsel, putting
part with part, so that when we see the connected whole,
the things that now seem most insignificant will shine
out in wonderful beauty and magnificence.

We are continually denying that we have habits which
we have been practising all our life. Here is a man that
has lived forty or fifty years, and a chance-shot sentence
or word lances him, and reveals to him a trait which he
has always possessed, but which until now he had not the
remotest idea that he possessed. For forty **or** fifty years
he has been fooling himself about a matter as **plain** as his
hand before his face.

There is many and many a man who thinks that he is
fighting the Bible and exalting morality when he says, " I
believe in such an old man; I believe in such a matron;
I believe in such a person." No, you do not believe in
them; it **is the grace** of God in them that you believe in.
It is, after all, those spiritual truths that God more gloriously writes in fleshly tables of the heart, than with ink or
on tables of stone, that you are bowing down before.

How many there are that use their ears as a bolting-
cloth, only to catch the bran, and let the flour go. How

many there are that hear everything that is keen and
pungent and salient in scandal, and nothing that is favorable, commendable, praiseworthy of men. How many
persons are, in regard to hearing, like sentinels who,
when set to take care of things that are good, are
always asleep, but who, when set to take care of things
that are bad, never go to sleep? How many persons
are there that form any conception of what the character of their life is in this matter? One man goes home
and sits down, and his companion says to him, "My dear,
what have you heard to-day?" and he commences to
descant on the things that he has heard; and it would
seem as if he had been carried by God's providence into
so many pleasant ways, as if he had heard so many pleasant things, that he had been signally blessed. Another
man goes home and sits down, and when he is asked,
"What have you heard to-day?" he says, "Heard! I
have heard some queer things"; and he goes on and tells
something that he has heard about this man to his dis-
credit; something that he has heard about that woman
that is derogatory: something that he has heard against
the judge; something that he has heard that implicates
his next-door neighbor; some story that a man should
never hear, or that having heard he should never repeat;
things that one would suppose he must have gone through
a pandemonium to hear. How many men take account
of their habits of hearing? I think it is important that
a man should examine himself for the purpose of coming
to some knowledge of his conduct in this regard.

I HAVE known many persons that, when they began to
feel a certain sweet joy in singing a hymn, would check
themselves and say, "Have I a right to this feeling?

does it proceed from the proper source ?"   It is exactly
as though a bird should commence to sing on a tree close
by your dwelling, and you should say to yourself, "I
wonder if that is the bird that I heard yesterday"; and
you should run to the window to see, and frighten it so
that it would stop singing and fly away.   If any feeling
begins to sing on the bough of hope, the moment you say,
"Stop, let me see the construction of its vocal organs,"
that moment it stops singing.   If an emotion of sympathy
with justice and conscience springs up in your bosom, the
moment you say, "Stop, let me see how it is coming,"
that moment it ceases to be.   If you begin to experience
love toward God, the moment you say, "Stop, let me
look at this," that moment it comes to an end.   The
moment you look at a feeling, the feeling stops, and in-
tellection begins, thus revolutionizing the whole process
of the mind.

"MAN that is born of a woman is of few days, and full
of trouble."   It comes to us all: not to make us sad, but
to make us sober; not to make us sorry, but to make
us wise; not to make us despondent, but by its darkness
to refresh us, as the night refreshes the day; not to im-
poverish us, but to enrich us, as the plough enriches the
field, — to multiply our joy, as the seed is multiplied a
hundredfold by planting.   Our conception of life is not Divine, and our thought of garden-making is not inspired.
Our earthly flowers are quickly planted, and they quickly
bloom, and then they are gone; while God would plant
those flowers which, by transplantation, shall live forever.

SOME of the most disagreeable persons that you meet

in the world, are these Christian people that are considering everything in the universe from the stand-point of their own culture. One of the most blessed things in this world is to be unconscious of self, and conscious only of God, the eternal sphere, and the great truths of the Divine government and human life. Happy is he before whom these things are so eminent that his own conscious self is gone. And yet how many well-meaning persons there are who are forever treating you to the various dish of their sensibilities, their struggles, their temptations, and their wants; with whom it is continually I, I, I, — me, me, me, — my, my, my; whose life is one everlasting habit of egotism, only basted and served up in religion !

WE part from this world strangers; we come together in everlasting acquaintanceship. We lose our friends that we may really find them. The husbandman loses his seed in the furrow, that he may gain a harvest. We lose our friends that we may really find them a hundredfold; for, that which we encircle here, that which our love cradles, that which flesh and raiment clothe, is not our friend. That which the body itself encloses is the friend. And who sees that through the composite flesh; through a life which is itself but disconnected and fragmentary; through toils and struggles, and intermitted purposes and mistakes; through griefs and heart-sorrowings; through dim ignorance; through yearnings and vague aspirations? Who more than suspects the cause that gives forth these intermitted effects? The soul, — who sees, who knows that?

A PLOUGH is coming from the far end of a long field, and a daisy stands nodding, and full of dew-dimples.

That furrow is sure to strike the daisy. It casts its shadow as gayly, and exhales its gentle breath as freely, and stands as simple, and radiant, and expectant, as ever; and yet, that crushing furrow, which is turning and turning others in its course, is drawing near, and in a moment it whirls the heedless flower with sudden reversal under the sod!

And as is the daisy, with no power of thought, so are ten thousand thinking, sentient flowers of life, blossoming in places of peril, and yet thinking that no furrow of disaster is running in toward them, — that no iron plough of trouble is about to overturn them. Sometimes it dimly dawns upon us, when we see other men's mischiefs and wrongs, that we are in the same category with them, and that perhaps the storms which have overtaken them will overtake us also. But it is only for a moment, for we are artful to cover the ear, and not listen to the voice that warns us of our danger.

MEN never can find themselves of themselves, but always in the touch of some other and higher one.

HE that knows how to die in his passions every day; he that knows how to die in his pride from hour to hour; he that has Christ in each particular thwarting and event of life; he that knows how, from the varied experiences of life, to bring forth from day to day a Christian character, need not fear the grand and final earthly experience to which he is coming. There is no death to those that know how to die beforehand. Those who know how to lay themselves upon Christ, and take the experiences of every-day life in the faith of Christ; those who see the will of God in everything that abounds, whether wounding or healing, — they have nothing left at the end of life except peace, translation, and the beginning of im. mortality.

———

It is the nature of Christ to awaken in us, and to bring forth, that which we should have no power to excite in ourselves. In all the fields there is not one flower whose root is not organized for the promotion of its growth; whose nature is not stored with all elements of development and of perfection. And yet, not one of them can lift up the clod, or struggle forth; not one of them can give birth to its leaves, or break forth in blossoming beauty, until the secret of their life, which the sun carries, is given to them. Then, when the light calls them, and the warmth; then, when the sun has wrought mightily within them do they come to themselves. Their life is in Him.

———

The loving women who followed Christ must have found a daily heaven. His serene nature; His beneficence; His all-encompassing sympathy; His disinterestedness, that gave everything but asked nothing; His supernal wisdom; His power over life; His regency over nature; His lordship over the winds that flew to His hand as a dove to its nest; His mastery over darkness and death itself, calling back the departed spirit from its far-off wandering to life again; His effluent glory, as He hung in mid-air, sustained by white clouds, or as He walked the night sea, carpeted with darkness; but, above all, that inspiration, that heavenly purity, that spiritual life which touched their life, and that aroused them as they were never before aroused, — in short, the presence of their God! — all these things, abiding with

4

them, travelling from **day to** day with them, measuring
out their golden year, gave them their first full knowledge of life as the soul recognizes it! And these were,
to their fond hope, doubtless, a perpetual gift.

WHAT is just, is more to us as we grow older. In
every new relation of life into which we come, we find
out finer shades, higher colors, nicer distinctions, and
wider circuits of justice. Justice is never so slender to
us as when we first practise it. It grows in the imagination. It is enlarged by experience. It includes more
elements, it touches things with a finer stroke, and it demands more exquisite duties, every single **day** and year
that a man lives, who lives at all right.

How many of my congregation have I seen in their
troubles! How many of them have I walked with in
their hour of anguish for sin! Every Sunday I look upon
a congregation, one in every six of whom, it seems to me,
I have gone down to the baptismal water with, or sprink-
led, and walked with, through all the stages of their heart-
distress. For how many of them have I spoken words
of consolation at funerals? Where are the children,
where are the brothers and sisters, where are the parents,
where are the kindreds of my church? Where are our
old friends and co-workers? Where are those that were
in the height of personal expectation ten years ago?
We have lived ten years together, most of us, — some of
us longer than that; and have we not tracked God at
every step, verifying His declaration, "Ye shall have
tribulation"? And are we to look forward to the time
to come with less expectation of tribulation? Let each
look upon his household. Who shall be unclothed next?

I desire to take it to myself. I desire to look at my plans and expectations in the light of this inquiry. For I too have made a garden, and have forgotten to put a sepulchre in it. I desire to commence a new survey. Let me go up to that central mound covered with flowers, and let me see if underneath those flowers there is not an opening mouth, — the darkness of the grave. And if there is, then let me rejoice; for I am sure that that is an unwatered garden which has no sepulchre. In so great a congregation as mine, where there are so many thousands that by invisible threads are connected with this vital teaching-point, sorrow becomes almost a literature, and grief almost a lore; and we are in danger of walking over the road of consolation so frequently, that at last it becomes to us a road hard and dusty. We are accustomed to take certain phrases as men take medicinal herbs, and apply them to bruised and wounded and suffering hearts, until we come to have a kind of ritualistic formality. It is good, therefore, that every one of us, now and then, should be brought back to the reality of the living truth of the Gospel, by some heart-quake, — by some sorrow, — by some suffering. Flowers mislead us, beguile us, enervate us, make us earthly, even if they assume the most beautiful forms of loveliness; while troubles translate us, develop us, win us from things that are too low to be worthy of us, and bring us into the presence and under the conscious power of God.

THERE can be no barrenness in full summer. The very sand will yield something. Rocks will have mosses, and every rift will have its wind-flower, and every crevice a leaf; while from the fertile soil will be reared a gorgeous troop of growths, that will carry their life in

ten thousand forms, but all with praise to God. And so
it is when the soul knows its summer. Love redeems its
weakness, clothes its barrenness, enriches its poverty, and
makes its very desert to bud and blossom as the rose.

A HOUSE built on sand is, in fair weather, just as good
as if builded on a rock. A cobweb is as good as the
mightiest chain cable when there is no strain on it. It is
trial that proves one thing weak and another strong.

I THINK that faith and much thinking do not dwell
well together; not in religion alone. I do not think it
does to think too much in friendship. Let a child think
about all the things he sees his father and mother do, and
see if he loves them any better after that. Let a friend
go about insisting upon reducing all feelings and instincts
to thoughts, and strive to understand the nature of emotion
by thinking, — let him, instead of giving liberty in his
heart, go to applying his philosophy to his friends, and
see if he will stand nobler in friendship or not. Let him
go out into the realm of thinking about eternal things,
and it would be just as foolish. Let a man begin to study
the relation of the race to God's government, and all the
mutations of government, all natural and civil law, and all
the ten thousand questions that rise up before the mind
that thinks and is inquisitive of such thoughts as these,
and the fact is that idea, stars, land, sea, everything, —
the more a man thinks upon them, the less is he strong,
and the more is he enervated. The great depths give up
their mists, and these banks of white silver hue are hid in
the fog. There are hours when it seems as though everything is swept away from us; that there is no heaven,
that it is all fancy and a dream; that there is no respon-

sibility; that there is no such thing as sin and virtue; that we are all so many animals, we are all following the instincts and circumstances that press without us; there is no God, or He would speak, or certainly He would give us some token in our extremest anguish that He is near; there would be some dawn of light. There are a great many men who strive to explain these doubts by reference to the natural laws, but no man has followed this line of thought to any satisfaction. There are a great many happy, genial, and hopeful theologians that think at last they have got up early enough to find out God, and so every generation you will find a man that explains everything. He does until the next man kicks it, and it all goes back to dust again. When you shall chain the waves of the sea that they shall not rise any more; when you shall fasten in the tops of the forest the winds that rock them, that make them sigh their dirges in winter and sing their anthems in summer; when you shall stay the courses of the stars and bind the earth that it shall not roll in its orbit, then you may take these great questions, and, by the bands of your thought and by the cords of your philosophy, you may fasten them; but so long as you cannot do that, so long will they have free course. And so with the thoughts of men. There must needs come hours when a man finds himself quite drifted away from old thoughts. Contagious hours they are, hours of great trouble, awakening hours of philosophy and of doubt. In such hours as this there is nothing for it but to run, and there is but one way to run, and that is Godward. A man in these hours that does not run for God, should run for the lunatic asylum. There is but one way in which a man can find any rest, and that is to say blindly but desperately, "There is a Thinker, there is a Controller, and if men have not drawn His lineaments right, and if the portraiture of the books is not right, one thing I know, my soul proclaims there is goodness and wisdom, there is control. Whatever it is I seize it, I hold by an anchor to that blessed hope." The very moment a man begins to hold by that, sometimes, as by an electric touch, the clouds fade away, the sweet beaming face of Christ shines again, and all the mists have gone as sometimes you have seen them in the morning disappear, you know not how; we are bright again, and have joy in Christ, and in all the blessed promises of His word; and the miracles recorded there are not half as marvellous as the miracles wrought in the sweet experience of Christians every day.

In cities, and in business, the proportion of men that have mistaken their calling is larger than anywhere else. I see men every day that are in situations for which they are not at all calculated. There are multitudes of young men that want to be rich in merchandise. They will not put their lily hands where the sun can brown them. They were born, they say, for better things. Many of them were born for the poor-house, and they will be there in the end! They may meet with a measure of success for a time, till the sap of youth is gone out of them, and then they will be fit only to be cast out, and to be trodden under foot of men.

If you transplant a tree in the spring, the sap in it will carry it half through the summer, though its roots may be dead. It will throw out leaves, and appear like a sound tree for a good part of the first year. But the next year it will die. And every man, when he starts in life, has enough of the sap of youth to carry him a certain way, though he may have mistaken his calling; but in the course of ten years, when that sap is expended, and he is rootless and branchless, where will he be? There is a whole deluge of white-faced, white-livered, imbecile, lily-handed men in the city, seeking wealth without toiling for it, — seeking honor without achieving it, — seeking place without deserving it. They are utterly useless to society, and yet of all men they are the most extravagant in their demands upon society. Do you suppose they will go unwhipped? God laughs at them; and so do angels, and everybody but themselves. They think that they are martyrs. They think that there is a mysteriousness in the providences of life, because such fair-haired, beautiful young men, who desired so much, and meant to have so much, got so little. And even what they did get was bitter.

Did not they get what they deserved? Was their experience anything but the inevitable result of the violation of a law of their being? Nowhere were cause and effect ever better vindicated than they are in the perishing of ten thousand, whose ill-starred ambition leads them into things for which they are unfit, and induces them to seek results which they can never attain. Do you ask what you shall do? Go to sea! — we need sailors. Go out to work! — we need farm hands. Go into the shop! — we need mechanics. Do not congregate and house in the city, where, when having made a few abortive attempts to be honest and succeed, and having failed, you will take the gimlet of craft and cunning, and bore your way through life, until, your consciences being gone, you will resort to more positively dishonest ways, which will bring you at last to utter disgrace and ruin.

THERE is a place where the glory of God shall be an uninterrupted stream which shall be so clear, so apparent, that we shall live in the presence of it. That is to say, when we stand so as to see God as He is, there will not be a single thought nor a single emotion that shall not fill the soul with rapture; there will not be a single emotion nor a single thought that shall not touch the soul as the hand of the musician touches the chord of the instrument; there will not be a single thought nor a single emotion that shall not vibrate with admiring joy. For God is the centre of glory, and He acts on a pattern of grandeur in moral attributes, such, that to stand in His presence and see Him, is to be ceaselessly agitated and affected by the wonder of such a Being. We shall see Him as He is,—the God of glory; and our eye will be so strengthened, that we can behold Him and not die.

IF a man has oil in his can, every drop he pours out makes his supply one drop less. There is no springing up from the bottom to prevent diminution in the supply. It is not so with the soul. The nature of that is to renew its supply, so that the more you draw from it, the more there is to draw; the more it gives, the more it has to give. Giving will make any man's soul richer.

WHEN a person becomes a Christian, it is not possible for him to have anything taken from him but that which he cannot afford to keep; and that which he does keep will be more fruitful of joy than anything which an unchristian man possesses. I know it is *living* to become a Christian, and *death* not to be one. It is liberty to be a Christian, and bondage not to be one. To become a Christian is to come to that for which God made you; it is to use your powers as God originally designed that they should be used. The object of Christianity is to restore man to the nature which he originally possessed. It was for this that Christ came into the world. And they that enter upon a Christian life earliest are the most blessed. I do not say these things to the young because I am a pensioned minister, and because it is my business to say them. I do not say them because I am a minister, but because I am a man. I would say them to my own son; to the dearest friend I have in this world. I say them because my inmost conviction is that they are true.

Do you suppose a parent dislikes to see real vigor, and joy, and elasticity, and genius, and attainment, and capacity, in his children? Is there anything that makes a parent happier than to see, so long as it is good, the utmost growth and development in his children? If their powers are not perverted, the more they expand, the more satisfaction does the parent derive from them. And does God, who is more than any earthly father, love dry and withered natures, or full and joyful ones, that are pouring out the freshness of their life? If ever you are going to be a Christian, do not set out to be a gloomy-eyed, twilight-faced, bat-like Christian, hovering between night and day. Do not be a Christian parsimonious of joy, and full of tears and sadness. Do not attempt to be a Christian after the pattern of the ascetic. "The kingdom of God is not meat and drink, but righteousness, and peace, and joy,"—righteousness of rectitude and integrity, peace which God gives by the regulation of man's nature, and joy which is the reflection of heaven from the burnished experiences of an enlightened soul.

4 *   F

I ask no young man or maiden to look upon a religious life as a life of toil and gloom ; I do not ask you to enter upon a religious life feeling that you are assuming a burden which you must bear till your nature is worn out. I come to where you are, and I strike on the rock, and say, "O ye dead, come forth into life!" I touch your blinded eyes, and say, "Look! behold!" I put my finger to the portal of your ears, and say, "Hear the Word of the Lord, ye that are deaf!" I invite you to manliness. Receive moral power. Use all the faculties which God has given you in such a way that they will give you the fullest liberty and the fullest power possible.

Is there anything in this world that grows so low as love? Is there anything anywhere that is so stunted? It grows as an evergreen grows in Nova Zembla, where the winter is long, and the summer is short, and where it can get but six inches from the ground. But when you carry it further south, it springs up and carries its stately growth full three hundred feet toward heaven, and stands emplumed and embowered there, showing what it should be, — and what love should be prefigured.

THERE are a great many Christian men that walk up and down our streets, shaking their heads, and talking to young men in a supercilious, worldly-wise way, saying, "Are we not deacons and elders? and do we not know what belongs to vital godliness? And do you suppose it is worth our while to be too scrupulous? My young friend, when you have lived as long as I have, you will have learned a good deal more wisdom than you know now." And so they wink at indiscretions and dishonesties essentially as mean as the Devil, — and the meanest thing in the world is the Devil. Do you not suppose that such men are infidels? Do you not suppose they are crucifying the things that are right, the things that are true, the things that are pure? They sacrifice every quality that belonged to the nature of Christ Jesus. They deride and sacrifice every moral attribute which He possessed. And in sacrificing these, they sacrifice the Lord that bought them. I think they are the worst infidels in the world. No, no; they are not, either, as long as they keep in the shop; but when they walk about, when they go into the homes of the poor, and begin also to apply the same wretched infidelity to public questions, to the rights of men, to great principles, — for principles are the lines of latitude and longitude by which God divides the events of time, — when they begin to apply that same withering selfishness to human proceedures, and attempt to bring questions of right and wrong down to the measure of the counter, rather than to that of the golden reed of God's sanctuary, they are even worse infidels than they were before.

I bid you, therefore, to beware of the infidelity of the counter. And I also bid you to beware of the infidelity of the Church ; or of the enlarging of a man's right to do wrong, under the cover of doctrines and ecclesiastical expedients ;— for never, since the world began, has there been more iniquity committed than under the priest's cloak, synodical or conventional. Christ has been crucified by religious men for religious purposes. The greatest wickednesses that have taken place in my life has the Church winked at, and winked at for expedient reasons. Religion has ridden the earth as a red dragon. It has been the torment of men the world over. Not the religion of Jesus Christ, but the religion of organized bodies

of men who take counsel of their own selfishness and
folly. I bid you to beware of all such religion as this.

———

SOME men seem to think that the glory of the Church
consists in being let alone. What they esteem above all
other things is *peace.* A green mantling pool of what
they call orthodoxy, with a minister croaking like a frog
solitary, — that is their conception of a Christian church
in a state of prosperity. But, according to the Bible, we
are warriors. The battles we fight, however, are not
battles of blood, but battles of love and mercy. We are
sent to carry, not the sword and the spear, not rude violence, but conceptions of higher justice, nobler purity,
wiser laws, and more beneficent customs. The weapons
of our warfare are not carnal. With these we contest,
and we will contest, against rage and wrath and bitterness, knowing that He that called us and sent us is the
God of battles, and will guide us and give us that victory
which, if worth anything, is worth achieving in the se-
verest conflict. For victories that are cheap, *are* cheap.
Those only are worth having which come as the result
of hard fighting.

———

HOW strange a combination of circumstances, that the
Cross should have been lifted up so near to a garden;
that the garden, of all places, should have held, amidst
its treasures, such a thing as a sepulchre hewn in a rock;
that thus a cold grave should have been unbosomed
among flowers, and waited, for weeks and months and
years, for the coming of its sacred guest! And now, how
striking the picture! A few words, and the whole stands
open to the imagination, as to the very sight! The two
women, side by side, silent and yet knowing each other's

thoughts, with one grief, — with one yearning, — with one suffering! Home was forgotten, and nature itself was unheeded. The odorous vines, the generous blos-soms, the world of sights around them, were as if they were not. There was the rock, and only that to them. There was neither daylight, nor summer, nor balm, nor perfume. There were no lilies by their feet, nor roses around them; for though there **were** ten thousand of them, there was to them only that cold, gray, sepulchral rock. **See** what **a life** theirs had been.

THE experience **of every fresh mourner is, "I** knew **that** Death **was in the world, but I never** thought that my beloved could die." Every one that comes to the grave says, coming, " I never thought that I should bury my heart here." Though from the beginning of the world **it hath been so**; though the ocean itself would **be** overflowed if the drops of sorrow, unexpected, that have **flown** should **be** gathered together, **and** rolled into **its deep** places ; though the **life** of **man**, without an excep-tion, has been taken **away** in the midst of his expecta-tions, **and** dashed **in** sorrows; **yet no man learns the** lesson **taught by these facts, and every man lays out his paradise afresh, and runs the** furrow of execution round **about it,** and marks **out its alleys and** beds, and plants **flowers and fruits, and** cultures **them** with a love that **sees no** change and expects no sorrow !

No man acquainted with men need **have any** philo-sophical scruple **in** believing in the **existence of evil** spirits. If there are any spirits **worse than some** men, I **am sorry** for them ! No man who watches what men do **to each other need have any scruple as to** the belief that evil spirits are occupied in tempting men. We can conceive of nothing done by a spirit, in the way of malignant temptation, that is worse than that which we see every day among living men. And those who doubt whether a benevolent God would allow a malign spirit to tempt His creatures, surely must have lived with their eyes shut. The question is settled in every street, the question is settled in every one hundred men, that God does allow men to live, whose business seems to be very largely that of pleasing themselves by injuring others. Those who have doubts on this subject cannot have weighed or considered the unmistakable and indisputable fact, that God does allow bad spirits in the flesh to tempt men to evil. Nor do I know why there should be any reason to suppose that He does not allow bad spirits out of the flesh to do the same thing.

NOBODY is without his equivalents. If a man is very impulsive, he says, "O, if I could be as cool as that man is!" The equator is always talking about icebergs, and icebergs are always talking about the equator. If a man is very phlegmatic, he says, "It takes me longer to get agoing than it does my neighbor to get through. I wish that I was quick." The other says, "I am like powder and I go off like powder. I wish I was cold like this man." Nobody, I say, is without his equivalents. If you are phlegmatic, you have disadvantages which an impulsive man has not; but you also have advantages which he has not. You have your platform, and he has his; and you are not to stand looking and coveting each other's peculiarities. You are to accept your nature such as it is, and study how you can carry it in such a way as to glorify God and serve your fellow-men.

Could that be a wise judgment that was founded upon the chaff, the husk, the stubble of the field, — ignorant of the grain, of the fruit? Can that be a satisfying judgment of men which includes only the instruments by which they grow, and leaves out the very fruits which these appendages and instruments were set to nourish? As the inward state does not represent itself in the outward life, so neither is the outward life an index of the inward state. The richest often are the poorest; the happiest often the least happy. The most sorrowful are fullest of joy. Misfortune is felicity; prosperity, bankruptcy. If you would know the meaning of these solemn words of infinite wisdom, — "He that findeth his life shall lose it, and he that loseth his life for my sake shall find it."

When the sun disappears below the horizon he is not down. The heavens glow for a full hour after his departure. And when a great and good man sets, the west is luminous long after he is out of sight. A room in which flowers have been is sweet long after the flowers have been taken away. They leave a fragrance behind. And a godly man who lives unselfishly and disinterestedly, and seeks the good of other men, cannot die out of this world. When he goes hence, he leaves behind much of himself. There have been many men who left behind them that which hundreds of years have not worn out. The earth has Socrates and Plato to this day. The world is richer yet by Moses and the old prophets than by the wisest statesmen. We are indebted to the past. We stand in the greatness of ages that are gone rather than in that of our own. But of how many of us shall it be said that, being dead, we yet speak?

MEN must not compare their own peculiarities with
their neighbors', and say, " Their constitutional tendencies
are such that they can easily restrain their faculties from
working in wrong directions, and they ought to do it; but
I am so organized that I cannot do it, and it is of no use for
me to try." I assure you that by faith and patience you
can do it. There is release for you from your evil inclinations, if you will but employ the powers which God has
given you with which to overcome them. The crooked
can be made straight. As a crooked piece of timber can
be made straight though its nature cannot be changed, so
a man's faults can be corrected though his natural disposition cannot be rooted out.

WE all know what is meant by a professional air.
The actor, the physician, the merchant, the sailor, the
schoolmistress, the minister of the Gospel, — any of them
can be told almost as far as they can be seen. You certainly can tell them if you talk with them. As men that
work in the midst of odors carry about in their raiment,
if not in their very persons, the savor of the things in
which they work, so there seems to be a perfume of the
business a man follows that strikes into him. When you
see a professional man, you feel that he is a professional
man, from his looks and his manners. We can easily distinguish the great sects which prevail in this country by
the peculiarities that mark them.

Now just such a stamp is apt to be put upon our piety.
It is a certain smooth-speaking; a pious way of talking;
a restricted, narrowed, measured thing. Men that are
Christians, or are trying to be Christians, seem to think
that Christian character requires suppression: not so
much opening out as shutting in; not so much the carry-

ing of a lion-like front that drives evil away, as the carrying of one's self in such a way that no lion can see him,
and nothing can get at him. There is a cowardly, white-
faced spirit of professional piety in the world. Thank
God, it is not as common as it was. It becomes less and
less common, I think, every year. We are in a transition
state out of it. Yet there are many things that tend to produce a want of robust, open-faced, upright, manly piety.

You have seen hedges, and you have seen forest-trees.
Of all formal things in the world, a clipped hedge is the
most formal; and of all the informal things in the world,
a forest-tree is the most informal. Now there are many
persons that think Christians should be hedges, and that
every spring and autumn they should undergo a Gospel
shearing, so that they shall have regular angular sides.
But the true idea of Christians is that they are to be like
cedars of Lebanon, — great rugged growths of centuries,
that never think whether this branch goes ten yards beyond that one or not, but which attain greatness of stature, and amazing strength and endurance. An old cedar
of Lebanon will suck more sap from among rocks, than
any of our hedges will out of the deepest ground ever dug
by the gardener's spade.

I UNDERSTAND by *law* nothing except an index of the
way in which God's own power acts all the time. When
we see a law, we see that which signifies the way in which
God invariably acts under certain circumstances; and
God's laws are nothing but words applied to habits of administration in the Divine Mind. And when you search
a law of nature, you search the way in which He reveals
Himself in certain administrative departments, and the
way in which He always acts in such departments.

GOD'S sovereignty is not in His right hand; God's sovereignty is not in His intellect; God's sovereignty is in His love. "I will have mercy on whom I will have mercy, and whom I will I will harden." He stands in the plenitude of all-comforting grace, — grace not to be given to those that have, but grace to be given as raiment is given to those that are naked; grace to be given as medicine is given to those that are sick; grace to be given as food is given to those that are hungry; grace to be given as charity is bestowed on those that are needy. God supplies, not the supplied, but the unsupplied; he strengthens not the strong, but the weak; he comforts not the rejoicing, but the sorrowing.

———

THERE are a great many persons that are superstitious of the Sabbath-day, of the Bible, of prayer, and of religious reading and conversation and institutions. Now these things are admirable. The Sabbath-day, the Bible, prayer, religious reading, religious conversation, and religious institutions, are indispensable to the present condition of the race and the world, and they are neither to be lightly spoken of, nor at all ridiculed or condemned. But then they are not religion. They are the means for educating men in religion. They are instruments merely for the production of a certain result, and not the result itself. A man may have flails endless, and not have wheat, although flails are the things for getting out wheat when you have it. A man may have pigments, and brushes, and canvas, and yet not have pictures, although these are the things for making pictures. Raphael, and Titian, and Correggio, would have had no pictures if they had not had fingers, — though I doubt not they would have come nearer to it than many do that have fingers and brushes.

Ploughs and harrows, and hoes and spades, are indispensable to the farm and the garden; but a man should not worship a plough, or a harrow, or a hoe, or a spade, as if it was the thing which it was made to produce. Many persons confound the means with the end in moral things, although they never do in ordinary things. Many persons have great scrupulosity of conscience about the use of means; but the absence of higher qualities of manliness, the violation of them, the total sacrifice of them, — these things give them little pain. Many men are exceedingly careful of the Sabbath-day. They are exceedingly careful of the Bible. The Bible, — why, it would shock them beyond measure if a child should handle it irreverently. It gives them great pain to see any disrespect shown to the Bible. They carry it as the old priests carried the ark of the covenant. About all the things that relate to religion as educating means they are very scrupulous. But when it comes to those qualities for which these were given, for which these are the machinery, for which these are merely the schoolmasters, — when it comes to unmistakable truth; when it comes to the most transparent sincerity; when it comes to faith in God; when it comes to courage, and simplicity, and unselfishness, and meekness, — when it comes to these, they have no scruples. The idea of striking the Bible gives them great horror; but the idea of striking a man, that is God's temple, has little or no effect upon them. And yet, when the round earth shall burn, the Bibles will burn too. But when the round earth shall burn, not one living soul will burn. All the wide world is but the tool of God for the development of the one fruit, — man. For man was that fruit which hung upon the tree in the garden, and man is to be the fruit issuing therefrom. This fruit, if plucked too soon, will ripen yet. It is the fruit which God means by the husbandry of time, — by all the institutions of the world. And what kind of piety is this **that** stickles for a Sunday, and does **not** care for a generation or a race? What kind of piety is this that stands tremulous with superstitious fear for church regulations, for religious ceremonies, and for days, but without concern lets world-currents flow deep as **the currents** of the Dead Sea over generations and races? **It is** that kind of piety which existed when Christ condemned the Scribes and Pharisees as hypocrites, and which consisted in putting the instruments above the end to be accomplished.

No man is prosperous whose immortality is forfeited. **No** man is rich to whom the **grave** brings eternal bankruptcy. **No man is** happy upon whose path there **rests** but a momentary glimmer of light shining out between clouds that are closing **over him** in darkness **forevermore**.

WHILE you are talking about distributing Bibles, really, in men's esteem, you are Bibles yourselves walking through the streets and in places of business. Do not you know that hundreds of men judge the truth or falsity of religion by what you **are** and what you do? Do **not you know that men are wont to** say, "O, the preacher drones **and drones** about **virtue**, but just see how his church lives. **As I** understand it, virtues are things that are to be looked for in the **life**. The doctrine that a man preaches is to be judged of by what his people are."

HUNDREDS of men fail by the nervous scrupulosity by which they mean to prevent failure. For we do best the things which we do without special thinking. Were a man to attempt to walk upon a beam six inches wide, lifted eighty feet above the ground, he would begin to think, " What would become of me and of my family if I should fall? He would endeavor to put forth skill in walking; and the moment he did that his steps would be loose, tremulous, and uncertain. But lay that beam upon the ground, and he would walk it from end to end as if it had the width of the whole floor in its six-inch face. In the one case he would fall because he took so much care, and in the other case he would succeed because he took so little care.

***

CHRISTIANITY does not disdain fear, nor conscience, nor circumspection, nor watchfulness against evil. It enforces these things heartily and often. But they are incidental. It relies mainly upon the direct energy of a man's faculties in things that are good. It seeks not to repress life, and keep down growth, because abundance of being is more difficult to restrain. Rather, it urges men to seek right things with such force, and with such persistence, that no strength shall be left for wrong ones. We are to overcome evil by doing good, and by being good.

***

WE blame no one that for his own sake he keenly feels the pangs of separation; but we do wonder that there is no more generosity in the love which we bear to our dear ones, and that the full and glorious certainties which illumine their condition when they have passed beyond us, do not cast back some light of joy upon our grief! We mourn as those that have no hope; whereas our mightiest griefs should be embosomed in hope and calm certainties of joy.

You sometimes see people who never impress you as having any depth of moral life, any richness of inward nature, any power of being, either in heart or soul; but who oppress you with such an intolerable conscientiousness about trifles, that you almost wish that they would break forth into violence, into anything that had life and grace of liberty in it! They step so many inches at a pace; they lift their hand in regulated gestures; they drop their sentences as if each word were a stiff metallic type, faced, and nicked, and registered. The tediousness of such men is almost beyond endurance. They are no more representative of true Christian conduct, than a dead and dry stake is representative of a living tree.

A MAN that is afraid is never a man. A man may have fear as a speciality, and yet be manly; but where that is characteristic, — where a man is always in fear, — he cannot be an example of true manliness. There is a kind of fear that is sweet. It is the fear which love begets; this is that "fear of God which is the beginning of wisdom." That tender, tremulous fear that we shall not do all that we ought to do, or all that we wish to do, for the honor and the pleasure of those whom we love, and whose life is more to us than our own, is exquisite, elevating, noble; but that fear which drops far below the sentiments, and moral feelings, and affections, and that produces a state of antagonism between a man's lower interests and his higher feelings, is paralyzing, demoralizing, unmanly.

Let all your things be done in love. As this great rugged globe, with all its jagged hills, hirsute with forests, shagged all over with bush and thicket, and rolling in an atmosphere of light, seems to those who look upon it in far-distant planets as round, and smooth, and radiant as their bright orbs seem to us, so the robust and rugged aspects of a true manhood, revolving in an atmosphere of Christian love, are smoothed and softened to the most attractive beauty. Strength in every part, and love round about all, is the receipt for manhood.

We are moving away, and faster as every cord is loosed that binds us to earth ; faster, as every heart that we loved draws us upward. Let us rejoice. And as in autumn the very earth prepares for death, as if it were its bridal, and all the sober colors of the summer take higher hues, and trees and shrubs and vines go forth to their rest, wearing their most gorgeous apparel, as ending their career more brightly than they began it; so let our spirits cast off sombre thoughts, and sable melancholy, and clothe themselves with all the radiancy of faith; with every hue of heavenly joy.

"Blessed are the dead that die in the Lord."

The problem of human life has in the natural world many illustrations; but it has no real analogies. We are set, at the first, to develop an animal nature, as a socket in which is to stand the spiritual, burning with a steady, guiding light. The progressive subjugation of the lower part of our nature by the higher, the harmonization of the whole round about a central spiritual power, — this has no parallel in the natural world. There are many tendencies which lead toward it, which point at it; but only that. The death of seeds, that they may give forth germs ; the absorption of seminal leaves, that the new plant between them may thrive from their stores; then the subordination of the leaves to the uses of the blossom and the fruit, so that from the beginning to the end all the lower organizations and functions serve and lead toward yet higher, and the very plant dies in ripening, leaving its fruit or its seed to go over to another season, — these things, I say, may *illustrate* the spiritual development of character out of a physical condition, but can do no more. They do not afford an analogue. Man is the highest divine creative development upon earth. That which is the characteristic and glorious element of manhood is our spiritual nature. The body is but the temple; the altar fire and holy service are within. That which is our real life can be seen only by its effects; never in itself. The reality of our life, the fulness of our being, the richness of God's gift to us, divine, immortal, glorious, is invisible. No one has ever seen the man that is in man.

MANY persons mistake the province of forethought and calculation, and attempt to carry themselves in the details and minute particulars of life by them. They rigidly inspect every act and experience, as though every act and experience must be taken up and looked at conscientiously, and narrowly, and watchfully. They go about with looks precomposed. They are sure to measure their steps. They will not laugh without a properly considered reason. If some wag surprises them into a laugh, they run back and look to see if they ought to have laughed. Everything in them seems to be drawn out as tape measures are, and seems, like them, to have a spring, which causes it to fly back instantly, and to be measured off into inches and fractions of inches. There is nothing about them which reminds one of natural clusters, or tendrils, or moss, or wild-flowers. Everything about them is after the pattern of yardsticks, and surveyors' chains. They are a sort of conscientious arithmetic. Their mouth acts, not as flowers do, obedient to the sap beneath; but as do the locks of safes full of gold, into which a formal iron key must needs be thrust whenever you open them. Can there be anything in this world so intolerable as the doing everything on purpose? He is a nuisance that is ever self-poised, self-conscious, self-measuring! that is forever studying and measuring God and the universe with reference to Self. Such complete addiction in thought and deed to one's self, and to what concerns him alone, is the quintessential idea of selfishness, instead of manliness.

THERE is an infidel "don't care," which is the Devil's net to catch the heedless; and there is a Christian "don't care," which is a cord of God to draw men toward heaven. A man who forms a purpose which he knows to be right, and then moves forward in its execution, without stopping to inquire whether the individual steps which he takes are just what they should be, and without caring what their immediate consequences may be, is a manly man. There are a hundred that will repair a mistake made by such a man where there is one that will repair a mistake made by one always fearing. There is something in human nature that responds to manly courage wherever it is found.

AH, what mean Christians coward Christians are!

5   G

They are not fit to be in my Father's house. A man that professes to be an heir of God, forever evading or backing out of difficulties, forever studying to know how he may avoid trouble, I am ashamed of such a relation! He is no relation of mine. He does not belong to my Father. He has none of my blood in him; for my blood is of Christ. A man that is afraid of right and its consequences, of justice and its consequences, and of manhood and its consequences, is so much a Christian, that, of all sinners, surely, he *is* the chief!

CHRISTIAN character can never be Scriptural or according to the Scripture ideal, which is only an inventory of negatives. **There is,** in Christian character, much that is negative. Unquestionably, "Thou shalt not" constitutes a very **large part of the** Christian teaching, but "Thou shalt," a much larger part. It is very important that a man should *not* swear; that he should *not* lie; that he should *not* gamble; that he should *not* steal; that he should *not* drink to intoxication; and that he should *not* eat to gluttony. We are to build these negatives along evil ways, like fences along precipices. And I do not ridicule nor dissuade from negatives. But some seem to abide in them, and to think that they have met the requirements of religion when they have withheld themselves from positive wrongs; whereas we are to develop the actual graces. There is to be a forthputting in things that are right.

It is not good husbandry that keeps the plough going so that no weeds can grow, nor anything else. Good husbandry keeps down the weeds, to be sure, but does it for the sake of letting corn grow. And there must be a positive crop developed of virtue before all the conditions of religion are fulfilled. No man can have a manly Christian character who is merely reserved, restrictive, conservative; who avoids evil, but does not produce much positive good.

THESE qualities of truth and honor, which the world appreciates and admires, and which the Bible recognizes and commends, constitute one of the developments of a Christian character. If you have these qualities, men, after they have associated with you for years, will bear this testimony respecting you: " He is like a glass beehive. You can always see what his motives are. He is full of honey. The more you know him, the better you will like him. He is true and honorable." But there are men who are like another kind of beehive, — one in which the bees are all dead, and there is nothing left except empty comb, and miserable moth-millers.

THE soul is formless, is shadowless. No eye beholds it; no hand handles it; no pencil may draw its lineaments. The mother that gave birth to her child; that overhung the cradle; that carried her babe imbosomed; that studied the girl's girlhood, youth, and womanhood, till the cloud of love opened and hid her in the wedded life, — even the mother does not know the girl nor the woman. Nor does he that takes her know her, when she is taken; nor even she herself. Our life is hinted, but it is hidden. It gleams out at times; it flashes in sparks upon us. None has seen the full orb, or known the full measure of it. We stand before each other as volumes of books. The binding and lettering are plain enough; the contents are unknown, or but dimly suspected. We are like books in which some things are to be hidden

from the common reader as unsafe, and at every few par-
agraphs the critical things are expressed in a dead language. So in human life, the simplest things are read;
the interior **things are not** legible.

THE very slender hold which Christ has taken of our
life is nowhere else shown so much as in the wantonness
of our grief and surprise at the death of our beloved ones.
Why should they not die ? Were they given to us that
we might sequester them? Does no one else love our
children **but** ourselves ? Are we to employ our love as
chains and bonds, that we may bind them forever to
the earth ? Shall **we girdle** them with our selfishness ?
Were they sent into **life as** into a campaign ? and shall
we mourn that the battle is quickly fought, so that it be
victorious ? **Were they** sent into life scholars and ap-
prentices ? and shall we mourn **that** their apprenticeship
is so soon ended, **and their indentures broken; that they**
are so soon graduated and their diplomas awarded ? I
have never seen any man hanging crape **upon trees** because the blossoms had fallen, that the fruit might swell ;
but I see people putting crape upon their doors, and
upon their own persons, because summer has come sooner **to** their children and their companions than they
thought.

WHEN **men** have lived long, and outlived strength and
activity, we do not marvel that they die ; but we think
that early dying is mysterious. That God might en-
wreath the year, and leave not one moment without a
blossom, He hath appointed flowers for every period.
Some things are made to blossom in earliest spring, some
in latest ; some in early summer, some in midsummer.

Multitudes are appointed for the autumn, and some God sets to put wreaths on the very brow of winter. In like manner, there are different periods of blossoming out **of** life.

You have probably noticed that when men walk across a stream on stilts, if they look at their feet to see where they step, their head begins to swim, and very soon they have to swim or drown ; whereas, if they fix their eye upon a single object on the opposite bank, and never look at their feet at **all**, they reach the other side in safety. Now, if a man stands looking at this world, he gets dizzy and intoxicated, and falls ; whereas, if he fixes his eye upon the bank of the eternal world, he walks straighter in this world, and is more sure of reaching the other side in safety.

I send to you, my congregation, the tidings of the departure of one who a few years ago was gathered, with a great multitude besides, into the membership of our church, but whom God hath lifted up and glorified in the church of the first-born in heaven. She is separated from you ; but even more from me. From her very youth she was reared under my eye, and in such endearing intimacy, that it is like the taking of one of my own. She went forth into a far land, but hath gone still farther. Most fair was she in going, but now still fairer. A pilgrim, she sought for knowledge and for beauty in a distant land. Better knowledge and higher beauty she hath found in a better land. For her the gate of heaven opened forth from Italy. The old city of Milan has always been reverend to me, with venerable associations of history ; but hereafter, when its name is mentioned, not first will come to my mind **its** galleries rich in art; its architectural structures; that wondrous cathedral, that lifts up its white and glittering spires and pinnacles against the background of the Alps: hereafter, **to me, it is** the city from whence God called **Annie** Howard to that more glorious city whose builder and whose maker is **God.** Her earthly work is done. The education of tears, of strifes, of sorrows and griefs, is suddenly **ended.** She was nearer perfect than we knew, since God saw that it required but to change the climate, and the fruit was **ripe.** A character that seemed destined to long life for its necessary development is now rounded up and completed in the bliss and blessedness of the eternal state. Mourners there are, but we are not of them. We stand and look upon that shore unwet with tears, and see that nothing **hath suffered harm. That which has** fallen is that which **was made to fall. That** inward life hath blossomed and ripened far beyond the reach of our earthly knowing.

THE promise of God is not this: "Do you declare what you want, and be pious, and I will see that the plan which you mark out is filled up." He does not promise that if we will draw a check, filling up the blank **with the** sum which we want, He will sign His name to it. **And** for this simple reason; men are fools, and God is wise; **and He** will not permit men to destroy themselves. History has shown that if men could have their own way, if they could have their wants fulfilled, it would be the undoing, I will not say of ninety-nine in a hundred, but, probably, of every one of us; and therefore, God, who loves us so well, will no more permit us to mark out the things which we are to have, than a parent will say to a

child, " What do you want?" and then promise to give it
what it asks for. It would want the razors, the tempting
bottles of medicine, the wine and brandy, (till it had
tasted them!) and such like things. Therefore, the parent knows that it is not best that it should be allowed to
have what it wants. Till it ceases to be a child, the parent must decide what it shall have.

I HAVE no doubt that the Devil overreaches himself
and cheats himself; but in any transaction between you
and him, he is longer-headed than you are. And if a
man sells his principles for secular prosperity, he shall
find in the end that the writings drawn and the promises
made were all spurious. Honesty is the best policy;
and of honesty, that which has the most of God in it is
the best.

IF you are to spend your life as a poor man, you can
better afford to be poor if you are a true Christian, than
if you are not. If you are to spend your life in moderate
circumstances, those circumstances will be a thousand
times better to you if you are a true Christian than if
you are not. If you are to attain to wealth, or to emi-
nence in literature or statesmanship, or to power, or to
influence, it will be better for you to be a true Christian
than for you not to be one. Wherever you are to be,
and whatever you are to be, in the ordination of God's
providence, a spirit of Christian manliness will be a help,
and not a hindrance, to you. No man need feel that he
cannot take upon himself a Christian life because it will
stand in his way; no man need feel that it is necessary
for him to attend so exclusively to his external affairs
that he has not time to look after religion; for Christ

stands, saying, "A spirit of righteousness such as God's kingdom propounds and demands is every way favorable as a condition of success and of happiness in human life."

———

MEN that reject religion in favor of indulgence, do not stand any chance of permanent prosperity. Such men are like gypsies that, by some freak of fortune, are turned into a magnificent mansion, well built, well furnished, and well stored with works of art. These gypsies go to work and break to pieces the exquisitely carved furniture, pull down the rare pictures, and strip the house of all the valuable things in it, and burn them, in order to make their pot boil, and thus to serve their lower nature, until, by and by, the whole dwelling is desolate, and bleak, and barren. And men who reject religion and serve their passions, are doing the same thing. They are kindling those lower fires at the expense of everything broad, and fine, and beautiful in their higher nature. And though the process may go on with some sort of success for a little time, it will not be long before they will be as bankrupt in secular things as they are in spiritual. The cases that are exceptions to this are rare.

———

IT was a remarkable saying of one of the Revolutionary heroes, when Congress, instead of passing a bill for more soldiers, recommended a day for fasting and prayer, that there might be a good deal in fasting and prayer, but he had noticed that God's providence was on the side of strong regiments. I have noticed that God's providence is on the side of clear heads. I believe that there is a good deal in God's providence in this regard: that wherever a man walks faithfully in the ways which God has marked out for him, *providence,* as the Christian says, — *luck,* as the heathen says, — will be on that man's side; and I do not believe that fire and water, and wind and earth, and all the seasons, will work into the hands of a man who refuses to walk in the ways which God has marked out for him. In a long run you will find that God's providence is in favor of those that keep His laws, and against those that break them.

As we know the odorous vines of rare and exquisite flowers which are grown behind high, opaque garden walls only by the fragrance which they waft to us through the air, while they themselves are invisible; so are we conscious of the heavenly and spiritual elements of noble natures about us, rather by their effects upon us, than by any open spectacle of them.

. I HAVE taken notice that upon the tops of our churches which have steeples they put weathercocks; and I have taken notice that those weathercocks run their nose around hither and thither with the wind the whole year. You can tell by our churches which way the wind blows. But I have taken notice that while these weathercocks revolve around, there is an iron rod on which they are fastened that stands pointing, in storm and sunshine, by night and by day, straight up toward where God lives. Men are the weathercocks in human affairs, and we are apt to look at them, and not to see the heaven-pointing iron finger. Men that look only at these weathercocks are always shifting in their moods and expectations. If we would but look higher than these, to Him that lets the winds blow, and holds them in His hands, we should

not be subject to such mutations, such fears, such expectations of disasters, such troubles.

No truths that are distinct from matter, and are in
their nature spiritual, ever seem so full and perfect when
you have embodied them in words, as when they exist
merely **in** the form of ideas ; and we are forever restat-
ing them, hoping to clothe them in stronger words **and to**
present them to the mind and heart with yet clearer
impress. But you never can do it. You never can incarnate a thought perfectly. It is too much for words.
And much less can you incarnate one principle that un-
derlies another.

THERE is no such thing as immediatism. Immediatism
is the fool's philosophy. **Cause and** effect are universal ;
and between **all growths there must be** room for the lev-
erage of causation. There is nothing **to which this truth**
is more applicable and important than this : that all **de-**
velopment of the soul toward character takes place little
by little. To-day in one direction, to-morrow in another ;
to-day by one instrumentality, to-morrow by another ;
and what the whole of these accumulating parts and
results is to be doth not yet appear. It is an invisible
process. It is a growth by **parts** toward a whole ; but
a growth which to **the end of this life will** still remain
fragmentary.

Look upon some building in **process of** construction.
All round about it are stones disconnected. The architect knows for what they were cut, but you do not. **Wheth-**
er it is cornice or window-cap, whether it is top of this
column or of that, you do not know. Vast timbers, in
the framer's mind fitted for their places, and brought

together here, give to your eye no indication of their function or their position. They lie around in their several heaps. As the workmen hoist them to their places, some order seems to begin. Yet it doth not appear what the whole is to be; nor will the beauty and fairness of the whole appear until it is completed. And what a building is whose materials are gathered and gathering ready for construction, that is man in this world, — a creature whose parts are yet under the hammer. This virtue, that grace; this self-denial, that restriction; this courage, that patience; this faith, that love; this sentiment, that affection, — all these varied elements, touched now by one instrument, and now by another, form, little by little, but never shaped into a whole in this world, that structure which is to rise into perfectness in the other life.

No man is a Christian in any typical sense of the term; no man presents a type of Christianity, who lives simply by force of duty. If there is no love in you; if there are no bubbles that reflect heaven before they break; if there is no singing joy; if there is no cheerfulness; if there is no spontaneousness; if there is no automatic life, then,.although you may be a Christian, you are a Christian in the same sense in which a chicken is a bird when it is just breaking the shell, when it cannot run, nor fly, nor do anything except peep. You are like an unfledged robin in the nest. And how different is the robin that is grown, and that can mount up and make circles through the air in its flight. The peculiarity of Christian life in its characteristic elements, is, that it has so taken God to be its Father, and Christ to be its elder brother and Saviour, and the service of God in all purity and nobleness to be its delight, that it becomes spontaneous. It is joyful living! not drudgery, nor even duty.

BEFORE **you** can tell whether a man is prosperous or not, you must go into the man himself; you must go and see how he lives in his soul; you must go and see what his secret thoughts are. I tell you there is more joy to many a pauper who looks at the sun and the **grass and** the flowers, and listens to the birds from the almshouse window, than there is to many a millionnaire. I have known a good many of these rich men. I always make friends with them, that I may find out what sort of men they are, what kind of a life they live, and how they enjoy themselves. I was very much struck by a fact that was related to me of a very rich man — he is well known **in New York, but I will not** mention **his** name — by his agent. Said he, "**I have often heard** him turn in his **bed** in the night, saying, 'O God! O God! O God! When will it be morning?'" It did me good! When a **man** has built his bed out of hard gold, he does not sleep any easier than he would if he had built it of iron or stone. When a man builds his life out of metals, he must have a metallic life.

HE is rich who is inwardly rich. He is poor who is inwardly poor. He is prosperous for whose spiritual culture all things work together. In the vineyard, we measure the cluster; not the leaves and the rank-growing vine. And it is the fruit that we must measure in men. They that care for the body only, are like gardeners who fill their conservatory with flower-pots, and these with compost, but forget to put seeds therein, or, flowers. Dirt and pottery are all the flowers they have.

For the most part, natures rich in moral elements have risen only so far above the world as to be able to brood over it; to cloud it with sadness; to **rain down** upon it some drops of cheerless sorrow. It is doubtful whether it be a blessing to receive such an endowment as makes the world too poor to live in, and yet reveals no other world, and no better sphere.

"Stand fast in the faith." There are some men who, because they want to grow, are continually being transplanted; and they think that, because they keep moving from place to place, they are gaining; but they gain nothing at all. Trees that grow fastest stand stillest. Running after every new thing that presents itself does not increase the growth of Christian graces, or anything else that is good. If a man would grow spiritually, he must have a stand-point, a fixed root-place, for **his** religious convictions.

What do you want? Torpor? listless indifference? the quietness of men that preludes spiritual death? **or** times when there is such a sensibility of conscience, such **a rousing** of universal attention, when the hearts of men **are waked up by the** presence and power of God, until men feel that life is earnest, and realize that there is tremendous sweep and importance in moral principles? Are not these times in which men ought to wish to live? What if, here and there, trade and property go down? Nothing goes down till manhood goes down; and **nothing** goes up that does not take manhood up. **It is a** painful thing to lose property, and it is a painful thing to be in disagreement with our fellows: but these are not the **worst things that can befall a** community, if they lead to nobler citizenship, a higher public spirit, a purer administration of affairs, and a more universal justice. Are not these the things for which we have been living? Have you not, many of you, been praying, "Thy kingdom come"? And when God's kingdom comes, crowns go down. The king said, "Thy will be done," and down went his throne. The aristocrat said it, and down went his aristocracy. The old inquisitor said it, and down went the Inquisition. They prayed, "Thy kingdom come," and God took them at their word; forth came the people, back shrunk their oppressors! They ran to hold the kingdom down, while yet they prayed, "Let it come." Tyrants would be infidels if they knew what the New Testament really means. When priests read it, they find much in it that God never put there. The Bible is like a noble mansion built for God's people. It has been wrested from them. It has been held by cunning priests and plotting despots. It is full of the slime of their wicked interpretations. Priests that believe God's Word to be a bulwark of oppression, are jealous of its authority. They pray for its spread. They pray for that kingdom in which they are to be terrific kings and priests. But God sends them insurrections, revolutions, democracies, and free states.

No man has known himself until he has known Christ. Our own will has no potency, and our own affections have but little power to develop our spiritual life. This is a Divine work. No man has ever known himself except through the experiences of faith, of ecstatic love, of holy aspiration, of that self-renunciation which comes with the higher forms of love.

If God should refuse to interrupt the course of men, they would scarcely know the strength of their resistance to Him. It is not when the cable lies coiled up on the deck that you know how strong or how weak it is ; it is when it is put to the test, and is made to sing like the chord of a harp, in times when the ship is imperilled, and the waves are beating fiercely against it. And it is only when men are brought to the test that they can tell what their real nature is, or how strong their instincts and passions are.

————

There are a great many persons that want to be Christians, who have no idea of Christianity, except that it is something sombre, which is to be endured, rather than to be enjoyed. They think they would prefer being Christians to being damned. They are so afraid of the future, they have such a sense of immortality, that the thought of venturing upon the other life without some hope of salvation, is terrible to them. So they say, "I am willing to undergo whatever there may be that is unpleasant in religion, for the sake of securing my eternal welfare"; and they go to priests, and humble themselves before altars, and avail themselves of every conceivable means of grace that is presented to them, that they may escape into the purity and liberty of life hereafter.

O, poor, misguided man! You are called, not unto bondage : you are called unto liberty, — only use not liberty for an occasion to the flesh. God summons you, — and he summons you, not as a master summons his slave, but as a father summons his child. That voice which sounded on Calvary, having gone up to heaven, comes inflected back in tones of cheer and love, and hope and gladness, and calls you: and Christ — ever-living, not now on earth a man of sorrows, acquainted with grief, but in heaven a Prince and a Saviour — says, "My son, give me thine heart"; and this being given, He says, "Now enter into all the royalty .of my possession and domain. Thou, as my child, art also heir with me to an eternal inheritance. Thou art to **be a** king and a priest before God."

Yes, when you are called to be a Christian, you are called unto liberty. You are not called as convicts **to** do penal service **in a** spiritual penitentiary. You are called, rather, to the freedom, the largeness, the sweetness, and the manliness, of a nobler character than ever dawned on the imagination of heathen poet. **To be a true** man according to the ideal of the New Testament, is to have a heart full of faith and confidence in God, and to have all that liberty which love begets in a child that dares to look his father in the face, and call him **by** the most familiar names.

––––––––

A MAN cannot do his duty because he must save the Church! Now the Church is of no more account than a straw, except for the justice and the truth that are in it. When you have sacrificed real piety for the sake of saving the Church, you have killed a man and got a corpse.

––––––––

A GREAT many have a superstitious feeling about reading the Bible. **It is** the effect that reading the Bible has on a man's life and conduct that makes it beneficial to him; but there is an impression that a man has but to read it to be benefited by it. So men carry texts **as** Indians carry amulets, with the superstitious idea that God will bless them to their good. The mere reading **of** the Bible, or carrying of texts, will not do you any good. A man may own a farm, and yet go to the poor-house. A man may be so rich in land that a tenth part of what it is capable of producing would be sufficient to support him, and yet want the necessaries of life. His land must be cultivated, or it will do him no good.

A MAN is not prosperous because he makes money, because he is skilful, or because he has knowledge. That man who is happy; **that** man whose mind is like a well-**chorded harp, and is** responsive to enjoyment; **that man** who knows how to enjoy with his intellect, with his moral sentiments, with his taste; that **man** who knows how to reap joy from **all his** social affections; that man who knows how to stand strong without being debauched by his animal passions; that man who knows how to regulate his physical life; that man who has supreme use of himself all through; that man who is happy in the broad-**est** way, and with the greatest number of fountains of enjoyment, — that man is prosperous. On the **other** hand, a man may be **a ripe** scholar and a rich man, and not be prosperous. A man may be a millionnaire, and yet be so miserable **as to groan all** day and curse all night. **A man may** have all the outside **things** which **the** world affords, **and yet not be a happy man.** One man may have a chest full of excellent tools, and be a bungling workman; while another man may have nothing but a jack-knife, and be **a** skilful workman. One man may have ever so many external means of enjoyment, and be miserable; while another **man** may have scarcely any external means of enjoyment, and be happy. You **must not,** therefore, argue that **a man** is prosperous because he has influence, or power, **or** money, or any of these things. If you want to know **who** are prosperous, find out who are happy.

You would think to look at that bell up in the belfry, "O, such a bell, lifted up so high, — it only needs that some one should pull the rope to make it sound gloriously through the air!" Well, pull the rope; it sounds for all the world like a tin pan! It is cracked. I see men in the old belfry of prosperity; and other men are looking up at them and saying, "O how happy they must be!" You will find them to be good for nothing the moment you subject them to that test.

WE know that the gifts which men have do not come from the schools. If a man is a plain, literal, factual man, you can make a great deal more of him in his own line by education than without education, just as you can make a great deal more of a potato if you cultivate it than if you do not cultivate it; but no cultivation in this world will ever make an apple out of a potato. It can be developed, but it must be developed according to the laws of its own nature. Education will make it more, but will not change its nature. If a man was not born eloquent, he cannot be bred to eloquence; if a man was not born to a sense of color, he cannot be educated to a sense of color; if a man was not born to a sense of form, he cannot be educated to a sense of form; if a man was not born to a quick creative genius, he cannot be trained to it. Where these things exist, they are gifts in the beginning. Education makes them better and more usable; but it cannot create in men what God did not create in them when He started them in life.

THERE is not a man that cannot be made to sin in one way or another. Some men can by lust; some cannot by that, but can by avarice; some cannot by that, but can by ambition; some cannot by that, but can by vanity; some cannot by that, but can by pride; some cannot by that, but can by superstition; some cannot by that, but can by the weakness of sentiment; some cannot by that, but can by the scruples of conscience. Even men that are in the most propitious circumstances, even men that are hedged in by Christian organizations, and moral sentiments, and Gospel sentiments, and every instrumentality calculated to shield them from the evil influences of the world, are perpetually breaking through and over these safeguards, and yielding to temptation.

THE vital difference between heathenism and the worship of Jehovah, as established and recorded in the Old Testament history, was in reality the difference between lust and virtue; between gross, sensuous indulgence and a moral, pure, economic life. The vital force of idolatry was its orgies, — not its theology or mythology.

WE live in the midst of vulgarities; little petty troubles; a thousand mechanical things that have not much juice in them. The greatest part of our life is spent in contact with things that have very little in themselves to reward our sensibility. We must, therefore, have something in the soul to make them glorious.

Walk in the midst of sunlight, and find me, if you can, one thing that is homely. The vine that has lost its leaves, and is without beauty; the leafless tree, that stands homely; the bare post; the dry stick; the moss-covered stone; the old tumble-down rookery, — these are luminous and beautiful in the sunlight.

Now, the sun can pour beauty on things that have no beauty of their own; and there is nothing that has not

the power to take beauty when poured upon it. And
God makes the human soul that loves Christ to be filled
with such a power of hope and faith and love and joy and
enthusiasm, that when they pour it out on daily life it
makes things luminous and beautiful.

WHERE a man turns from evil, and takes hold on good,
there is to be more than meditation or wishing or willing;
there is to be expression. Even thinking cannot be clear
until it has had expression. We must write, or speak, or
act our thoughts, or they will remain in a kind of half
torpid form. Our kinder feelings must have some expression, or they will roll out of the mind as clouds roll
out **of a** hemisphere. Our kinder feelings must *rain*, or
else they will never bring up fruit or flower. So it is
with all the inward feelings; expression gives them full
development. Thought **is the** blossom; action is the
fruit right behind it.

O, HOW easy it is for a man's lips to **say,** " Thy will
be done on earth as it is in heaven!" A red-hot plough-
share running among the roots in your garden, would not
be more blasting to them, than the will of God — if it
were done in your nature — would be to your pride, your
avarice, your idolatrous affections, your lusts, your appetites, **your passions.** And would you dare to open the
doors and chambers of your soul, **and** say, understanding
what you did, " **Walk in,** thou Prince **of** glory, thou holi-
est One, and let Thy **will be done in me!**" Would you
dare to go home to your household, **and ask** that God's
will might be done there? Would you be willing to have
God come into your business, and to have His will rectify
your journals, and ledgers, and bargains? Are you pre-

pared to submit your papers, and plans, and ambitions to God, and say, " Thy will be done in all these things "? Could you take the infinite crookedness of your daily life, and say to God, " Straighten this "? Have you come to that state in which you can say to God, " I am blind, and Thou art all-seeing; Thy will be done concerning me "? It would be like hell and damnation to men, to let God's will come with power and rectification into their practical lives!

EXPEDIENTS are for an hour; but *Principles* are for the ages. Just because the rains descend, and winds blow, we cannot afford to bond on shifting sands.

THE child that is at school, in the beginning of the term, jealously prepares his little bow and arrows, and traps, and springs, and riddles, and puzzles, and what not. Then, they are choice treasures to him, and he mourns if anything befalls them. But when the last days of the term come, how generous he is in distributing them. He tosses them to one and another of his companions, saying, " Here you may have them if you want them : I do not want them any more." He is glad to get rid of them. The things that a month or two ago he guarded sedulously in his treasure-chamber, now have no value to him; for the hunger of father and mother is on him. He says to himself, " Day after to-morrow I am off "; and he cannot eat, nor sleep, nor play, such is the excitement which he feels at the prospect of going home so soon.

Now what home-sickness is to the child away at school, that to the soul is heaven-sickness, which sets us free from the ten thousand joys and sorrows of this world, if we really *are* heaven-sick.

How little you know what will be the effect of what you do when you cast that little black seed of a poisonous plant into the ground. It looks as fine as a seed of the most harmless flower; but how little do you know what it will come to. How little do you know what the plant will be from the seed. And so shall it be with the human soul that grows and grows in pride, in selfishness, and in hostility to the Divine will. Such a soul drops into **death as** the seed drops into the open furrow. **Its root shall** come forth again, it shall lift up its trunk again, it shall grow again; but, oh! who can **tell** what that growth may come to? To what will the unregenerate man come when he grows in the soil of another life? If in all our developments here **we are but seeds,** to what states of wickedness shall we come in that land where all restraints are removed from men, and they **are left to be** swept on by the whole force and impetus of their **depraved natures?**

I think that many people take their troubles by the imagination. I think that more than half that we suffer through fear of troubles, is that which we are made to suffer by magnifying them. You suffer ten times as much in thinking about having your tooth drawn as you **do** in having it drawn. I do not think the surgeon's knife, in whipping through the flesh and around the bone, gives half as much pain as the patient suffers in thinking about having the operation performed. We take our troubles, and turn them over, and look at them; we imagine what form they will assume under such and such circumstances; we make an inventory of them; we muster them, and call the roll, and put them in order, **and march them first this way and then that; we annoy our-**

selves with them as much as possible. Men are infernally ingenious in tormenting themselves with troubles which, ninety-nine times in a hundred, have no existence except in their imagination. For although there are such things as troubles, generally speaking those things that hurt are things that we do not imagine are going to hurt. When grief puts its harness on a man, the place where it rubs and binds is not where there are pads, but where there are no pads; the place where it bears **heavily is where he has make no provision for it.**

THERE is a point of application to persons who suppose that mere reformation is all that is required of a man that is sinful, and that the more radical doctrine of being born again is characteristic of olden times, and is not needed **now.** If the very direction of your life is wrong, if the very cast of your character is wrong, if you are wrong to the very foundation of your being, then no mere varnishing no mere whitewashing, no mere changing of external decorations is sufficient for you. You need to be built over again from bottom to top. **It is the** testimony of Christ, the mild speaker, the sweet **and loving One,** " Except a man be born again he cannot see the kingdom of God." The change that must be made in you is one that starts a man over again in life. And how blessed to me **is** this fact. My heart leaps up, sometimes, at the thought of it. When I see men reeling and staggering with wickedness, striving with vices and crimes, struck **through** with the leprosy of sin, how blessed it **is to me** to be able to say to them, " You can have another chance **in life;** you may throw away all the past, and begin anew; you may be born again, like a little child, and start afresh, **in spiritual life, as if you had** never lived ! " How

blessed and encouraging to those who are weary of the
burden of their sins, and discouraged at every attempt to
make themselves better by successive upbuilding, is this
doctrine of a new birth, **so** deep, **so** efficient, that it
changes a man's will, from one of insubordination, to one
of submission, to the Divine will! **We are** diseased with
sin, and we need a remedy as comprehensive and thorough
as our sickness ; and that we have in the grace of the
Lord Jesus Christ, — that we have in the gift of the Holy
Spirit of God.

It would be a very small thing for the captain of a
piratical vessel to show that he kept it perfectly clean,
that his men were orderly, and that he and they were
guilty of no special violations of the etiquette of life. If
a vessel is a piratical vessel, and at war with every civilized nation on the globe, that is enough to condemn it.
Its organization, the purpose **of it,** is radically and atro-
ciously wrong. And these single virtues **of a** man's
character are of little account, so long as the very foundation of his being is corrupt. It is a small thing for a
man to show that he has never committed any memorable,
flagrant sins. It is far better, of course, for a man to
cultivate virtues, and abstain from vices. **I** would say
nothing to discourage from any virtue, or to encourage in
any vice. But I say that mere right-doing, and absti-
nence from wrong-doing, is not all that is required of men.
A man's whole life is more than any individual act. The
opposition of the heart to God is **of** itself a thing merit-
ing judgment-day condemnation. Nothing more than
this is required to exclude a man from the glory of the
eternal heavens.

WHENEVER you see flowers, understand that there is a meaning in them; and remember that Christ has said, with reference to them, "Consider." You have no right to pass by the smallest, the tiniest, the most inconspicuous flower, and say, "O, it is a little common flower." A common flower? It is God-opened, and God-built; and Christ has said respecting it, "Consider." Yes, there is a meaning in flowers. It is a precious meaning, — one that you need, and one that will kindle up your life, and make your soul glow with radiance. Take it, and profit by it.

————

MEN say, "It is impossible that I should have an emotion of hatred toward God, and never know it. Do you suppose I should not know fire if it touched me? Do you suppose that if a man were to put caustic on me I should not know it? And do you suppose I could have a feeling of hatred toward God and never be conscious of it?" There is such a thing as latent hatred, that must be inflamed before it will manifest itself. Men say, "Do you suppose I could carry fire in my bosom and not know it? I have felt myself a hundred times, and I am not hot." But there may be fire raked up, as well as fire in full glow. There may be a susceptibility of heart that stands prepared, like powder in magazines, to be ignited. A man may be like a military fortification, with implements of war of every kind ready to be brought into requisition the moment the signal gun is fired. But it is a military fortification, though the signal gun may never have been fired, and though not one of these implements has ever been brought into requisition. It is a military fortification, though a particle of powder may never have been exploded in it. It was built for war

6

from foundation to turret, and all the implements it contains were made for war, and they are in readiness to be applied to the purposes of **war** when **the** proper **time** shall come.

Now look at the soul, — castellated, fortified, provisioned, armed. Though the day may not have come when its mighty implements have been used, yet they are ready to be used at any moment **when** the proper circumstances arise. A man may have qualities of mind **which do not** manifest themselves in his life, because the circumstances necessary to bring them into action do not exist.

It is charged, **not that every man has come to a** flagrant outbreak in opposition to the **Divine** Being, but that every man has elements that are opposed to the Divine Being, which, the **moment he is** brought to a realization of God's authority, **will develop** their real character. You are not obliged, **in order to be at enmity with** God, to say to Him, in so many words, "**I will not have** Thee to reign over me." Whether spoken **or not,** that **is** the natural language of the unconverted human heart.

To a resilient nature nothing can be more trying **than** to lie aside from usefulness and be worthléss. If it please God to say to us, "I lead you through dark and critical ways where ordinary and unsustained manhood cannot walk, because I want an example there"; it fires the soul with such a conception of the mission of suffering, that we are able to endure it, and to endure it cheerfully.

THE tree of life, whose **leaves were for the** healing **of** the nations, has been evilly dealt with. Its boughs have been lopped, and its roots starved till its fruit is knurly. **Upon its** top had **been set** scions of bitter fruits, that grew and sucked out all the sap from the better branches. Upon its trunk the wild boar of the forest had whetted his tusks.

But now again it blooms. Its roots have found the river, and shall not want again for moisture ; the grafts of poisonous fruits have not taken and are blown out; mighty spearsmen have hunted the swine back to his thickets, and the hedge shall be broken down no more round about it. The air is fragrant in its opening buds, the young fruit is setting. God has returned and looked upon it, and behold, summer is in all its branches !

In our social intercourse we perceive how differently children behave under restraint. If you attempt to govern one child, you meet him face to face, and he flames at you like a little volcano. The next child you attempt to govern is not one whit more willing to be subdued, but he draws a veil of tranquillity over his rebellious spirit, and glides away as if to obey you, simply to get out of your reach. One colors in the face, and waxes hot, and openly violates your commands ; the other says, " Yes," and goes and does as he has a mind to. Both of them are fractious, and both of them disobey you. It is not always the most obstreperous natures that are hardest to be subdued ; it is oftentimes these soft, gentle natures. There are persons that are amiable, and that go purling through life as little brooks do through meadows ; but no brook runs up stream. There are persons that are worldly and notoriously without God in the soul, whose dispositions are soft and tranquil, simply because their nature works by softness and tranquillity : but they are just as much opposed to the Divine will as if their opposition were more open and declarative.

It is not in vain that I have preached that this life is but God's school-house, in which we are being prepared for an eternity of blessedness **in His** presence. The things that are flying backward and forward in this world are God's shuttles, that carry the thread out of which are to be woven the garments that we are to wear hereafter; and blessed are they whose shuttle carries a thread which shall glow in garments of white evermore.

PAUL had brought near to him — nearer than the things which the senses ministered to him — the eternal realm of blessedness beyond this sphere, the habitation of God's sons, where Christ is ever present with them, inspiring them, and rewarding them, and leading them to higher joys and nobler enterprises **of** usefulness forever and forever. This **was so near to Paul** that he lived in sight of it, and said, "O, these little distemperatures, — this being beaten with rods; this receiving stripes; **this** being shipwrecked; this being in perils of sea and of land; this being cold, and hungry, and thirsty, — these things only tap and hit the body; they do not go inside; they do not strike through. I live in such a nearness to my coming glory, in such a nearness to the invisible and **the** eternal world, that I regard these things as of no account when compared with that. I do not care for them."

And why should we? **We** see the same principle at work every day in little things. If in Kansas the careful husbandman, **whose** starving cattle have but a faint chance of living the winter through, sees a wisp of straw, a handful of stalks, or a particle of hay being wasted, it sorely grieves him. He is so near to the edge of starvation that he cannot afford to have anything wasted.

But go into Illinois and Indiana, where all these things are abundant, and where the herds are their own harvestmen, and tramp down a thousand times more than they eat; and the farmer, when he sees the stack gnawed, and scattered around, knee deep, and being wasted, says, "There is no need of my saving such little things, they are mere trifles; I have so much that I do not know what to do with it."

The apostle, arguing according to the same principle, says, "What is a little waste here? The rinds and crumbs of life, — a little sorrow; a little loss; a little contempt; a few persecutions, and afflictions, and troubles, — what are these in the great circle of God's eternal world? There I am rich and honorable; and what difference does it make if here I am the offscouring of the world?"

———

"I HAVE learned in whatsoever state I am, therewith to be content. I know both how to be abased, and I know how to abound: everywhere and in all things I am instructed both to be full and to be hungry, both to abound and to suffer need; I can do all things through Christ which strengtheneth me." It is as if Paul had said, "I have absolutely subordinated the physical and the temporal, and I regard them as but instrumental to that which is greater, — to my own inward state. I have achieved a complete victory over them. I have overcome all things, so that with my mind fixed upon Christ and upon the image of Christ that is formed in me, I count nothing to be unendurable which tends to build up the manly character of which I have an ideal. And I know when I am hungry to be hungry, and not to care; and, on the other hand, when I come into circumstances of abounding luxury, I know how to accept that and not be harmed by it. I can sit with the barbarian and eat a crust, and be contented and happy; and, on the other hand, when swept by a current of prosperity I am taken into a rich man's house, I do not sit and pout, and criticise, and censure, with lordly stoicism. I understand that there is good in fruit, and bread, and things like these. I love luxury; and I do not fear the want of it. I can go up and I can go down. I can be swept like an ever-swinging pendulum, with riches in one tick and poverty in the other, with joy resounding in one and sorrow in the other; and I know how to take them both in quick succession, and yet to feel that after all such things are mere outward accidents to a man's life, and that in the soul is where the life itself resides." Was there ever a more perfect human nature than Paul's?

"SEEK ye first the kingdom of God, and his righteousness, and all these things shall be added unto you." Christ was speaking to those who were sawing, and hammering, and ploughing, and sowing, and toiling in every way, and trying to get bread, and clothes, and fuel, and the various things that are indispensable to physical comfort. He was speaking to just that sort of men who were accustomed to say, "Self-preservation is the first law of nature." Christ said, "The highest carries the lowest; the greater includes the lesser. Seek first the moral element, — the element of truth and righteousness, — and in seeking that, by the very law of your creation, you cannot help taking the other things with you. They will follow of necessity." If you take the top first you leave the bottom; but if you take the bottom first, that carries the top with it. You can lift the roof and not the founda-

tion, but you cannot lift the foundation and not the roof.
And the foundation of human life is rectitude, righteousness.

WHATEVER men may say, American slavery is not
Hebrew slavery: it is Roman slavery. We borrowed
every single one of the elemental principles of our system
of slavery from the Roman law, and not from the
old Hebrew. The fundamental feature of the Hebrew
system was that the slave was a man, and not a chattel;
while the fundamental feature of the Roman system was
that he was a chattel, and not a man. The essential
principle of the old Mosaic servitude made it the duty of
the master to treat his servants as men, and to instruct
them in his own religion, and in the matters of his own
household; while the essential principle of Roman servitude
allowed the master to treat his servants, to all intents
and purposes, as chattels, goods.

IT seems very strange, — this economy of God, in
which He thrusts into the door of life a million of His
children, saying, "Go, live, and find out how to live."
That is the very point of the Divine economy. The finding
out how to live, you know, is what whets a man
sharp. That is the ordained law of existence.

Whole ages may live and die and not know how much
God has stored up for men through natural laws. We
do not understand their full power and office. We have
an idea of what light is, but we have only a blush of a
knowledge of its entire nature and all its functions. We
hardly suspect the capacity of solar light. Who would
have dreamed twenty-five years ago that the sun was a
portrait painter? Who would have dreamed twenty-five

years ago that every man could possess the portrait of his
friends? Who would have dreamed twenty-five years
ago that the poor soldier, when going to battle, could
carry with him likenesses of his mother, his sweetheart,
and his brothers and sisters, at the cost of a few shillings?
And yet all these powers of the sun to paint pictures
which have but lately been disclosed, it has carried in its
bosom from the beginning of the world. Telescopes
existed in possibility long before they existed in reality.
And all that the sun has yet concealed you do not know.
No man knows what things are still to come to the world
from the sun. The sun is crammed full of blessings to
be unfolded when we have found out the things that are
in it. And all the great natural laws of the globe have
existed from eternity. The fact that they have not developed themselves does not militate against the fact that
they have existed, that God made them, that He has con-
trolled the earth by them, and that they were designed to
work out a great history.

I STAND to declare that justice is worth more than the
cornfields of the continent. I stand to declare that right
between man and man is worth more than all the freights
of all the ships that whiten the sea. I stand to declare
that there is not in the king's crown, nor in the sceptre
of any monarch, such a power as there is in simple
mercy between human beings. I stand to declare that
the secret of national compactness is in national conscience, national affection, and national faith in moral
ideas. And I stand to declare that the period in which
men scoff at moral laws and moral truths is a period of
rank infidelity and utter apostasy. The form of religion
may stand in such a period, but it will be worm-eaten;

it will be dead ; it will be rotten. And if you want to know which way nations are to go to find prosperity, let me tell you that every nation that means to be prospered must steer straight to the light-house of the universe. And what is that? God's heart. Any nation that steers for any other thing will run upon shoals and rocks.

Do not be afraid because the community teems with excitement. Silence and death are dreadful. The rush of life, the vigor of earnest men, the conflict of realities, invigorate, cleanse, and establish the truth.

THE Bible says that everything was made for the sake of righteousness. Men generally feel that perhaps it is so. They hope it is. They do not exactly see how it can be. They do not understand it. They sometimes hope and sometimes despond concerning it. Let us look a little at it, then.

We ought to understand beforehand, that a law may not seem to be enforced which is absolutely enforced.

When the ground breaks, and the grape comes up, I say, "The law of that plant is to develop grape sugar. That which this vine is going to reach after is grape sugar. Grape sugar is what it will tend toward all through its life." I may interfere with it and stop its growth, or maim it, or kill it, or hold it back, or graft upon it some other grape that will not develop sweetness. Or, I may watch it through the first, the second, and the third periods of its growth, and laugh to scorn any man that says it is tending to grape sugar. I may be looking for sugar in a bowl, sugar in lumps, and, looking at the vine, may say, "That's what you call sugar, is it? Great sugar!" And yet, after it has grown for four or five years, and come to maturity, and developed clusters of fruit, then in October, when the berries are ripe, pick one and taste it, and see if there is not sugar in it. See if it has not at last come to sugar. When the vine is growing you can stop, pervert, or check the law, but that does not alter the fact that the law is to seek grape sugar; that if unimpeded it will come to grape sugar; that it was organized to develop grape sugar; and that you cannot change its nature so but that it shall tend in that direction.

So it is in respect to all the great laws of nature. They are so established that they will fulfil their functions in part. They may be held back, they may be masked, they may be perverted, but this does not alter the fact that they are laws.

THE peculiarity of many of the afflictions of life is that they take out a man's marrow, they take the strength out of him; he is left collapsed and feeble, and there is nothing in him to rise up against these troubles. It is quite in vain to stimulate such persons by telling them what others have suffered, giving the old accustomed comfort, telling a man that he is not suffering more than anybody else has suffered, or that the longest night has a dawning. All these truisms of consolation do not help anybody, but hurt a great many. There is but one thing under such circumstances that ever has consolation. When, by reason of afflictions of any kind, life is paralyzed, and there is no sensibility left, if the soul can lift itself up to feel that there is life in God, that there is a vital connection between itself and the life of Christ, that though it die, it shall live, — the simple thought that Christ lives and so shall I, that is an anchor, and that holds a man in this extremity and emergency of grief.

THERE is tonic in the things that men do not love to hear; and there is damnation in the things that wicked men love to hear. Free speech is to a great people what winds are to oceans and malarial regions, which waft away the elements of disease, and bring new elements of health. And where free speech is stopped miasma is bred, and death comes fast.

I WOULD die myself, cheerfully and easily, before a man should be taken out of my hands when I had the power to give him liberty, and the hound was after him for his blood. I would stand as an altar of expiation between slavery and liberty, knowing that, through my example, a million men would live. A heroic deed, in which one yields up his life for others, is his Calvary. It was the hanging of Christ on that hill-top that made it the highest mountain on the globe. Let a man do a right thing with such earnestness that he counts his life of little value, and his example becomes omnipotent. Therefore it is said that the blood of the saints is the seed of the Church. There is no such seed planted in this world as good blood.

AMONG the most exquisitely delicate of human experiences are those which the young child goes through when it begins to quarrel with itself because it cannot help thinking that the parent is imperfect.

WHEN night is on the deep, when the headlands are obscured by the darkness, and when storm is in the air, that man who undertakes to steer by looking over the side of the ship, over the bow, or over the stern, or by looking at the clouds or his own fears, is a fool. There is a silent needle in the binnacle, which points like the finger of God, telling the mariner which way to steer, and enabling him to outride the storm, and reach the harbor in safety. And what the compass is to navigation, that is moral principle in our affairs. Whatever the issue may be, we have but one thing to do, and that is to look where the compass of God points, and steer that way. You need not fear shipwreck when God is the pilot.

Our children come to us in all the seeming of angels. How sweet is the dawn of life! How is the cradle like the opening of the gate of paradise! And yet, who can overhang the unformed, yet shadowy, dreamy beginnings of life in the child, and remember that it comes by sinful parents into a sinful world, bearing a sinful disposition, without feeling that there is a counterbalance to the pleasure which it brings?

The value of things is measured in the great world by their price in market, by their relation to pleasure, by their power to win praise, or to gratify and confirm ambition. Worldly men are perfectly sure of that which they can see, and which their hands can handle. Money is a certainty, and pleasure is a certainty. There can be no question about the reality of power, place, and influence. Houses and lands, ships and stores, goods and stocks, silver and gold, certainly make men rich among men. And these, to worldly natures, are the great truths of life. For these they yield up affection, refinement, honor, virtue itself. Beyond these, and above them, all is shadowy and uncertain. For worldly harvests their sun comes up, their seasons rule. The only providence which they recognize is that which remunerates industry, economy, frugality, and shrewdness. They laugh to scorn the intimation that all these things are but the covers that, like hull and husk, drop away so soon as the grain is ripe, and are of worth only while they serve *it.* But the whole realm of nature is administered for the purpose of evolving and establishing this secret and inward life of man. The true history of the world is to be found in the relation of the outward world to the inward.

IN estimating the dignity of men, the volume and the vastness of their being, we are not to measure them by the use to which they have put themselves, but by the nature of those faculties which God gave them. Insphere man in the infinite realm, project him by the mighty power of his infinite Father, and then, moving along the ways of eternity,— then, when ages have nourished him, and **the full measure of** Divine beneficence hath showered **its** seasons numberless upon him, — then, when stars **have** worn out and weary worlds have ceased their circuits, — then, when God hath wrought out in full **literature of** wondrous wisdom the whole of **that** of which earthly life **was but** alphabetic, —then measure him if you can! **It** is from this foreseen **and** imagined destiny that **we** bring back a light to glorify the cheerless way of rude and un-replenished men.

THE spirit and the letter of Christianity require us habitually to regard man in his essentials, and not in his accidental relations. "Be ye of the same mind one toward another. Mind not high things, but condescend to men of low estate." To be of the same mind one toward another, is to have a feeling of community, a feeling of common universal sympathy; and we are expressly forbidden to do what every one in the proportion in which he is educated tends to do, — to aspire to the exclusive association of those who have risen in the world by reason of the same privileges. They, too, are our brethren, who are undeveloped, unpolished; who perform the menial offices of life; who live narrowly upon slender means. At one blow this command demolishes the customs of the world. It is for the Christian to separate men from their external, transient relations, and to behold them in those greater relations in which all men are alike. Our brethren are not above us nor below us, but on the same level with us. All men are upon one platform and level who stand upon the redemption of Christ, who subsist upon the mercy and sympathy of God, who reach forward to immortality and glory equally and alike. The example of Christ ought to be deeply pondered. It stands in marked contrast with the habits of all classes of men in His time. He does not seem to have thought of men as they stand in societies grouped in classes, separated or united by various customs, nor even as they were separated and classed by the result of their moral conduct. He seems simply and quietly, but always, to have beheld them in their original and spiritual relations, to each other, to God, and to eternity. He approached men from a different point of view from that from which others started. He looked at them from a law of sympathy not ordinarily employed. His example teaches us that our thought is not to be, "Is this man educated? Does he stand high in social life? Is he strong? Is he acute? Is he skilful? Is he rich?" There is no evidence that these questions ever arose in the mind of Christ with reference to any human being. He looked at men in their higher and holier relations. They were the children of His Father. He was elder Brother, and was not ashamed to call them brethren. They were destined to the same eternity which waited for Him. They were **all weak**, vincible by temptation, in need of help, of instruction, of moral stimulus. Their poverty, their rudeness, was the accident. Their **Divine nature was** the characteristic element.

SOME of God's noblest sons, I think, will be selected from those **that know how** to take wealth, with **all its** temptations, and maintain **godliness** therewith. It is hard to be a saint standing in a golden niche.

WHEN the Bible prescribes Christian graces, it always implies love as the motive power; as when we speak of rearing harvests it is always implied that there is a soil. Without love there is no soil for any Christian grace. **If** there be little of it, the fruit of Christian feeling will **be** poor and scant. If there be much, there will be great fruit, and easily **grown. All things are easy to love. It** tames all passions, inspires **all affections, feeds** every generous sentiment, gives both softness and potency, **as its** needs require, to the will, makes the understanding luminous, and by making the whole man like God, makes it easy for him to be godlike to his fellow-men.

IF earthly analogies may at all guide us, there can be no more direct and offensive assault upon God than through His children. A man may draw near to my dwelling to rail at me; may assault my reputation; may lie in wait and plot against my secular prosperity; may overreach me in the market, and hinder me upon the roads of life; may steal from my substance, and mar my enterprise; but he has not yet reached *me*. But let him sully the name of my child, and clothe her with ignominy before the community, and all the globe, were it a ball of fire, would not be hot or vast enough to express the indignation **I should feel.** Through my child he has reached me.

The feeling of justice is **terrible when** stirred up in us in our own behalf; but **we never know the full power of** the feeling until it is stirred in us in behalf of others. I have never felt such indignation in my own behalf as I have for the weak, for the poor, for the enslaved. When great wrongs fall upon them that are ready to perish in **their helplessness, the soul is like Mount Sinai, and its thunderings and lightnings are full terrible! What,** then, may we suppose to be the indignation of Almighty God, who carries in his heart the well-being of every living creature, when He beholds the numberless torments and wrongs inflicted upon **them? What must be the** grandeur of that experience **of Love-wrath,** (such as mothers feel, such as stirs fathers, such as raises lovers for their imperilled ones to the fiery zeal of heroes,) when it exists, not in the small circle of a human soul, with fitful impulses, but in the great rounds and deeps of the Divine nature, with calm intensity, with unchangeable fervor, and with infinite outreachings **of power!**

"THOU *shalt love the Lord thy God with all thy heart,* AND *thy neighbor as thyself."* . That conjunctive particle is a rivet that holds these two sentences together inseparably. Each element is necessary to the completion of the other. But men turn the feint of Solomon to a reality, and cut in two these vital members of the one life. Thus

we have devout men full of religiousness, but caring little
for their fellow-men ; while over against them are superficial philanthropists, full of fussy zeal for humanity, without love for God, **or** solemn depth of reverential sentiments.

As a body of men, the Scribes and Pharisees were not
men of bad morals, more than are many church-members
of the present day. Neither were they men who lacked
fidelity to the religious principles in which they were
educated. The Pharisees were in some respects the
Puritans of their time. They were that portion of the
Jews who stood up for reformed Jewish worship. They
brought back the faith of Moses from its heathen wander-
ings, and strictly adhered to it. They were the Puritans
of the Jews. But they preferred the church to the people, the state to the people, the temple to the people,
their denomination to the people : and their guilt was
simply this : a contempt for human nature ; utter heart-
lessness about the common people. And because they
put burdens upon other men which they would not bear
themselves ; because they were without humanity, and
mercy, and sympathy, notwithstanding they had personal
power, and were faithful to their theologic faith, and were
the most enlightened of the times in which they lived,
Christ crushed them with mountains of denunciation.
There is no such invective as came from the lips of
Christ Jesus against men who were utterly devoid of
sympathy toward their fellow-men.

Do not criticise men's callings ; do not measure between one and another ; especially disarm yourselves of
that infernal tendency to make men discontented in their

various avocations, by comparing them unfavorably with
your own. Arrogate nothing to yourselves or to your
sphere. Avoid carrying yourselves in such a way that
men shall feel hurt by the shadow which you throw
across them, by the snuff of pride, or the chill of indifference.

"In honor preferring one another." This is contained
in the twelfth chapter of Romans, and the tenth verse.
It enjoins an honest desire, springing from unfeigned
sympathy with others' welfare, to see them put forward
in life instead of yourself. There be some to whom
other men's advancement is always a fret and a burden.
There is a spirit of selfishness which leads envious and
covetous natures to esteem another's good so much de-
traction from their own. This is an admirable illustration
of the nature of benevolence by its converse. A truly
benevolent mind is made happy at the prospect of another's good. A mind which is made miserable by another's
benefit, is truly malevolent. The father covets nothing
from the son. She must be a miserable mother that
is jealous of a daughter. Nay, in the mother's heart
there is a glow of triumph, suppress it as she may, as the
child's beauty rises on the one side to take the place of
the beauty that is sinking on the other. As one star
goes below the horizon, its last rays of light are cast in
cheer toward the star that comes from the other. Fathers' and mothers' hearts do these glorious things spon-
taneously, and teach us how easy to those that love are
the most recondite and apparently impossible Christian
graces.

We hear people say, "What makes you preach doc-

trinal sermons? Why do you puzzle our heads with
things that we cannot understand? Why do you not
preach to us the balmy gospel of love? Why do you
not preach about the mild and lovely Saviour?" There
are a great many men that like to hear the sentimentali-
ty of love, who have not the faintest conception of what
the effect and the power of it is to be in them.

I look at the life and disposition of these men who cry
for the lullaby of love, in the family, in the shop, in all
departments of their life, and I find that they abhor love
except on Sunday when I preach on that doctrine of
God's moral government. But if I were to go to them
at their places of business, and say, "I understand that
you take advantage of the circumstances of your workmen, and employ them at one quarter of what they ought
to have, so that they can scarcely subsist on what you
pay them; and as you wanted me to preach about love,
I thought I would come and tell you what the doctrine of
love is as applied to matters of this kind," they would
say, "Religion is religion, and business is business. Go
home, and when I want you to come to my shop and
preach to me I will let you know." In other words, they
want sermon love, poetic love, theoretic love, love that
makes them feel good during the insurance day, — for
Sunday is the insurance day of the week! And they
want me to talk of love because it subdues their fears,
soothes their hearts, and makes them feel pleasant. But
there is a way in which they do not want love preached
even on Sunday, and in the pulpit. They do not want
it preached as a rod of iron, that says, "I am sovereign
and supreme; I stand in you for all; and, in the name of
God, I command that every part of your being, — your
thoughts, your feelings, and your actions, — shall be sub-

ordinate to me." When men have love presented in this way, they do not like it. They like to have it presented so as to allow them to have their own way, and so as to quiet their conscience in their selfish courses.

THERE can be nothing more a violation of the spirit of the Bible, of the law of God, of the feelings of Christ; nothing more an affront and offence before Heaven, than feelings of contempt, bitterness, or hatred toward men. Even indifference and coldness are culpable. Sympathy with mankind is a universal duty. Christ taught us that every man is our neighbor. We are commanded as we **have** opportunity to do good unto all men. There should be an abiding disposition of benevolence out of which should spring incessant acts of kindness. When the **waters** of an inexhaustible spring have been conveyed through pipes to your dwelling, it needs only that **you** should open the vent, and it will gush forth with **power** and copiousness by its own native **force**. Even when **it** is not flowing, it is pressing and urging itself, and longing to flow. Left to itself, night and day it would gush. It must be hindered, it must be stopped, but it needs never to be solicited. There is a well-spring of love which God sinks in the human soul, which throbs without ceasing, and strives to give itself forth. From such a reservoir we need no slow-descending and heavy-rising bucket, **we need no** forcing-pump, nor instrument of power of any sort. **It is its** nature **to** rise **up, to go out.** The kindness **is** always there, always ready and waiting. Only opportunity is needed.

A MAN is, as it were, a **cask** of wine. The figure would have been allowable in the days of Christ, — more allowable, perhaps, than it is in our temperance days! A worm gnaws through a stave. It is a small worm, not half so large as a knitting-needle. The moment he comes to the wine he draws out his head, — for worms are not so fond of wine as men are! — and a drop follows him, — only a drop. Another worm, on the other side of the cask, gnaws through another stave. He gets a drop, and draws back. On each end there are a dozen or twenty other worms eating their way to the wine. Not one of them is as big as a mite; but fifty or sixty of them together, if each makes a hole large enough to allow a drop to pass through it, are sufficient to cause the waste of all the precious contents of the cask. After the lapse of a day, a week, a month, or six months, the vintner goes to see his treasure; and behold, the cask sounds empty as a hypocrite's heart! There is not a drop in it. And yet it looks like a cask of wine. Where have the contents gone? Not one pint has been surreptitiously drawn by the servant that gets blamed, or by the thief that the vintner accuses without knowing who he is. The wine has all leaked out at holes not large enough to admit of the discharge of more than one drop at a time.

Now, ten million little meannesses, ten million selfish- nesses, ten million pettishnesses, ten million waspish dispositions, pierce and puncture the heart, and all its graces are drawn out. You are empty because you leak all over!

One of the most difficult faculties to subdue is that of reason. The pride of reason, the vanity of reason, and the selfishness of reason, are among the last things in a man that are subdued, as well as being among the last things that men understand that they ought to subdue. And yet, the pride of reason, in the days of Christ, was an object of the most terrible denunciations. And in the days of the apostles it was the chief obstacle to the spread of the Gospel. But men have got, first or last, to bring it into subjection to love as a dispositional element in the soul, before they can be said to have true piety.

A BOUNTIFUL mother sits in her house, and says, "Mary, go down to that dwelling, and carry this food. Julia, go down to the dwelling on the other side of the street, and carry this tea and this sugar. Charles, take this money to that man: I promised to pay his rent. James, take this clothing down to that woman: she is sadly in need of it. Elizabeth, take this book to that child." Elizabeth, and Mary, and Julia, and Charles, and James, are so many names of the messengers sent on these various errands of mercy; but the mother was back of them all, and sent them all.

Now the soul has its mother, Love, and she says to Conscience, "Here, do such and such things"; to Veneration, "Here, do such and such things"; and to Reason, "Here, do such and such things"; and Conscience and Veneration and Reason, and all the other faculties, run to do as they are bid: but it is the mother, Love, that sends them. · They all represent her, and perform her errands. Though each one walks with a separate name, Love sits behind them, and they obey her mandates.

You can imagine thistle-down so light that when you ran after it your running motion would drive it away from you, and that the more you tried to catch it the faster it would fly from your grasp. And it should be with every man that when he is chased by troubles, they, chasing, shall raise him higher and higher.

It is scarcely needful to exhort men to sympathize with those of their own kind, or with those whom they recognize as superior to themselves. Our selfishness would inspire it in the one case, and our ambition in the other. Men are quite willing from a subordinate rank to reach up to and sympathize with men of superior stamp. The student will sympathize with the ripe scholar; the cadet with the veteran soldier; the clerk with the millionnaire. If Humboldt should take us into his library, show us the maps which he has consulted, the works which he has written, spread before us specimens of his cabinet, — rock, earth, plant, — he would not need to crave our interest and sympathy. Among men of our own rank, who dress as we dress, who spread their board as we spread ours, who occupy themselves with the very things which engage our time and attention, we find no difficulty of sympathy. Are we merchants? We honor a man that can drive a smart bargain, because we do such things ourselves, — or try to do them. If one understands how to build a splendid house; how to invest money to a good advantage; how to get rich by dealing in stocks, or by wide yet circumspect enterprise; how to enter into the hurly-burly of life, and make his way through all difficulties by the force of will and wisdom, — if one is what we are ambitious to become, if we are not like him already, we find it easy to sympathize with him. But when at sundown the sweated laborer comes trudging weary from the field; when the blacksmith, smouched and grimed, stands cooling himself in the door while we drive past; when the subterranean collier emerges into our sphere; when men forever stooping to the spade, back-bent, in laying stone, delving, groping, toiling men, whose **extreme necessities have consumed all** their hours with hard work, leaving little leisure, and no disposition for reading and improvement, — when this great army, I say, that immensely populates the world, and represents nine-tenths of the whole race, are brought before us, how seldom do we find working in us the quick response of relationship! We thank God and bless ourselves that our lot was not like theirs. Where there is one man engaged in the things in which you take interest, there are a million of blood-bought men, eternal spirits, that are groping, yearning, longing, in the midst of scenes far below you. And what is the command of God to you with reference to these uncounted and innumerable ones? "Mind not high things, but condescend to men of **low** estate. Honor all men."

"THE SABBATH WAS MADE FOR MAN, AND NOT MAN FOR THE SABBATH!" That sentence is passed upon every usage, custom, law, government, church, or institution. Man is higher than them all. Not one of them but may be changed, broken, or put away, if the good of any man require it. Only, it must be his higher **good, his virtue,** his manhood, **his** purity and truth, **his life and progress, and not his mere capricious material interests.**

Do you suppose that religion is like a bird in a cage, and that you can lock it up in the church, and that the keeper will take care of it, and feed it, and have it ready to sing for you whenever you choose to come here and listen to it? Is that your idea of religion? Very well, then: your Bible and mine are different. We read different translations!

———————

IT is not selfishness in themselves, but selfishness in others, that men hate. Every man wants his wife, his children and his neighbors to love him supremely. Everybody thinks that everybody else ought to keep their temper. He is the only one that has a right to indulge in ill-temper. Every man draws the reins tight in regard to other people, but allows himself the widest latitude.

———————

I WOULD much rather fight pride than vanity, because pride has a stand-up way of fighting. You know where it is. It throws its black shadow on you, and you are not at a loss where to strike. But vanity is that delusive, that insectiferous, that multiplied feeling, and men that fight vanities are like men that fight midges and butterflies. It is easier to chase them than to hit them.

———————

WHO ever passed the tomb of Abelard and Heloise in the ground of Père la Chaise without a heart-swell? There is no deep love which has not in it an element of solemnity. It moves through the soul as if it were an inspiration of God, and carries with it something of the awe and shadow of eternity.

———————

NEVER was the conflict of a soul, lifted by yearnings and aspirations on one side, and pulled down by sinful impulses and habits on the other, better described than in the seventh chapter of Romans. There is a solemn tenderness in it that leads men to love it, as one loves to hear the minor chords of music. It is not the voice of

7   J

one that declaims, or of one raging. It is sad, deep, solemn. It is the *Miserere* of the New Testament. I have seen, in the hill country, a little stream gathering from the springs, and holding its way with deepening water, until it enters a gorge. Dark evergreen trees make the place gloomy. Rocks and fallen timber hinder the stream. It falls headlong upon some stone, and is dashed to spray; it trickles back to a channel, only to be caught and whirled in a dark pool; and boiling out of that, it shoots now to the right, still embroiled, and now to the left, but whether forward or sideways, always hindered, broken, and made to cry out and roar by its plunges and innumerable interruptions. No flowers edge it. Its way is too sunless for beauty. But when, at length, far down, it sees beyond a glimpse of field and meadow, it takes cheer, and speeds on, until at length the broad sunshine strikes it, its cascades are fewer, its course evener, and at length beneath bending grasses, and simple flowers, and ruffling shrubs, and over smooth shining sand, it steals tranquilly on, undisturbed, beautiful, and the cause of beauty on either bank.

Such is the seventh chapter of Romans, — the soul in the cleft rocks of the mountain gorge; and such the eighth chapter of Romans, — the soul flowing deep in the fair fields of heavenly joy. The experience of this seventh chapter may often have been as deep and as wonderful in the souls of men as in that of the Apostle; but the expression of it has never been equal to his.

I do not know of anything that vanity does not desecrate. I think the probe would scarcely reveal more hideous results in the lusts themselves than in vanity. Who would dare to say that among those whom they know there are not those whose sickness is a kind of oblation to vanity; a part of whose capital is how much they suffer; and who, if you were to deny that they suffer more than anybody else ever did suffer, would feel that you were despoiling them of their legitimate trophies? **Who** would dare to say that in the circle of their acquaintance there are not those whose bereavements are oblations to vanity; who take a vain pleasure in being the objects of the attention of the neighborhood for the hour, in seeing the preparations for the funeral, in numbering the carriages, and in witnessing the sympathy that is excited for them throughout the community? Who would dare to say that there might not be cases in which, if it were their own child, there would be a mingling of this heathenish feeling with their grief? I tell you, if you sit down and look at your life in its reality, you will find that there is not much poetry in it. The poetry is given to clothe life so that it will not look as hideous as it really is.

IF a man is living a true Christian life, and says of himself, "I was convinced of my sinfulness in this sudden and most miraculous way," there is no reason why you should not believe him. But if he should say to another man who has not had such an experience, but who is living a godly life, "You can scarcely have been truly converted, because you had no such experience," I would say to him, "You have no right to tyrannize by your experience over another man. Your experience may have been genuine; but that is no reason why this other man's experience was not genuine, though it was different from yours."

We have no right to forget God's sovereignty, and

limit Him, or our expectations, to this one way. Christ entered Jerusalem by many gates, — not by one only. The human heart has more gates than Jerusalem had; and God enters it by that gate which, in view of the age and circumstances and condition of the person, it seems to Him wisest to enter by.

It is better that a man should be convicted of sin terribly than that he should be lost; but a man ought to be ashamed to be obliged to be swirled and sweltered in heart and conscience before he will abandon that which is evil, and take hold of that which is good. When a man is in the wrong, how little it takes to make him repent and go to the right, indicates how manly he is. When a man is in the wrong, how much it takes to make him repent and go toward the right, indicates how manly he is. It is characteristic of a noble nature, that, the moment he has done an injustice to a neighbor, and he sees it, he says, "I must put that man right." Why? For his own sake? For the sake of his own reputation? No. He says, "There is something in my own manliness which tells me that, having wronged that man, I must right him"; and he makes haste, he leaps with eagerness to do it. A noble nature is always anxious, if he has done wrong anywhere, to have it made known to him; and when it is made known to him, he is restless day and night till the wrong is made right.

Many persons are waiting for conviction. They are desirous of becoming Christians, but they think they have no right to discharge Christian duties until they have gone through certain appointed steps of conviction. They wish to be Christians, and to feel like a Christian, before they live like a Christian. Is there a man who says, " If I had been convicted and converted, and was a Christian, I would live like a Christian?" Begin to live like a Christian! that is more important than any preliminary steps you could take. Do you think you would pray if you were a Christian? Pray now! Do you think you would **instruct** your children if you were a Christian? Instruct them now! The very way to become a Christian is to do Christian duty. Would you praise God if you were a Christian? Praise Him now, then! Do you think you would talk to men of salvation if you were a Christian? Talk to men of salvation now! The doing of these things will make you a Christian. Being a Christian is no mysterious thing. If you would feel like a Christian, act like one, — live like one. The way to be a Christian is to do as the scholar does, — go to studying; as the traveller does, — start on the journey; as the workman does, — take hold and work; as the farmer does, — put in the spade and the plough. The way to be a Christian is to let alone the thing that is wrong, and take hold of the thing that is right. Go and pray for faith. If you gain but little, do not be discouraged; you will gain more next time. Watch for it. Strive for it. Make up your mind in the beginning that you are but a child in these things. Say, "I am a beginner, and am ignorant; but I desire to learn, and I never will leave off my efforts to become more and more enlightened. By prayer and reading I will seek to know my duty; and so far as I know it, I will endeavor to perform it." If you can say this truthfully, you need not be troubled about the evidences of your Christianity; they will take care of themselves. Only let there be spring in the air, and there will be crocuses under the fence, and violets in the garden; and let the Sun of righteousness shine on the willing soul, and ere long it will blossom with Christian graces. And these will be the best evidence that you have been convicted, and are a Christian. And in all your Christian career, never think of getting beyond that state in which you will be under conviction of sin.

THERE are many who think they are Christians because they have had a wonderful conviction : not because their lives are so good, not because they have such a sensitive conscience, not because they perform their duty as Christians with such fidelity; but because they had a wonderful conviction. If you sit down to talk with them, they always go back to the time when they passed through the Red Sea in coming out of Egypt. That on which they base their hopes is the circumstance that once they were slaves to the Egyptians, that God sent Moses to bring them forth, that when pursued by the thundering Egyptians God opened a clean path in the sea through which they crossed to the other side, and that, like the Israelites, they wandered forty years in the desert afterwards! Now, where a man's only faith is based upon the fact that he felt bad once, you may be sure that he will act bad all the rest of his life. A man is good because, under the influence of God, he is living a righteous life. What your conviction was is of no account at all; it is the fruit of to-day that is of importance.

I SUPPOSE there never was an exactly pure and natural experience of mind in the world. Every experience, every inspiration of genius, every conception of the artist, every rapture of the poet, every impulse of the orator, is imperfect, springs from an imperfect source, arises from an unbalanced state. Therefore, I do not undertake to say of any conviction of sin, that the circumstances attending it were normal and necessary. But I do undertake to say that men are suddenly overtaken by a sense of their personal sinfulness, which almost absorbs their life from its ordinary channels, which pervades them, which fills them, which controls them, so that they sit as a man under black clouds beneath Sinai, **and** pass out of that state with triumph, up into a life of certainty and joy, their after-life, consistent in divine holiness **to** the end, giving witness that the first experience **had in it** benefit and propriety.

When a man organizes purely for this world, his every step away from the life and spring of youth will be apt to be a step away from enjoyment, and his old age can scarcely be other than barren and miserable.

Ordinarily rivers run small at the beginning, grow broader and broader as they proceed, and become widest and deepest at the point where they enter the sea. **It is** such rivers that the Christian's life is **like.** But the life **of the** mere worldly man is like those rivers **in** Southern Africa which, proceeding **from mountain** freshets, are broad **and deep at the** beginning, and grow narrower and **more shallow as they advance.** They waste themselves **by soaking into the** sands, and at last they die out entirely. The farther they run, the less there is of them.

Men are afraid of extremes. They think the "golden mean," as it is called,—and oftentimes it is *mean* enough, —is the safest. It may be where the question is one of mere expediency, where no moral principle is involved. But where it is a mean that stands between right and wrong, where it is a mean that stands between honor and dishonor, where it is a mean that stands between courage and cowardice, where it is a mean that stands between selfishness and benevolence, where it is a mean that wants the benefits of both sides without the responsibility of either, then it is a point of unmanliness. Zero begins half way between right and wrong; and when a man is enthroned on zero in moral things, you may understand about where he is. He is in that point in which — changing the figure — God is pleased to say to him, " Because thou art lukewarm, and neither cold nor hot, I will spew thee out of my mouth." So much for a man's popularity in heaven who takes the "golden mean" between moral extremes!

It is a small thing for that fool to walk across a cable with the roar of Niagara under him, carrying some booby like himself on his back, though ten thousand other fools go to gape and stare at him. But for a man to walk across the thread of daily life, carrying not another fool, but a soul with immortality in every faculty, potent, wonderful in scope and power and susceptibility, so as to keep it in balance, is not a small thing.

Since the earliest periods of which we have record, the staple scepticism has arisen from the apparent unregulation of human affairs. Men have doubted whether there were an observant God; whether He cared to make distinction between virtue and vice in this life; whether by law and its inherent penalty, or by an active interposition of His hand, He rewarded virtue and punished vice.

This arises from a total misconception of the relations

of this world to its work. This is not God's show-room, but His workshop. It is not at all surprising that rudeness and dust and confusion should prevail here. If one should go to a watchmaker's, and look upon an exquisite watch, should know the regularity of its pulsations, the exquisite framework and adjustment of every part, the completeness and finish of the whole instrument, would he be wise in saying, "The shop where this was made must be rarely clean and exquisitely adjusted?" Let him go back and search for its beginnings; let him see its beginnings; let him see the gold smelting; let him listen to the clatter of hammers and files; let him see the confusion of much-used tools, — the furnace, the bellows, the vice, the anvil, — and learn that infinite apparent confusions may conspire together to the production of perfect symmetries. While it was being made, the wheels of the chronometer were separated; were in different degrees of finish; were formed even in different shops; were brought together one by one, and fitted by manifold plyings. And when each part had found its place, the most difficult labor was yet to be done. Its regulation and its adjustment for perfect time-keeping are more difficult than the mere construction of its parts. Thrust into an oven, it was left to throb in high degrees of heat. Then, with sudden change, plunged into ice, it was demanded of it with equal beats to measure time in this opposite condition. Nor will the adjustment be complete and the regulation perfect, until the instrument bears itself substantially even and alike under all temperatures, in all positions, and in all conceivable circumstances. How little would one, inexpert and ignorant, looking upon the place where this watch-construction proceeded, conceive of the admirable fitness of the instru-

7 *

mentalities to the work to be done! How simple and foolish is he who, seeing the watch without having seen the shop, imagines that so much perfectness must needs imply regulated harmony, cleanliness, beauty, in the instrumentation!

The very idea of this life is that it is a place in which to prepare men for perfectness in a life to come. Perfectness in the individual, still less perfectness in society, is no part, apparently, of the Divine economy of this world. The Great Artificer, we may hope, discerns, in the conflict of passions, in the rudeness of violence, in the attritions and raspings of men; in hope, in despair, in love, in hate; in joy, in sorrow; in yearnings, in disappointments; in bafflings, in victories;—but so many influences which, working slowly, with seeming disconnection, and without obvious results here, are, nevertheless, shaping innumerable souls, to revolve in eternal harmony and regularity in that sphere above all misrule, above all rudeness and imperfection, where God's heart beats time for the universe, and every living creature throbs sympathetic.

———

It is with men as it is with machinery. Everybody that knows anything about machinery, knows that it wastes faster when it is allowed to stand still, than when it is worked, if it is worked right. If a watch stands still a year, it wears out as much as it would in running properly two years. But where machinery runs without oil, and squeaks and grinds, it gets hot, and wears out speedily. Now anxiety is in human life just what squeaking and grinding are in machinery that is not oiled. In life trust is the oil. Confidence in God is that which lubricates life, so that industry and enterprise de-

velop the things we ought to have, and do it in such a
way that they bring pleasure with them.

It is no small thing for a man to have a rule in his
mind by which to judge every part of his life, even
though every part of his life may not always conform
to that rule.

If you have stood by the pilot of a ship, and watched
him as he steered it, you know that such is the build of
the ship, such is its equipoise, and such is the unequal
motion given to it by the waves and winds, that no man
can hold it exactly to its course. No sooner is it brought
into steering line than it is carried to the right or to the
left. One minute it is too far inland. The next minute
it is too far in the opposite direction. The pilot is
obliged to be constantly turning the wheel to meet the
various forces that oppose him. The steering of a ship
is marked by a succession of imperceptible zigzags; a
man's life certainly is, whether a ship's steering is or
not; but where the voyage is as wide as the breast of
the Atlantic, where it is the whole of our earthly existence, and where a man has a definite purpose which
constitutes his steering line, and he comes to that in the
end, it amounts to a straight voyage.

We see the same thing demonstrated in daily life.
We see supreme purposes which men have formed running through their whole career in this world. A young
man means to be a civil engineer. That is the thing to
which his mind is made up: not his father's mind, perhaps, but his. He feels his adaptation to that calling,
and his drawings toward it. He is young, forgetful, in-
experienced, accessible to youthful sympathies, and is
frequently drawn aside from his life purpose. To-day he

attends a picnic. Next week he devotes a day to some other excursion. Occasionally he loses a day in consequence of fatigue caused by overaction. Thus there is a link knocked out of the chain of this week, and a link knocked out of the chain of that week. And in the course of the summer he takes a whole week, or a fortnight, out of that purpose. Yet, there is the thing in his mind, whether he sleeps or wakes. If you had asked him a month ago what he meant to be in life, he would have replied, "I mean to be a civil engineer." And if you ask him to-day what has been the tendency of his life, he will say, "I have been preparing myself to be a civil engineer." If he waits and does nothing, the reason is that he wants an opportunity to carry out his purpose. That purpose governs his course, and he will not engage in anything that would conflict with it.

Now, this sovereign purpose of a man to live for certain great moral principles and moral ends ; this sovereign purpose of a man to live for the eternal world ; this realization by a man of God's existence and God's government ; this determination of a man to be governed by God's law, — this is itself a settling of the soul in a way that lays the foundation for satisfaction and for peace. It gives singleness, simplicity, sincerity, — for these three words cluster around the same central idea. It brings the whole life to aim at one thing ; it brings the whole mind under one government ; and however much the separate parts may rebel, it yet holds a man to one direction, and reduces all things to simple tests of right or wrong by a given and acknowledged standard ; but as age advances, victories are gained, education ripens into fixed habits, the very conflict ceases, and the whole body is full of light !

WHEN we come in contact with men we do not know what they leave upon us. I have noticed that when spiders spin their webs in bushes they leave none that you can see at midday. But the next day the dew that has lodged **upon** them reveals them, and then you can see that the bushes were covered with them. And the influences which men exert upon you, you cannot see when you receive them. It is only when they are subsequently revealed **in** your life that you become aware of them.

I THINK that a man who is attempting to live a Christian life on one side, and a worldly life on the other, is like a sick man who has made up his mind that what the doctor says is all folly, and that, since he does not like the medicine and regimen, he will do that which is most agreeable to him. When the nurse and physician are out, he steals into the pantry, and loads his stomach **with** things aggravating to his disease. He deceives everybody but Nature; Nature is never deceived. You may call food what you please, but if it is contrary to the law of digestion, when the stomach takes **it,** Nature knows it. You may call your course in life what you please, but when your conscience takes it, and its effects are evolved, its real character is disclosed.

SOME feel religious teaching because it falls upon a certain sort of susceptibility; but they are only susceptible, **not soft.** There are people who have ripples, but **never waves;** who have surface feelings, but never depths **of** feeling. They **never** have deep convictions or deep emotions; yet they are always shimmering and moving. There are persons that are like farms that have only had surface-ploughing three or four inches deep, under which is a hard pan through which neither root nor moisture can break, so that what is planted thereon has a sprinkling growth, and a meagre existence.

A MAN goes into a community that has been under Puritan teaching for many years, and teaches what he conceives to be a better doctrine. The people there are living good lives, and after he has been among them a short time, he says, "See the effect of my doctrine." It is not the effect of his doctrine. These people were indoctrinated in right views before he came among them. And righteousness is as hereditary as vice, and godly men transmit moral qualities to their children and their children's children. Therefore the character and tendency of a new doctrine cannot be determined from what can be seen of its effects within a single man's lifetime.

THOUGH you have a straight line of apostolic successors, if your work is poor, you are not in the line of succession; and if your church does not make full-grown men, it is not. I do not care anything about the line of succession of my grapes, if my vineyard brings forth better wine than your vineyard does. You may say that yours came from those that Noah planted; but they are not so good as mine after all. For by their fruit ye shall know them. And the test of all churches, as of all orthodoxies, and all doctrines, and all usages, and all governments, is this: What is their effect upon the generations of men?

No princely fortune could be such a boon to a man as a disposition or grace which should lead him to say,

"God is my Father; I am heir with Christ of an eternal inheritance; and I cannot be poor, I cannot be forsaken." How valiant a man is who can say that!

WHAT is the essential idea of Puritanism? It is this: God, everlasting, sovereign, immutable, eternal; God, glorious in holiness, and fearful in praises; God, the whole heaven full of Him; God, the whole earth full of Him; God in the past and God in the abounding ages of the future; God the universal Father, and man, God's child! O, the dignity, the power, the glory, the sacredness that there is in every individual man's life, the moment you fill the heavens, the earth, and all time, full of God, and take every single living creature, and say, "Each creature born is God's child!" How it makes every man more massive than kingdoms! How it makes every man's conscience more authoritative! What breadth it gives to the conception of the individual! That is the reason why Puritanism always goes toward liberty. In Switzerland it did; in the land of the Huguenots it did; in old Scotland it did; in New England it did.

THERE has been a great deal of dispute as to whether men should say their prayers extemporaneously, or precompose them, and read them. That question is altogether secondary. It makes no difference whether the service is of one shape or another shape. The question is, What is the spirit in which it is administered? Is it for the sake of supplying men, or for the sake of teaching men to supply themselves? Is it for the sake of bringing men's hearts into bondage to forms and ceremonies, or for the sake of organizing independency in the hearts of men? Many churches are like conservatories, in which the members are like a flower in a flower-pot. There it is in the flower-pot, and it cannot get out. And little sticks are put down beside it to keep it in a particular position. And every branch that attempts to go beyond a given point is instantly snipped off, in order that the flower may assume an ideal shape. And the members of many churches are like geraniums trained for show, tied up, and constrained in root and branch and stem. There are thousands of people in churches that sit around in their respective rows, and take whatever nourishment is dealt out to them, and grow in just the shape that is prescribed for them by those that have them in charge, and have no voice in determining what kind of a structure shall be made of them.

WE speak of the crucifixion of our passions. In one sense, so far as a sinful indulgence of them is concerned, they are to be crucified and slain; but in no other sense are they to be slain. We are to use them so that there will be no need of crucifying them. For there is not one primary desire or appetite in the human system that was put there to be taken out again. Everything that is in a man was put in him for no other reason than because it was necessary to the symmetry of the whole; and the attempt to crucify any of our normal, lawful desires, is an attempt to mutilate God's perfect work. We have a right to every one of our appetites and passions; and that, not for suppression, but for use, so that we use them in subordination to the higher moral sentiments and affections.

THE world is full of imbecile men whose parents' pride or vanity was such that they would not allow them to do the things which they were fitted to do, and who try to do what they never had a function for. Their life is one long failure, and they are forever complaining because life is so misadjusted.

THERE are many children that are brought up with care and assiduity, who, when they are deprived of the sustaining influences of their parents, seem bankrupted; and, on the other hand, there are many children that are brought up without any care or foresight, who make splendid men. And people say, "There is no use of family government." The first example does not prove that family government tends to the destruction of children. The parents took care of their children, and would not let them take care of themselves. They did not give them the idea that they could take care of themselves. They did not teach them not to need to be taken care of. They would not let them stand alone. They were afraid that if they put them on their feet they would run away, and so they did not put them on their feet. They were afraid that if they allowed them to use their hands they would do mischief, and so they kept them tied. The consequence was that when they were eighteen, or nineteen, or twenty years of age, — just at that critical period when reaction is most apt to come ; just at that critical period when the child passes from boyhood to manhood ; just at that critical period when the parent throws the child on his own responsibility, — the consequence was that then these children did not know how to stand, or walk, or take care of themselves, and they went to the devil! And people said, "That is what comes of Christian teaching. That is the way the children of religious parents turn out."

On the other hand, how was it in the other case, in which people seemed to neglect their children entirely, and in which, notwithstanding this, the children turned out well? The parents neglected the children in **some** things, but in some things they conformed to God's **funda-mental** law of letting every man take care of himself to the extent of his ability. The influence of the neglect was therefore superficial. **The** parents were practising self-reliance, and the children, gaining confidence from their example, practised it also. **The** consequence was that the children, when the parents died, or when they went out from under the parental **roof,** knew how **to** stand on their own root, and were saved.

Do not go **back to** monkish days, and **take on ascetic** ideas of religion. If you *will* go back, **go back to the** Jewish times, where men worshipped largely in festivities; where, when they **came** to the temple, **they came with** such outbursts of pleasure, such uproarious **rejoicings,** that the writers who described the tumult **which pre-vailed** on such occasions, spoke of it as the sound of mighty thunderings, and the voice of many waters. The Jews were cheerful. They had not much mirth, but they had great hilarity. The Old Testament is **full of cheer-fulness,** of buoyancy, **and commands to it.**

MANY persons **suppose that when a man becomes con-verted,** he of necessity **becomes solemn.** They suppose that a Christian is like **a man who is looking in a dark** pit all the time. They think that there **must have been** a mistake made in the **creation of the mind.** But God, when He, in infinite creative **wisdom,** looked round about and selected **the traits for the human soul,** salient, mag-

nificent among them He put imagination, which is in the
mind what a diamond is upon the bosom, sparkling and
throwing its light upon every side. And when He put
imagination there, He meant that it *should* sparkle.
And wit, with its concomitants of humor, mirth, and
conviviality in intellectual things, was likewise placed in
the mind by Divine intention; as was also hope. And
these three traits — hope, wit, and imagination — go to
constitute what we call the buoyant temperament. But it
is supposed by many that while a man is a worldling,
while he makes no profession of religion, he may laugh,
and carry himself gayly, and sparkle in this direction and
in that, and indulge in his quips and witty sayings, and be
a radiant, entertaining man; but that when he becomes
convicted of sin, and converted, he must put a snuffer
over the imagination, shut the door on mirthfulness, and
repress all those elements which give hilarity or gayety to
life. They think that when a man becomes a Christian,
he must be constantly under the influence of veneration
and of awe, and that he must think of nothing but the
solemnity of the cause that he has espoused, and of his
awful responsibility before God.

Now, God wants the whole soul. If He had not
wanted your wit, He would not have put it into you.
If He had not wanted your imagination, He would not
have put that into you. If He had wanted no stars in
the firmament, no stars would have been there. If there
is a flower in the world, God wants that flower. If there
is a tree on the earth, He wants that tree. And if there
is a trait in the human mind, He wants that trait. You
may abuse it; you may employ it in infelicitous ways;
but that has to do with the question of regulation and education. I aver that the perfect man is the man that has

developed all the radiant, joy-breeding, and joy-dispersing traits of his nature. It is a shame to let these traits go to the hands of the adversaries, and exclude them from Christianity.

"EVEN Solomon in all his glory was not arrayed like one of these." I know he never was; nor has anybody else ever been; nor will anybody ever be. I can show one apple-tree that puts to shame all the men and women that have attempted to dress since the world began.

A MAN has lived in a cellar, where he has been a poor, dungeoned creature, striving to live a life which was prolonged death itself. At last, he goes up one story; and then one story higher; and then one story higher; and he continues to go up little by little, till by and by it seems to him **that** there must be some place where **it is** lighter. He keeps on exploring and going up for a time longer, and finally reaches the roof. There he beholds the heavens over his head, and the sun in the east, and he is entranced with amazement by the glory of the things which surround him. And yet, every single day during his existence, and for countless ages, the heavens have hung above the earth, the sun has shone forth in splendor, and the other creations which astonish his vision have been beheld by men. **For** forty years he has been in the cellar, and now that he has come up where he can see them, it seems to him that they have now appeared for the first time, because he **sees** them **for** the first time.

So it is with the disclosures of the love of God in Chirst Jesus to Christians. They think that the time when they first realize that **love**, is the time when it is first shed upon them. But as God pours abroad infinite breadths of His Being without an eye except His own to behold them, so He spreads over our heads an unknown, an unmeasured, and an immeasurable love, waiting for our recognition, but in nowise depending upon it. I know of nothing that is calculated to give more hope to the Christian in the midst of his discouragements, than this feeling, — namely, "I am not to be saved because I am so good, but because God is so good."

IT is argued by some that men will take advantage of the love of God. No, not *men*. You must get some other name for those lazar-house creatures that are capable of doing that.

If I were greatly in want of money, and I went for aid to an old, usurious, miserly man, who hated to give, and only gave for a consideration, and scolded when he gave, I do not know but I should take a little comfort in pestering him. I suppose there is a little relish of torment which every one feels in dealing with such a man. I presume I should enjoy going to him and getting out of him all I could. But if I went for aid to a man of a kind and generous nature, the case would be different. I get into trouble, and go to such a man, when he meets me with a face bathed in smiles, and says, "You have come again to give me the pleasure of assisting you." I say, "I have liabilities to the amount of ten pounds, which I am unable to meet." "What! is that all?" he exclaims, and gives me twenty. I attempt to express my obligations to him, when he says, "Not at all, — not at all"; and shoves me out of his house. As I start to go away, he says, "I shall see you again; I shall get another chance at you; I shall have more pleasure out of you!" By and by I go to him again, hanging my head, when his

first words to me are, "Ah! your pocket is empty and
your head is down. Come in! come in! You cannot
get away so easily." And again he gives me the money
I need. At length I get into deeper trouble. Sickness
enters my family, and my means run out. In my distress
I go to him once more. The moment he sees me, he
says, "What! spent your money so soon? I declare, I
do not know but I shall have to make you my son. I
must look after your affairs. I see you cannot attend to
them yourself." He sweeps away my debts, and supplies
my present wants, and urges me to call on him whenever
I find myself pressed for means. Now suppose I say,
when I get by myself, "This old fellow is so kind and
good that I can practise on him, and I will take advantage of his kindness and goodness," what ought I to
be baptized? Toad? snake? No, I will not so slander
savage animals! I ought to be baptized *devil!*

———

THERE is something unspeakably affecting to me in the
thought of — what may I call it? — the solitude of Divine love for men, and its patient continuance in God
without consciousness on our part. There is something
sweet in interpreting the nature of God from the family.
Now, who can tell the sum of the thoughts which the
mother bestows on the child? All through his infancy
he is scarcely out of her mind. She watches him as he
sleeps in the cradle. She wakes at night to go and see
if all is safe in the room where he is. All day long, as
he plays, her eyes are upon him, to see that no harm
comes to him. And all through his boyhood her love
and care surround him. And yet he is unconscious of
most of her solicitude concerning him. He knows that
she loves him, but he only feels the pulsations of her

love once in a while. I think we never know the love of the parent for the child till we become parents. I think that when we first bend over our own cradle God throws back the temple door, and reveals to us the sacredness and mystery of a father's and a mother's love to us. And I think that in later years, when they have gone from us, there is always a certain sorrow that we cannot tell them that we have found it out. I think that one of the deepest experiences of a noble nature in reference to loved ones that have passed beyond this world, is the thought of what he might have been to them, and what he might have done for them, if he had known, while they were living, what he has learned since they died.

Now, when I think of the love of Christ, and the love of God in Christ, overhanging my life; when I think of the long period during which I had no conception of that love; when I think of the long period during which I resisted and struggled against it; when I think that during these long periods God, unchanged and unchangeable, brooded over me and yearned for me without my knowing it, — when I think of these things, they are inexpressibly affecting to me. And, moreover, they bring the nature of God into such reality and form that I feel that I can comprehend Him and worship Him.

Not only does God think of us constantly, and love us steadfastly, but there is a healing, curative nature forever outworking from the Divine mind upon ours, although we may not coöperate voluntarily with His will. My impression is that all those moral tendencies we feel, all those yearnings we have, are the crying out of the soul for God, under the influence and ministration of His love to us. I think that every throb of our spirits that an-

swers to spiritual things is caused by the influence of
God. We are attracted by Him, though we may not be
conscious of it. As the child that is sent away from
home to school, under circumstances such that it does not
know its friends, gets home-sick, and sobs, and cries for
brothers and sisters, and father and mother ; so there are
many home-sick men who feel in themselves strange
yearnings for they know not what. It is their soul crying out for God because He is working upon them by the
power of His thought and love, — only they do not know
its language.

And that is not all. It seems to me we have testimony in the workings of the providence of God in the
experiences of our daily life, that God's love is still shed
upon us, although we may be unconscious of it. I recol
lect to have read the case of a man in a city of southern
Europe who spent his life in getting property, and
became unpopular among his fellow-citizens on account
of what seemed to them his miserly spirit. When his
will was read after his death, it stated that he had been
poor, and had suffered from a lack of water, that he had
seen the poor of the city also suffering from a lack of
water, and that he had devoted his life to the accumulation of means sufficient to build an aqueduct to bring
water to the city, so that forever afterwards the poor
should be supplied with it. It turned out that the man
whom the poor had cursed till his death, had been laboring to provide water for the refreshment of themselves
and their children. Oh! how God has been building an
aqueduct to bring the water of life to us, He not interpreting His acts, and we not understanding them!

If you had gone to Wesley's room, when John and

Charles met in the University, and Whitfield and others met with them, and looked upon this handful of men who were derided as the offscouring of the earth in their day, would you have suspected what a fair fabric was to arise through their humble instrumentality? You never would have dreamed of it. For God seemed to be everywhere but with them. No flaming chariot came down to them, no silver trumpet sounded before them; no messengers from heaven led them; no angel choirs sang to them as **they** sang to shepherd ears when Christ came. They **were poor,** hated, bemobbed **men. It was** on that very account that they became the men they did. The same elements were with them which accompanied the advent of the Babe of Bethlehem. For whenever Christ is born into the world, He comes in as when He was first born. He came in at the bottom; He came in through a manger, with the poor standing round about Him; and whoever, professing the name of Christ, comes in in any other way is a thief and a robber.

WHEN a simple child is by his father first taken out to sea, and the storm arises, and terrible waves run in upon **the** ship, **and** winds smite **it, and** it reels and careens, and **the** groaning timbers strain, and the sails and cordage fill **the** air with clack **and** clamor, the child is sure that safety **is at an end, and that** destruction is upon them; and he **is amazed** to see the captain, his father, going about **sternly** resolute, but without quailing; the man at the **helm calm,** watchful, but not afraid; and the sailors alert **and hearty in** obedience. After a while, the **child begins to gather** confidence, too; not so much because he sees how they are to be kept safely,—**for every time** he looks **over the side of the** vessel his fear takes possession of him again, — as by the conviction that his father knows how to save them, if he does not see how. He puts confidence in him. Instead of trusting in his own sense, in this matter of danger, he trusts in this being who seems now to him almost superhuman. And we praise the child for doing so. We admire in the child those qualities which lead him to have such confidence in his father as to rebuke his own senses. And we think that such distrust of one's own inexperience, and confidence in another's experience, is not only heroic, but almost divine. It is in a child; and it is in everybody, if it be exercised toward One that holds the same relation to him that the child's father does to the child.

If you look in detail into the history of the Puritans it seems hard that they should have been treated with such contempt as was heaped upon them. Well, it depends upon what was to be made of them. If it was desired to make puff-balls of them; if it was desired to make imbeciles of them; if it was desired to swell out their skin with fatness, and put them into the high places of the earth as idols, and worship them, and make them the recipients of passing enjoyment, then the worst things that could have befallen them, were the things which befell the old Puritans. But when a man wants to make a sword, he does not deal with it as you would deal with a baby that you wanted to soothe. He takes the ore, and plumps it into a red-hot furnace, and melts it, and takes it out, and puts it back again, and stews it over, and subjects it to a series of other purifying processes, and at last it comes out steel. Then he puts it under a trip-hammer, which smites it as if the thunder were kissing it, until every particle that flies off from it is like a spark of fire. Then it is good to make swords that will stand in the day of battle. It must go through fire and water if you would have it make a sword that will not betray you in the hour of trial. And when God made the Puritans, he made them as we make swords. And I tell you, they were swords of God. And men that pulled them out of their scabbards wished they could push them back again!

IT does me good, sometimes, to see all things going just right, and everybody crying about them! It does me good to see things moving forward with God at the helm, and everybody offering prayers, and burning wax candles, and making vows, and telling what they will do if they can be saved! It does me good to see men racing about as if all creation was after them, and they were on the point of being devoured by dragons! It does me good to see men who profess to be Christians; who accept every one of the thirty-nine articles of faith, and would accept forty-nine if it were necessary; who are all the time talking about God and heaven; who are all the time singing such hymns as "When I can read my title clear"; who are active in prayer-meetings, delightful in revivals, charming in conference-meetings; who are very devout and trusting on Sunday, — it does me good to see such men, the moment they get into Monday or Tuesday, and hear the least rustle in the heavens, forget Bible, and prayers, and hymns, and God, and eternity, and ask, "Where is my chest? where are my customers? where are my prospects? where are my notes? where is my prosperity?" When men look after God, they generally look in the way in which their real god is; and when I see men in times of trouble running after worldly things instead of looking to God, I say to myself, "These are your idols; these are what you believe in." Let them take counsel of such things, if they will.

But, are we to be among that puling crew? **Are we to be children of fear,** — we that are descendants of men who lived without sight, purely by faith; who steered through stormy seas and ages, with faces turned upward; who were **wise toward** earth, **because they** were wise toward heaven? **Are we to** be degenerate children of such **ancestors, and to quake with fear lest God** shall **now** abandon or forget His own purposes, **or** let go the interests that are as dear to Him as **the** apple of His eye? **I am** ashamed **of** anybody that is afraid. Let us sing when other people cry; **and laugh when** other people scowl; and walk **elastic when** other people trudge **with** lead in their **shoes.** For men **that have** lead in **their** shoes generally have it in their head, too! **It is not for** us to be without hope and comfort. It is for us to ask, " Which way is righteousness going, which way is justice going, which way is humanity going, which way is truth going, which way is social purity going, which way is love going, among a great people?" **I do not** care which way the earth is going. I want to take my direction **from** God's brightest constellations, and steer by them.

———

No man would suspect what the kitchen was from the banquet; and certainly no man would suspect what the banquet was from the kitchen. **No** man seeing the dyevat, would suspect what **the** finished silk was; and no man seeing the finished silk, would **suspect** where it came from. And the peace and prosperity of the world come from causes in which, when you look at them, you see no prophecy of their results; because God, working in the great sphere of the universe, and in the vast sweep of time, by so many instrumentalities, and instrumentalities of such largeness — working in one century for the next, and in that for the next — outruns the proportions of our working and our following. But if you go back and look at past ages, you shall find that those things which have seemed the most prosperous, have been the least so; and that those things which have seemed the most disastrous, have been the most prolific of good.

If men begin to preach the gospel in its relations to a better state of society, if men begin to apply the Gospel to questions of war, questions of slavery, questions of usury, questions of national intercommunication, people start back, and say, "The Gospel was ordained for the salvation of men's souls; and you are going out of your way when you preach of these extrinsic things." The publishers of religious books publish those which are for the conviction and the conversion of men, for their souls' salvation, and let all other questions alone. It is right that they should publish such books; but the implication that the only end of the Gospel in this world is to be a wrecker's boat, to be sent out to a ship rolling dismasted on the tempestuous sea, and take off those that are in danger, the crew, and save them, is not right. While it is a boat sent to a ship rolling dismasted on the sea, it is to save both the ship and the crew. It is the design of the Gospel to bring the old ship into port, to rig her again, and to send her out with crew after crew, and maintain her on the water, and not let her founder nor go down. Or, to drop the figure, the Gospel of the Lord Jesus Christ, while it has a special reference to the condition of each generation, has also a comprehensive refer-

ence to the condition of successive generations of the
world, from the earliest periods down to the dawn of that
millennial day in which the race, regenerated, shall yet
stand. The Gospel contemplates something more glorious than the mere individual salvation of men from
period to period; it contemplates the salvation of the
world, as well as of individual generations of the world.
And while it does possess an individual application to
each class and period, while it does seek to convict and
convert men, and build them up as far as it can in their
day, it has a larger purpose, — the augmentation of future
world-character. The Gospel, then, is to save, not indi-
viduals alone, but the race; and to save them, not by
plucking them out of the world from generation to generation, but by making each successive generation higher,
and stronger, and nobler, until the world shall be like a
bride dressed for her wedding, that God, the Husband,
may embrace it and lead it to the bridal altar. The par-
tial idea, glorious as it is, becomes narrow when you
compare it with the fulness of the whole. I think the
salvation of each individual generation is a work worthy
of the blood of the Saviour, and of His death; but for
the race to be disenthralled, and enabled to stand amid
the waves and storms of time, — that is more glorious
yet. And that is the Scriptural ideal.

God is united to us, and we are united to Him, not by
any form of matter, not by physical conjunction or con-
tiguity, but by the intersphering of soul-life. It is that
which knits us to Him. Our thoughts reach out and
thread themselves to His thoughts, and thus bring us
toward Him.

Hence, God's union with men is not a shadow, is not a

figure, is not a dream: it is the statement of a fact as literal as any law in nature. The union of sunlight with vegetables is not more real. The flow of nourishing sap in fruits is not more literal than the interfusion and soul-union of God's soul with men's.

What a wonderful and glorious doctrine is this, that the soul of God touches the soul of man! As there is no babe cradled and rocked that has not its mother, in the ordinary course of life, to overhang it by night and by day, to kiss it as it sleeps, and to cover it with smiles and caresses when it wakes; so every creature that is born into life has a God whose ever-watchful soul broods tenderly over it by day and by night, and who inter-spheres it in His own radiant thought and feeling.

———

CHRIST was not so much with His disciples when wearing a human body, and walking with them, as after His ascension. He did not go so much away from them when taken into heaven, as He had done while on earth. He had been separated from them, as it were, in the body. The spirit has its poorest chance in this world, where it has to work through an untransparent body. And it was needful that He should be taken up, that He might con-summate that spiritual union which was possible to a less degree in the body than out of the body.

The eye, the ear, the hand, cannot connect us with each other; for although we gaze, although we listen, al-though we clasp electric hands, it is something within the flesh to which the eye makes its report, to which the ear makes its report, to which every sense makes its report. Every man is conscious of something inside that is not of the body. It is the soul that finds the soul. It is spirit that recognizes spirit. Inward spiritual unity is first;

and the unity of sense is but its representative or symbol. The only substantial union of affection is that which comes from the touching of soul with soul. It is invisible and spiritual.

Christ ascended is nearer to the world, more apprehensible, and more at one with the soul of every believer, than if He stood clothed in a body, visibly, before men. It was needful, perhaps, for the disciple, that Christ should disappear from the sense, in order to reappear to his inward life and spirit.

WHAT is the doctrine of the Holy Ghost? It is the doctrine of the interworking of the Spirit of God upon the souls of men. I have no philosophy about it. All I say is this: that God knows what is the secret way in which mind reaches mind. I do not, — you do not. I do not know why words on my tongue wake up thoughts corresponding to those words in you. I do not know why the soul of man, like a complex instrument of wondrous scope, is played upon by my words, so that there are waked up in it notes along the whole scale of being. I do not understand why these things are so, but unquestionably they are so. I do not know how the mother pours her affection on the child's heart; but she does. Two stars never shone into each other as two loving souls shine into each other. I know it is so, but I do not know why it is so. I do not know how soul touches soul, how thought touches thought, or how feeling touches feeling; but I know it does.

Now that which we see in the lower departments of life, — that which exists between you and your friends, and me and my friends, — that I take, and by my imagination I lift it up into the Divine nature, and give it depth and scope and universality; and then I have some conception of the doctrine of God's Spirit poured upon the human soul.

THE moment a man's heart touches the heart of Christ in living faith, he becomes, whether he knows it or not, the brother of every other, in heaven or on earth, who has come into the same relationship with Christ. Whoever is united to Christ, is brother or sister to everybody else that is united to Him.

THE whole brotherhood of Christian men, in all the earth, that now live, are mine. And in this great household there is to the soul no division such as, from the weaknesses and imperfections of life, exists in external matters. Every good man is, so far, of my faith. Every Christian man is therefore mine, simply because he is Christ's. I am Christ's, — though most unworthy, — and He is mine. Wonderful, that my lips should be permitted to say that I own God! Nor would I say it if it had not been said, "All things are yours." I would not say it if it had not been said that I was heir with Christ, because He became my brother. I would not dare to say it if these things had not been said. But now I dare go to God, unabashed and undaunted, and say to Him, "Since I am thine, whatever thou ownest in man throughout the universe, I own. All men are indeed mine. I am united to them. I am related to everything that has got my nature and thine."

I wish I knew more of them. It comforts me to believe that the silent ones are sometimes as rich as the noisiest ones, — that the unfruitful in outward things are contributing to the nations more than external labor.

There are men in dungeons that the world could not do without. You know the dungeon is the oracle of God, and speaks most precious things to men. The best things that ever came into this world came when Christ was riven, and immortal life flowed out; and men are riven, and immortal truths and examples flow out.

THERE is a most unutterable gladness and sweetness in singing together. We are so much under the dominion of the body yet, that in prayers, where there is the silent accompanying by thousands of the utterances of one voice, there seems less indication of this union than in singing. I never see my congregation singing, that I do not feel, "There at last goes the breath of their soul and mine; and that hymn is the chariot that is taking us together up before the throne of God."

THE process of being born again is like that which a portrait goes through under the hand of the artist. When a man is converted, he is but the outline sketch of a character which he is to fill up. He first lays in the dead coloring. Then comes the work of laying in the colors; and he goes on, day after day, week after week, month after month, and year after year, blending them, and heightening the effect. It is a life's work; and when he dies he is still laying in and blending the colors, and heightening the effect. And if men suppose the work is done when they are converted, why should we expect anything but lopsided Christian characters?

ALL men that have had a noble ancestry feel a joyful sympathy with them. We like to trace our name, even if it ends in some honest farmer. We like to know our origin. We like to go to the mountain and find the very hole in the rock from which the spring spirts, whether we are the river or the morass! We are fond of tracing **our** ancestry, if it have glory, and if it have none. It gives us pleasure to trace our forefathers to colonial days, and **to** the *Mayflower*, — that ark of the covenant for America. Moses carried the **ark** through the sands; our fathers carried it through the **waves**.

We love to trace our ancestry to early houses and families in England. **We love to** trace it to Huguenot or Hebrew blood. Neither is this vain or foolish. It may become **so through** abuse, but it is not so of necessity. It is right. **A man** may take something from the loom of the past to cover the nakedness of the present with.

But mere bodily ancestry is the lowest form of a great truth. **The** soul gives relationship. All who have lived, and, by God's help, poured their life as a soul-wine forth for the refreshment of the world, are **my ancestors, my** relations. All the patriarchs are mine. **Not to the Jew** alone are **Abraham** and Isaac and Jacob; but to every man that knows how to feel like them, and revere them. All judges of Israel; all prophets and holy priests; all religious kings and patriotic men; all apostles, ministers, and confessors; all holy men of the cloister, — in ages when the cloister benefited society; the heroes of dungeons and scaffolds; the witnesses for liberty in every age, and everywhere, — these men seem to us dim and shadowy; but we love to go back and make them more substantial. We love to search those long forgotten, and give them resurrection, and claim them as our own. I go back to them with fervent joy. Their blood is mine. It beats in me; for the blood of Christ it is that makes of one blood all good men on earth. I am blood-kindred to all that have been blood-sprinkled from on high.

I do not know how much this seems to you. That depends upon circumstances. If you are as hard as a tenpenny nail, and have no more heart than that, probably it is not much. You may be a nail, and that in a sure place; but to any one that has any considerable imagination, and any considerable enthusiasm of affection, I think it will be a source of great comfort and joy. I, for one, would not for anything give up my heritage in the past. I ask no roses, I ask no titles, I ask no estates, except the revenues which my own heart can bring forth of sympathy and inspiration and joy from the past. To every man that ever did a noble deed, to every man that ever thought a noble thought, to every man that ever achieved a noble purpose, to every man that ever dared to suffer for the right, to every man that ever laid down his life for truth, I am related. I am related to all that is good in the past.

I DO not distinguish men one from another merely by the difference of their thought-power. Still less do I distinguish them by the difference of their executive power. There must be a deeper gauge than these. Still less do I distinguish them by their external differences, as where one is high and another is low; where one is rich and another is poor; where one is wise and another is unwise. The point where true manhood resides is in the neighborhood of love. In the copiousness, the variety, the endlessness, the sweetness and the purity of the element of love, you shall find the measure that God applies, discriminating between one and another.

As I sat and looked to-day at the meadows and at the trees, I thought within myself, " What message have they

for me of my God, and from my God?" And all day long
I have felt that never was there such an interpretation of
munificence ; that never was there anything that so indi-
cated what it was to give without money and without
price, — to give out of a nature whose spontaneity is
generous, profuse, magnificent.

As, in wandering from one thing to another, I looked
at the freshness of nature, and the multitude of her children, — those hidden in coverts, those under dark, cool
rocks, those laid in where mosses are, those growing in
the broad fields, those springing up under the shadow of
forest trees, and those suspended upon their boughs in
the air, — as I looked at all these things, I found I could
scarcely estimate in one square yard where I sat, how
many notes God had rung, how many thoughts He had
bestowed, how much care He had lavished, how much
power He had exerted, and how much wisdom He had
displayed. And there came to my mind such a sense of
God's overruling providence and presence, as has made
the whole day one of unexampled sweetness to me.
There was not a single bird that I had time to hear, or
rather that I was awake to hear, — for you must wake
early or you cannot hear the birds sing in chorus. From
four to five o'clock is the time for family prayer, and
they always have congregational singing then! If you
miss that, you will not hear anything like it during the
whole day, although during the whole day there is not
an hour in which they are silent, — there was not a single
bird that I heard that did not direct my thoughts to God.
And all through the day, in the singing of the birds, in
the blossoming of the trees, on the broad green sward,
along the sides of the walls, skirting the edges of the wood-
lands, through the glades, in the air, on the earth, every-

where, it seemed as though God were almost so near that I should hear Him, and see Him, as certainly I felt Him.

And what a joy there is in knowing that the earth is not merely something that God thought of when He made it, and, as it were, spun out of His hand, saying, "Go, take care of thyself"; but that it is God's daily care, that it is His estate, that He works it as I work my garden, and that He watches all things in it with that same anxiety and interest with which I watch one plant after another that I mean to see blossom, and mean to help to blossom! To us, nothing makes the world so precious, nothing makes it so profitable, nothing makes it so little barren and so much rich, nothing so takes away its sordidness, as the knowledge of God's solicitude concerning it, and His care over it.

———

WE are branched on every side with faculties exquisitely susceptible of influence. The whole world is striving, and moving about us, and upon us. And no man can prevent dents and scratches, unless he looks before and provides beforehand. If a man allows his body to come into collision with rock, or tree, or hedge, or wall, it is too late for him to avoid injury. He should have kept off. We protect the eye, the nerve-woven skin; we learn to be vigilant without volition for the body, and even when absorbed in thought there is yet a subtle piloting of the body by the mind, I know not how; we see the stone without seeming to see it; we avoid the ditch without knowing that we noticed it; we lift the foot with a regulated gradation to meet the varying surface of the road, quite unconsciously; we instinctively discern the qualities of things, and accommodate ourselves to them.

But the soul is more sensitive than the body. It has a greater surface, it has more branches, it has more arms and feet, it has more nerves, it has more injurable attributes, than the body. It carries them, too, amidst flying missiles countless, endless in succession. When the fire touches gauze, it is too late then to interfere; you must not let it touch it. When the rap is given to the crystal vase, it is too late then to save it; you must keep it free from the blow. When the frost has struck the flower, watching is then remediless; you must keep it where the frost cannot reach it. We must keep sensitive things free from rude contacts. That is true wisdom in practical life. And so of hundreds of moral things. We must keep them away from evil, so that it shall not overtake them. A man must carry himself, not so as to repent of harm, but so as, by constant vigilance and forethought, to prevent harm from befalling him.

———

PHILOSOPHERS go to the glaciers,—those frozen rivers that move with a slow and steady pace down the mountain-side,—and set stakes on the firm rocks, and measure how far the whole body moves within a given length of time. By means of these unmoving stakes they can detect its almost imperceptible but continuous motion, through day and night, and summer and winter, which the heedless never observe, nor believe in.

Now, if you take your stand on the firm rock of God's truth, and watch men, I think you will see that they move with a slow and steady motion. I take sight at a good many men. I see where they start from, at what pace they are moving, and in what direction they tend. Their motion is slow and steady, like that of the everlasting glacier; and every moment they are moving downward! They are not law-breakers; they are not bad citizens, — it does not take much to be a good citizen; they are not men addicted to lust or drinking. But if to transform one's whole being into the love of money; if to set before one's self, not God, not immortality, not justice, not purity, not faith, not any of the ethereal virtues of the eternal realm, but the acquisition of property; if to seek, above all things, to become money-strong, to build pyramids for men to see, whose broad base shall cover acres, and every stone of which shall be solid gold; if to think golden thoughts, and measure forces by a golden measurement, and estimate men thereby, and value customs, laws, institutions, sanctuaries, books, everything, by the amount they will bring in the market, — if that is to move downward, then there are men who are going down the sides of Mount Sinai as surely as the glaciers move down the sides of the Alps! And I tell you it is time, not that men should watch for each other, but that every man should wake up and watch for himself.

———

A LAW, to be of any use to you, must be higher than your practice under it. There is no use in your attempting to learn to write, when already you can write as well as the copy. There is no use in your going to school when you know as much as your master. There is no use of your sitting before a drawing-board to learn to draw, when you can draw better than him that teaches you. And no rule, no principle, is of any great use to a man unless it is in advance of his attainments. From the lowest forms of physical industry up to the highest spiritual virtues, the indispensable requisite for growth is the conception of something better than has been, or than is, in us. All industries are prosperous as they are striving toward something better.

An orchestra that should play through the whole of Beethoven's Eighth Symphony and only chord five or six times from beginning to end, would hardly be considered first-class performers. An occasional discord can be tolerated, but such an absence of concord that perfect harmony is touched but five or six times in the playing of the whole piece, is intolerable.

Now, our life touches concord only once in a while, and all the rest of the time it plays in discord; and when a man who is striving to live according to God's law begins to find this out, he says to himself, "I am perpetually coming short of my standard; I not only do not love right, but I hate it often; I not only do not obey, but I positively disobey: I not only do not seek the strait path, but I rejoice to walk in the broad road; I not only do not control my temper as I should, but I allow it to scourge and torment others; and how can I call myself a Christian?" He strives for a month, for six months, for a year, to live aright, and finds that in spite of all his strivings his life is still imperfect, — wofully imperfect.

And then what happens? Oftentimes under such circumstances a man says, "The standard is too high. One never can reach it, and therefore it is too high. It ought not to have been put so high." Now, the worst thing a human being can do is to bring down his standard. That does not bring up conduct. The conduct will be about so far below the standard, whether it is high or low. Many a Christian insensibly falls into a self-indulgent state, and has in himself this unexpressed feeling: "It does very well to hold up these exaggerated ideals in preaching, but it is impossible for men to live as ministers tell us we ought to live; and it is of no use for us to make ourselves think that Christianity demands that we should." And so he gets ease by lowering the standard, instead of attempting to carry conduct up to the standard.

Do I, when I open my house as a refuge for orphans, require that they should be perfectly clean before I take them in? No; the dirtiest ones I take first. Do I require that they should be well clothed? No; their very rags are their invitation. Do I take them in because they are ready to graduate? No; they cannot read a letter. Their only education is profanity. The reason I take them in is because I am benevolent, and they are needy. And the reason that Christ accepts us is because He loves us, and we are in need of His loving-kindness. It is only those who hug their sins, and refuse to give them up, that He rejects.

God's greatness and supremacy have been taught so as in effect to produce the impression of solitary and unsympathizing sovereignty. I hold and teach that God is supreme; that in thought and will and government He is sovereign; and that, from the very necessity of His being, He takes counsel of none, asks permission of none, and is obliged to carry Himself above all government and all suggestion. I hold that this is a glorious doctrine which flames abroad not less in nature than in revelation; and the Divine superiority, supremacy, and sovereignty cannot be taught too much for my rejoicing. It may be taught in the wrong way; for if it be taught that God is sovereign in the sense that He is lifted so far above men that He is out of sympathy with them, and that they of necessity are out of sympathy with Him, then we have lost our God. It is not necessary to make orphanage among men in order to make God sovereign. It is not necessary, in order to make God radiant and glorious, to make Him like Mont Blanc, which is beautiful, to be sure, with its snow-white covering, but which is cold and forbidding, nevertheless. Men seem to have lifted God up into such solitariness of supremacy as to make Him unsympathetic, careless of men, and regardful of nothing but Himself. Men have seemed to think that there was an entity called government, by which God so separated Himself from men that their thoughts could not find Him with any joy, hope, or pleasure.

THE great incarnation mystery, the peculiar mission of Christ, is this : that He brought God down to us, that He revealed God to us in His example, while walking the streets of Jerusalem, — while going about the highways of Palestine, — while sitting on the mountain side, — while in the vessel, — while raising the widow's son to life, — while distributing all things, reserving nothing for Himself, so that He had not where to lay His head, — while using His whole being for others, and not for Himself. The example of Christ was, as it were a section of God's eternal life let down into this world, that men might see One whose nature it is to administer forever and forever on the principle of making His own being subservient to the welfare of those over whom He presides. And when He was caught up again into heaven the same blessed work went on, only in a higher sphere.

Christ is spoken of as " the Lamb slain from the foundation of the world." That which men saw of God during the brief space of thirty-three years was only a specimen of His life before and after. And that being God, to give Himself perpetually for the good of His creatures; that being God, to eternally love and succor the intelligences that He has made; that being God, to bestow the vast stores of His nature in endless benefaction; that being God, blessed be His name that He does live for His own glory, that He never does stoop from the lofty altitude to which He is lifted, and that He never does swerve from the purposes of His administration.

One man has kindness deep within him; and when the occasion comes, the rind or shell is cracked, and the kernel is found. Such a man's heart, too long clouded, like a sun in a storm-muffled day, shoots through some opening rift, and glows for a period in glory. But there are other natures that are always cloudless. With them, a cloud is the exception, shining is the rule. They rise radiant over the horizon; they fill the whole heavens with growing brightness, and all day long they overhang life, pouring down an undiminished flood of brightness and warmth.

Whether other men have received more or less than you have, is not the question at all. Have you not received all you have earned? Has there been any opportunity withheld from you? You desire ease; but where is the evidence that you have earned it? You desire pleasure; but where is the evidence that you have earned it? You desire comfort; but where is the evidence that you have earned it? Does society owe you these things before you have earned them? No more than the wilderness owes me harvests which I have not sown, or fruits which I have not planted. Society owes you what you have gained, achieved, — nothing more.

If you say there are men that have not worked half so hard as you have, who have got ease, or wealth, or honor, there may be a question to be raised as to why they have got it, but there is no question to be raised as to why you have not got it. You do not deserve it. And if you say, "Neither do they," it may be so, and it may not; but that does not touch the question at all. "Is thine eye evil because I am good?" Has God defrauded you because He has dealt bountifully with other men? If I give one beggar a penny, and pass by the next one without giving him anything, do I cheat the one to whom I give nothing? Have I not a right, on the ground of generosity, to give to one when I do not give to the other? Is it not optional with me to do what I will with my own? Is it not my privilege, where I violate no pledge, and where I am left simply to the dictates of my feelings and judgment, to give to one, and refuse to give to another? And are a man's own feelings to measure my conduct in this matter?

"I could wish that myself were accursed from Christ for my brethren, my kinsmen according to the flesh."

I wish you could see what stupendous ingenuity of folly has been employed in finding out what that signifies; how men have put on spectacles, and double spectacles, and quadruple spectacles, to pry into its meaning, saying, "Did he really think he would be willing to lose his soul for the sake of his brethren?" thus screwing the words up to exact measurement. It is as though an old hard-hearted bachelor should hear a mother, in anguish

of soul, exclaim, "I would give my life a thousand times
over to save my child?" and he should stand and say,
"A thousand times? Two hundred and fifty would be
a great many. A thousand times?" Why, feeling is
always, in its nature, full of overplusage. It defies and
scorns measurement. Such extravagant expressions mean
simply *much*. When a man's heart is full, and he wants
to rise to a royal conception, he disdains measured language. The apostle says, "I could wish myself accursed
from Christ," and nothing else could indicate how strong
his feeling was. He did not stop to think what the literal
interpretation of these words would be.

"To the intent that now unto principalities and powers in heavenly places might be known *by the Church* the
manifold wisdom of God."

When God sets forth His manifold wisdom, what are
to be the leaves of the book that shall be revealed?
Palpitating hearts are to be the leaves of that great book.
From the beginning of the world to its last day, men
shall go up in order, and every human soul that has lived
and yearned for help, and received help, shall recite its
experience; and it shall be an experience manifesting the
wisdom of God in this world. And every Christian will
be a new page, a new history ; but not one written with
ink nor cut in stone, but one that has been experienced
in the living soul. When God shall make manifest what
has been His wondrous wisdom, martyrs, and confessors,
and holy prophets, and apostles, and humble Christians
will rise up in thousands and tens of thousands, yea, in
multitudes without number, chanting and speaking that
wisdom.

IF you bring me a basketful of minerals from California, and I take them and look at them, I shall know **that** this specimen has gold in it, because I see there little points of yellow gold; but **I** shall not know what the white and the dark points are that I see. But let **a** metallurgist look at it, and he will see that it contains not only gold, but silver, and lead, and iron, and he will single them out. To me it is mere stone, with only here and there a hint of gold; but to him it is a combination of various metals.

Now, take the Word of God, that is filled with **precious stones** and metals, and let one instructed in spiritual **insight go through it, and** he will discover all these treasures; while if you let a man uninstructed in spiritual insight go through it, he will discover those things that are outside and apparent, but those things that make God and man friends, and that have to do with the immortality of the soul in heaven, will escape his notice. No man can know these things unless the Spirit of **God** has taught him to discern them.

THE mother suffers most for the child and is nearest like the Saviour to him, — for we are nearest those, and most glorious in **the esteem** of those, for whom we suffer most. Do not you know how things will loom up and magnify when you see them through a haze? So when you see persons through tear-drops which they have shed for you, and the things that they have suffered for you, they are magnified, and seem more saintlike to you.

RESPECTING the whole tendency of men here, this is true : that the less you develop them, the more content they are in regard to immortality. The nearer a man is to a stone the less discontented does he feel. We talk of punishing men by withholding joys from them. Men say that misers are punished because they have not the joys which spiritually-minded men have. You might as well say that a toad is punished because he does not know what the philosopher knows. If a man has not got a thing, and does not know that such a thing exists, and does not want it, is he punished by not having it? Do you suppose a leaf is punished in the measure of the things that it does not have? Do you suppose a man is punished in the measure of the things that he has.not got? Do you suppose a coward knows what he lacks in courage? Do you suppose a mean man knows what he lacks . in magnanimity? The lower you go down in the scale of human being, the less discontent you will find. And the moment you begin to bring a man up, his every step is taken with aspiration, susceptibility, yearning, and longing, all of which point in one direction, and lead him to feel in his whole inward experience, " I am not of this world. There ought to be another place for me to live in."

WE carry something of God in us. It does not exist in such a form that we can define it. If the logician says to me with reference to it, " State your position : prove what you say "; if, like an apothecary, he wants that I should weigh it in scales, and give him the result in drachms and scruples, I cannot meet him. Nevertheless, I think there are thousands of witnesses who will say, " I have an undying certainty in my bosom that I am allied to God in such a way that I shall not be extinguished when this life is ended ; that I shall not die when

I die." I think there is a forelooking into the life to come. It seems to me that there are in the lives of many — certainly there are in the lives of the more favored — hours in which they seem to themselves to stand with only the filmiest separations between them and the spirit-land. Some think that they can pierce it and discern it. I hope they can. We cannot say much for each other. But I think all of us have known hours when we have said, "A little more, the least bit more, and I shall see and know." I think there have been times when it seemed as though **voices spoke to** you out of the great concave; when it seemed as though you almost felt the touch of a shadowy presence ; when it seemed as though your soul was caught up, so that you did not know whether you were in the body or out of the body, as the apostle declared that he did not.

———

SOME think that a Christian life is like a canal, with proper locks to lift men **up and drop them down** as occasion requires. There may be a sluggish, lazy, puddle-life of that kind ; but there is no such Christian life. No man can live a Christian life that does not avail himself of all the power given him on every side. There is work for the thought, work for the imagination, **work for** every moral sentiment, work for every affection, work for all the combinations of the faculties, in their different moods, and through all the varying periods of life, — youth, middle age, and old age ; and if a man would be a Christian, a child of the all-working, unslumbering God, he must be awake and vigilant.

———

MALARIAS, you know, are dangerous because they do not address themselves **to any sense.** We can put up

9 • M

lightning-rods to ward off thunderbolts; but no man can put up rods that will protect him from a poisonous atmosphere. You can drain morasses that you can see; but you cannot free the atmosphere above them from impurities that you cannot see. The sweetest and most beauteous days in New Orleans are those on which death strikes most terribly there, in times of pestilence. It is on such days that it is the most insidious. It has no visible or perceptible exponent. It cannot be detected by sight or by touch. And that is what makes it so dreadful.

Now, we are walking in a malarial atmosphere all the time: not one that attacks the body; not one that penetrates the heart; not one that congests the liver; not one that crazes the brain; but one that infects the soul. The soul is poisoned all the time by pride, vanity, the love of money, greed, competitions, rivalries, and the various other noxious elements by which it is surrounded. Human life is one vast Campagna, and there are, in the atmosphere round about men, silent, corrupting forces of which they are quite unconscious. And nothing but this inward spiritual vigilance will make a man a match for these things.

—————

IT is not the quality of the thing, but the quantity. Too much watching becomes disease,— not watching, but *too much* of it. Too much bread is as bad as arsenic, only in another way. Too much fruit, too much water, too much light, too much of anything, *is* too much, and is oppressing, and not nourishing or serving. The simple overacting of good makes it mischievous. In respect to the body, although the signals of trouble are hung out, and the uncomfortableness of sensation reveals the im-

prudence of our indolence, yet it is sufficiently difficult
for men to keep within the lines of moderation, in the
body. How much more need of watchfulness, when the
gradually-growing excess is in a thought-faculty, or in
the disproportionate use of a feeling; when the excess is
not in the nature of the thing felt, but in the continuity
or degree of it! We never sin by evil faculties, but
always by good ones misemployed. There have been
men that have used good faculties evilly, and that continually; but God never made a bad thing in a man.
He made him well; and every blade was to be good,
every instrument good, every quality good; and the evil
that proceeds from him comes from the wrong use of
things that are good.

———

A DULL axe never loves grindstones, but a keen workman does; and he puts his tool on them in order that it
may be sharp. And men do not like grinding; but they
are dull for the purposes which God designs to work out
with them, and therefore He is grinding them.

———

I NEVER saw a man that did not believe in the immortality of love when following the body of a loved one
to the grave. I have seen men under other circumstances that did not believe in it; but I never saw a
man that, when he stood looking upon the form of one
that he really loved stretched out for burial, did not revolt from saying, "It has all come to that: the hours of
sweet companionship; the wondrous interlacings of tropical souls; the joys; the hopes; the trusts; the unutterable yearnings, — there they all lie." No man can stand
and look in a coffin upon the body of a fellow-creature,
and remember the flaming intelligence, the blossoming

love, the whole range of Divine faculties, which so lately animated that cold clay, and say, "These have all collapsed and gone." No person can witness the last sad ceremonials which are performed over the remains of a human being, — the sealing down of the unopenable lid; the following of the rumbling procession to the place of burial; the letting down of the dust into dust; the falling of the earth upon the hollow coffin, with those sounds that are worse than thunder; and the placing of the green sod over the grave, — no person, unless he be a beast, can witness these things, and then turn away and say, "I have buried my wife; I have buried my child; I have buried my sister, my brother, my love."

God forbid that we should bury anything. There is no earth that can touch my companion. There is no earth that can touch my child. I would fight my little breath and strength away before I would permit any clod to touch them. The jewel is not in the ground. The jewel has dropped out of the casket, and I have buried the casket, — not the jewel. And you may reason, you may say what you please, you may carry the case before the supreme court of my understanding, but there is something higher than reason, and something back of the understanding. All that is in me revolts at the decision, and spurns it, and says, "You must try heart cases before the heart. We will not believe but that there is life somewhere else; we will not believe that life is buried here; and the soul goes out and cries, like a child lost in the woods, to find itself in this strange world, saying, "Where am I? and who shall guide me, that long and yearn and reach upward?"

It is not so much the stalactites as the stalagmites that

I am looking after. Those crystalline columns that hang down from the roof of the cave are stalactites; but there rise up also from the floor equally crystalline columns, which are stalagmites. Now, in my thoughts spring up the longing of my soul for honor, the longing of my soul for perfect love, the longing of my soul for a sense of rectitude and purity, the longing of my soul for the society of spirits of just men made perfect; and I know that these longings spire upward; and in clear days, exceptional days, I think that I can see the light of heaven glisten, and that my thoughts go to the gate, and almost within the sacred precinct. I know not that their thoughts are able to reach down to me. I hope they are; and when there is evidence that they are, I shall be glad to receive it.

I SUPPOSE that there are hundreds of men that are exceedingly sceptical in regard to the Bible who have a certain hidden reverence for it. Why? God sent them an angel, and let her walk with them two years, and then took her home; and they hold her memory with such sacredness, that they say, "If there ever was a Christian, my wife was one; and she believed in that book, and there must be something in it which makes it superior to other books."

GIVE me a hundred men, — not men that are glowing while they sing, and heavenly while they pray, though I would have them so, but men that are, morning and noon and night, born of God, and that so carry the savor of Christ that men coming into their presence say, "There is a Christian here," as men passing a vintage say, "There are grapes here," — give me a hundred such men, and I

will make the world believe. I do not ask to be shown
the grape-vine in the woods in June before I will believe
it is there. I know that there are grapes near when the
air is full of their odor; and the question under such circumstances always is, "Where is the vine?" and never,
"What is it that I smell?" You are to be a savor
of love, and peace, and gentleness, and gratitude, and
thanksgiving, so that wherever you go, the essence of
the truth that is in you shall go out to men.

NATURES that are constitutionally overprone to vigilance are apt conscientiously to redouble that which they
do not need in such measure. They are of the opinion
that fear is almost a positive Christian grace. They not
only set a needless number of sentinels about the dwelling
of their soul, but they seem to frequent the company of
sentinels without, more than that of guests that are, or
should be, served within. Many a man has little time for
Christ inside, because he is so busy watching the devil outside. Theirs is a religion which is more in fear of evil
than in enjoyment of good. There are a great many men
that have never yet known the profound philosophy of
the command, "*Be not overcome of evil, but overcome evil
with good.*" The way to overcome evil is, sometimes, to
be sure to watch it; but a man that does nothing but
watch evil, never will overcome it.

WHAT! does a man sin when he is a Christian? Certainly he does. If nobody ever came to the communion
of the Lord's supper except those who are void of sin, we
should have a great wilderness in the church. Do not
you sin? Is there a day in which you are not selfish?
What is selfishness? It is acting with any one of your

faculties so as to promote your own good at the sacrifice of the good of another. **And do** you not act so with your pride and vanity every day, — ten thousand times a day? Do you not act so with your very conscience and benevolence? Do **you** not with your love make an idol of one side, **and** cheat the other side? Does any man live an hour without sinning in some of his faculties? I do not suppose a Christian would be a burglar, or sin in the sense of violating a civil law, but in the sense of violating the law of God there is not a man who lives a single hour without sinning.

GIVE me the men, and I will write a commentary on the Bible that will **not need any** explanation, — for most commentaries are more troublesome than the Bible which they are designed to explain. I will put them, not in the sanctuary on the Sabbath, but at home, in the street, in their neighborhood, in all the intricacies of business, everywhere; and no matter where they may be, they shall be a savor of Christ, sweet as the odor of blossoms. They shall be garden-men that have some flowers for every month, and that are always fragrant and redolent of blossom and fruit. Give me a hundred such men, and I will defy the infidel world. I will take them and bind them into a living volume, and with them I will make the world believe.

FAITH in Christ has no tendency to make a man careless as to his conduct, or less eager to obey the law of God. Do you think that a boy taken out of the house of correction would be more in danger of picking the pocket of his benefactor than if he had not shown him a kindness? Would not the kindness be the surest guarantee against such an occurrence?

There was a man in Boston (I know not whether he
lives yet, — yes, he lives, but I know not whether he
lives in this world) who, though not rich, was accustomed
to go into the courts of justice every morning to give bail
for culprits that had no friends ; and it was his testimony
that of all those for whom he gave bail, not one betrayed
him, — not one left him in the lurch.   And do you suppose that those creatures whom Christ has helped, and
whom he has given a hope of eternal salvation, would
turn against Him, their best friend, and the one to whom
they are indebted for their choicest blessings ?   Would
that be human nature ?   Is there anything on God's
earth like gratitude to inspire a soul to act in the right
direction ?

Now, where a man sees all his imperfections swept
away by Divine love, has he not in this fact the greatest
stimulus that he could have toward holiness ?   No man
is so little tempted to sin, and no man has such victory
over sin, as the man that loves Christ because He died
for him, because He lives for him, and because through
His love his sins are washed away to be remembered no
more forever.

God is near to many men that are unconscious of His
presence.   The perfume of Divine love is round about
many men that do not perceive it.   You are like men
who have no sense of smell. ·You are in the garden of
the Lord, and you call it a wilderness.   But wake, O
soul! out of despondency.   If you are — as you know
you are — sinful, and you long for something better,
take hold of the hand of Christ, and go toward it.   He
will hold fast to your hand, and will lead you to the end ;
and then you will be saved, not because you are perfect,

but because He has swept you into that charmed and
blessed sphere where the flesh and the world shall drag
us down no more, but where our enfranchised manhood
shall lift itself up in ineffable glory, crystalline purity,
and perfect symmetry.

———

It will be with men's excuses in the day of judgment,
when God looks upon them, as it is with the frost-pictures
on a window of a winter morning, when the sun looks
upon them, — they will be gone with His looking.   The
excuses which you paint in this life to justify pride, and
selfishness, and disobedience, and recreancy, will, the moment you stand before God, melt away.

———

What is the Bible in your house? It is not the Old
Testament; it is not the New Testament; it is not the
Gospel according to Matthew, or Mark, or Luke, or
John: it is the Gospel according to William; it is the
Gospel according to Mary; it is the Gospel according
to Henry and James; it is the Gospel according to your
name. You write your own Bible. To every man that
sets up a Christian household, God says, "I am going
to reveal my grace through you." And if you have a
Bible in your family, it will be just so much of that grace
as you interpret to your children and dependents. And
do not you know that there is a Bible that has in it a
large Apocrypha between the Old and New Testament,
containing Esdras, and Tobit, and Judith, and Ecclesias-
ticus, and various other books. Now, there is in your
experience, besides the revelation of the Old Testament
and the New Testament, an intermediate revelation that
is false, that is untrue; and your children read that
living Bible, — particularly the Apocrypha. It is a

solemn thing for a man to be a Bible that is read by those about him.

Do any of you seem to yourselves to be useless, and say, "O that I was eloquent! O that I could wield the pen of a ready writer! O that it was given to me to go forth and be an apostle of Christ!" It is given to every one of you to be an epistle of Christ, known and read of all men. By your humility, by your truthfulness, by your justice, by all the things that make you like Christ, you become His minister, and you are known and read where you never suspect that you are being known and read. Take care, then, and speak right things of Christ. See to it that the testimony you bear of Christ is such as He would have you bear.

A CHILD is in a distant country, and there she talks of home; and people who hear her say, "I am glad I have not such parents as she had." It comes to her ears afterwards, and she says, in tears, "Did I leave an impression that my parents were bad?" She reproaches herself for having done anything to produce such an impression. She says, "My father and mother are noble and true, and I fain would have left an impression that they were so." And as children feel in reference to the impression they leave of father and mother, so ought we to feel in reference to the impression we leave of God and Christ. We are to live so that men shall be led by our works to glorify our Father in heaven.

THERE is a providence,— not a fatality, not a coercive necessity: but a broad, beneficent system which has, whatever it may be, such a relation to you and this world, that you cannot afford to be uneasy. You can afford, when you have done your best, to take things easy, and enjoy yourself. Think, if you want to think, as long as it is pleasant to think; plan, where you ought to plan; labor, where you ought to labor; achieve, where you ought to achieve; but thinking, planning, laboring, achieving, — let all be done in a spirit of confiding trust. As little children will frolic, and play, and talk to themselves, and sing, and be happy, if every time they look up they can see their mother's form or shadow, or hear her voice; so we are, in God's greater household, to have such a consciousness of our Father's presence as shall make us happy, cheerful, contented, in our sports and duties.

ONE reason why we are not trustful and cheerful is, that we believe that there will be fulfilments of the promises of God only so far as they are wrought out in the problems of our understanding. A great many persons have said to me, when I propounded this to them, in view of their adversities and extremities, " I cannot understand how there should be a special providence of God. I cannot reconcile the theory of special providences with my ideas of general law, and of God's agency in nature." That is to say, when God lays down an unquestionable command, of the most explicit kind, unless you can go behind that command, and can find out the philosophy of it, you will not accept it at His hands. Simply as a thing commanded by your Father, you will not, with the faith of a child, accept it. If you can spin it on your wheel, and then weave it in your loom, and make it conform to your pattern, you will accept it; but as simply from the hand of God, you will not accept it.

Now, I like to reason; I like to search out results from causes; but it is sweet for a man, in the midst of the turmoils and troubles of life, where he can, to rest himself on his faith in God. It is sweet for a man to be able to say, "I do not care for to-morrow. I do not fear what shall befall me. I will trust in God." To understand the philosophy of a Divine command, where I can, affords me satisfaction; but where a command comes from such authority, and with such variety of illustration in nature, as this one, I do not care whether I understand the philosophy of it or not. My soul is hungry for it, and I accept it because my God has given it. I trust and rest in God, simply because He has said, "You may, and you must." That is ground enough.

CHRIST says, "Are ye not much better than they?" Yes, I hope so; though now and then I feel mean enough to say "No" to this question. Now and then I have such a sense of the poverty and the miserableness of human life, that I am tempted to say that a man is no better than birds.

It is only when you come to consider not merely our relations to this world, but our relations to the future; not merely our imperfections and ungrowth here, but our immortality in the world to come, that we seem better than birds or flowers. When you take in the root, and the stem, and the everlasting growth, and the fruit of human life, then are we not much better than birds and flowers?

ONE text that hooks a man to God, and that makes him feel that in Him he has a Father who wheels the bright army of the stars, who carries the globe in its revolutions, who is the Controller of time and of eternity, who is the Creator and Sustainer of all mankind, — one such text, O, how it takes away care, and anxiety, and sorrow! How much food there is in your Father's house that you never tasted! In that house there is bread enough and to spare; and **yet** you go fretting and worrying through life, borrowing trouble about the future, with which you have no concern, and making yourself miserable in the present, with which you have concern.

OUT of every night God is making a path by His hand for the morning, and for you; and out of every day God is making a bed of darkness for the night, and for you.

"BEHOLD the fowls of the air; they sow not, neither do they reap, nor gather into barns."

I thought of that to-day, for when I was very busy sowing some seed, a bobolink flew over my head, with a wild, sarcastic descant, as much as to say, " Go on, old clod-crusher! you sow, and I will rejoice." He flew past, and I understood him.

O, IF this life were all that I could have, I should weep, it seems to me, from the present hour to the very end, unless I could say as the ancients did, " Let us eat, drink, and be merry. To-morrow we die, so let us make the best of the little time that is left us." I should be in a state of wanton, merry despair, on the one side; or of tearful, sad despair, on the other side. I must live again. I must make the experiment of life once more. I have made poor work here, but I have met with just success enough to feel that if I had a better chance I could do something. I am like a man that takes the first canvas to paint a picture. He does not know what he will do. He lays in forms in all sorts of ways without coming to any satisfactory result. At last he says, "I cannot make anything of that picture; but I have a conception. Bring me a fresh canvas, and I will try again, when I think I shall have better success." I have long been trying to paint a true life, and have only partially succeeded; but if God-Almighty will give me another canvas, I think I can paint better. And He will. He that brought forth from the dead our Lord and Saviour Jesus Christ, will bring me forth. And, thank God, when I go home to heaven, I shall leave behind many things that will be of no use to me there. When an engine is taken from one boat and placed in another, it is not necessary that the fastenings should go with it. The screws and clamps and feeding-pumps that belong to that peculiar ship from which it is taken may be left behind. The screws and clamps and feeding-pumps that have been necessary to keep my mind in this body, and that it has given me so much trouble to patch and mend, I shall leave in the grave. But my supremest reason, my divinest sentiments of religion, my affections and loves, my tastes, — these God, the blessed Pilot, shall carry safely through the grave and its darkness, and I shall be planted again in heaven, where snows never fall, where frosts never come, and I shall bring out leaf and blossom and fruit; and then, with leaf and blossom and fruit, I will present myself at the Throne of God, saying, "Thou hast given me life, and life again, and life forever: to Thee, and to Thee only, be praise and honor and glory, evermore."

WHAT is more beautiful that that centrality, that self-serving, that selfness, which God has given to every man, and which leads him to take care of himself? What business we would have if we were obliged to take care of each other! How wonderfully God has lightened the work of life by giving to every human being an instinct by which he is led to care for himself! This attribute of our nature relieves the world of a vast accumulation of painstaking. And yet how deep — no man can measure, — how broad — no man can estimate, — have been the mischiefs that have sprung from this element of selfness; for when selfness is carried beyond a certain point, it becomes selfishness, and therefore an instrument of evil. The evil does not proceed from the quality of the thing; it is simply the result of not watching to see where the thing ceases to be good, and begins to take hold on that which is bad.

A HUNTER scorns a pigeon-roost; because he would fain have some reward in skill and ingenuity; and he feels that to fire into a pigeon-roost is shocking butchery. But for that feeling I should like no better amusement than to answer the sermons of men who attempt to establish the right of slavery out of the Bible. It would be simple butchery! A man must be addicted to blood who would fire a twenty-four pounder into a flock of black-birds or crows!

As a boy that cannot write at all looks with wonder and admiration upon the performance of a writing-master who without thought can form the letters and sentences so as to make the page look like engraving, while the master himself has no idea that he is doing anything extraordinary; so men looked with wonder and admiration upon the miracles of Christ, by which He fed the multitude, turned water into wine, healed the sick, cast out devils, brought the dead from their shadowy land, and evoked victory out of defeat, while Christ himself did not regard these things as of very great importance. They were merely the authentication of His divinity. The real thing for which He came was that which lay beyond this. His errand was to bring upon the human soul a cleansing power, an inspiring power, a formative power. He was to set us free from sin, inspire in us a longing for purity, and form our character on that basis. Accordingly, Christ is presented mainly in the New Testament, from beginning to end, in His relations to the soul of man. Even when He is compared with His Father, it is always as a means of exhibiting with greater power His curative relation to the human soul.

ONE of the delicacies in this world is, that when two souls come together, and unite with each other, no one has a right to meddle with them, to know their most blessed intercourse, or to interpret their thoughts to each other. They are to be let alone. And when a soul goes up in the enthusiasm of its affianced love to unite itself to Jesus Christ, shall not its trust be respected? Shall anything separate it from Him? No, nothing. It is God that surrounds us, it is the eternal Father that rejoices in us; and at no time does He rejoice in us more than when we are giving our life and our being to Jesus Christ our Saviour.

THE very word "God" suggests care, kindness, goodness. The very idea of God in His infinity, is infinite care, infinite kindness, infinite goodness. We give God the name of good; it is only by shortening it that it becomes God,—a vulgarizing almost of the term.

In the exigences of business—in all cases where men are in doubt and perplexity as to what is right and what is best, as to what you may do and what you may not do—be sure to give the greater advantage to the moral element. If you make a mistake, let it be on the right side. It is better that a man should not avail himself of liberties that he might take, than that he should avail himself of advantages that he should not take. It is better for a man to be too careful and scrupulous, than for him to be unscrupulous and careless. Men that look at everything simply in the light of their own interests, grow narrow, mean, and foolish, and at last come to stand in their own light. I think there is nothing more foolish in life than this kind of selfishness, which really stands in a man's own way. I often see men that are so selfish that they cannot prosper. Men that settle all questions by reference to some higher standards—by benevolence, conscience, humanity—will find that these arbiters of duty will avail, in the end, not only for spiritual good, but for secular good also.

The broader the pattern which a man is made upon, the more will he have it in his power to control the conditions of success, even in this life. Therefore, let me say to every young man, always reason up. In every exigence reason up. Never reason down, under any circumstances. Never allow yourself to say, "But may I not do this?" Never say, "Has not this knot been tied too tight? Is there not too much moral restriction in this direction?" Always make your Christian manhood come between you and the endeavor to go down in the scale

N

toward perdition. Do not say, "What may I venture to do?" but say, "Lord, help me to rise higher than other men are, and to refuse the things that make men low. Let it be mine to go from strength to strength, and from nobility to nobility, till I become more pure, more just, more benevolent, than the customs and laws require me to be."

Men, instead of listening for a moment to this argument, say that a person who confines himself to such a course of life as I am recommending, cannot be as smart as one who does not; but I say he will be smarter. Goodness is smarter than baseness. Uprightness has more genius, more executiveness, more power, more real aptitude for business, than rascality. Give me a broad conscience-man, who looks over the field of life with an equitable regard for his fellow-men; who makes their interests his interests, because he loves them. Such a man has more statesmanship in his conscience than other men have in all their sharpness and discernment. Sharp men, like sharp needles, break easy, though they pierce quick. There is no fallacy more universal or more fatal than that which teaches that there is no temper except in wickedness; for I aver that God puts into a man's soul more temper, more executive power, more of the elements of success, than the Devil ever did by his craftiness, or than Mammon ever did by his selfish, wicked expedients.

Now, I should be ashamed to ask a man to be a Christian from motives drawn from the exchequer; but if it be true that godliness is profitable, the city is just the place where there are men that want to know it; and I declare my faith in this doctrine, not merely because God teaches it, (though that would be reason enough,) but because I see it exemplified in life. For these reasons, then, I say that a religious life, begun early, is the surest road to honor, prosperity, and happiness.

If I understand the words of Jesus Christ, He says, " You had better lose your life than do wrong." If you stand where a man says to you, looking with open eye on that which is wicked, " You shall do this or forfeit your place in my establishment," Christ says, " Forfeit your right hand before you do it." And suppose he does kick you out, where does he kick you to ? Into the bosom of God Almighty's providence. You think of the man who gives you permission to sleep under the counter in his shop, and to draw one hundred pounds this year, and one hundred and twenty-five next year, and deem it worth your while to court his favor; and are you not to regard Him who sits on the throne of the universe, and gives you your existence, and promises you eternal life ? Are you not to regard Him who holds the earth in His hand, and gives life to the wicked man that employs you, and would pervert you for his own selfish interests? He declares, " Give up your eye, your foot, your hand, nay, even life itself, rather than consent to do evil. For what shall it profit a man, if he shall gain the whole world and lose his own soul ? "

Now, I say to every young man, Go out of any establishment where it is insisted that you shall do wicked things, quicker than a shot goes out of a cannon when it is fired; and not only go out of it, but keep out of it: unless you made a bargain that when he bought your services, he bought you. In that case I have nothing to say, — I do not speak to slaves. If, however, you went into an office, a manufactory, a carpenter's shop — no matter where — as a man, and engaged your services, no one has any authority to control you in moral things. There you stand a free man, and there you are to produce the charter of your liberty, and say, " God Almighty made me to be His son, and shall I throw away my son-ship? No; I will stand for that which is right, though life itself shall fail." And I tell you, this is a salt of fire, a baptism of blood, which no man can experience without coming out a saint; and a man who has experienced it, is as much stronger and better than one who has not, as a man who *is* a man is better than one who only *pretends* to be one.

————

I say to every man you ought to have a conscience so active, so sensitive by daily communion with God, so bathed in the sweet ways and meditations of a Christian life, that you shall be misled and deceived by no example, and by no specious reasoning. A man who has a correct watch learns to trust it. After he has thoroughly tried his faithful servant of the pocket, and knows that through months and years it has given him true reports, he places great reliance upon it. He may ask the time of the town clock, but if it gives a different report from that given by his watch, he at once says to the clock, " Thou liest." He may ask the time of his friend whom he meets in the street, and he takes the report of his friend's watch till he looks at his own, when, finding that they differ, he says, " Mine must be right, for it never deceives me." Every man should keep an account of celestial time; and setting his own heart and his own conscience by the beats and throbs of God Almighty's heart, he should take counsel of, and believe in, no other. He should compare himself daily with this standard, and should take no testimony against that. He that has an open face, and looks into the open face of God, shall be a child of light, a child of liberty, and a child of glory.

I was living in the West, and was in straitened circumstances. I think that, for a period of four years, there had not been a time when some member of my family was not sick from the malaria which prevailed in that part of the country. I did not expect or desire to be anything except a missionary. I was contented, but quite poor, so far as money was concerned. But there came a time when it seemed to me that I should be ousted from even the humble berth I occupied; and I made up my mind that if I was, I should go to some smaller place where my services would be acceptable. The reason why I expected to be ousted was, that I had attempted to stand up against the leading men of the vicinity where I was, on the slavery question, at a time when the people of Indiana did not dare to say that their soul was their own, or that the negro's soul was his own. It seemed to me that my church would be shut, and that I should be deprived of the means on which I depended for the support of my family. And I recollect that on a certain day, while reflecting upon the unhappy state of my affairs, I read this passage, — "Let your conversation be without covetousness," — that is, Do not borrow trouble about where your salary is coming from, — "and be content with such things as ye have." "Why, yes," I thought, "I have not many things ; but I will be content with them." And now for the royalty of the reason for contentment: "For he hath said, I will never leave thee nor forsake thee." These words, as I read them, seemed as really a message from God to me, as if the

white form of an angel had spoken to me, saying, " Henry,
I am sent to tell thee from your God, I will never leave
thee nor forsake thee."   And the rest of the passage is
this, — " So that we may boldly say, **The Lord is my**
helper, **and** I will not fear what man shall do unto me."
I then thought, " Now, Mr. Elders, shut up the church if
you have a mind to.   I am not afraid of any man that
lives, since I have this message from my God."   It sank
like a seed into my soul, and it has never been rooted
out.   If there is any text of the Bible that has been an
anchor to me, it is that one.   I have swung with it
through many a storm.   It has held me a thousand times
if it has once.   I never think of it that it is not to my
soul like a touch on the keys of a piano.   There is always
music in it to me.   " Let your conversation be without
covetousness."   Do not fidget, and worry, and vex yourself about how the ends are going to meet.   **You** may be
sure that they always will meet, though you may not
always see how they can meet.   If they do not meet in
this life, a man dies ; and then they meet.   I used often
to think, " If they do their worst, they can only kill me ;
and I shall thank them for that."   When to shove a man
through a door is to shove **him into heaven, you** cannot
do him any great indignity.

WE cannot come to the conviction of the divinity of
Christ so well by the intellectual and philosophical method as we can by the **spiritual** and experimental method.
This latter method is the method of the New Testament ;
and I think, that in the wisdom of the ages to the end of
the world, it will be found to be the **true method. We**
are first to employ Christ by faith in all the offices which
He sustains to the soul ; and then, I hold, no other argu-

ment can produce such a conviction of His substantial and glorious divinity, as will come from His effects upon the soul. In accepting Christ in all His glorious offices, as prophet, priest, and king, we have the best conceivable evidence of His divinity.

WHAT do you suppose Baron Humboldt would have been to an Indian boy fifteen years of age, if he had come before him with all his astronomic, geometric, and geographic knowledge, — with all his scientific knowledge, — with all the boundless wealth of his great mind? Why, the largeness of Humboldt's being, his power of thought, everything that made him the philosopher that he was, would have fairly eclipsed the poor Indian boy. You might as well bring the sun down before my eyes, blazing me blind, to give me a conception of that mighty orb, as to bring the fulness of such a mind as Humboldt's before the mental vision of an undeveloped Indian boy, to give him a conception of that mind. It is dark where there is too much light, as well as where there is too little. If being is to help being, there must be some proportion between the being helping and the being to be helped.

Now, if it had pleased God to come to earth in all the fulness of His glory, man could not, according to the declaration of Scripture, have looked upon Him and lived. He not only could not have understood Him, but he could not have borne the shock of contact with Him. Christ therefore veiled Himself, laid aside the glory of the Father which belonged to Him, to such a degree as to bring Himself within the ordinary reaches of the human mind.

CHRIST comes to every man, and demands of him love.

He presents Himself in every aspect in which a greater mind can be presented to a lower; He presents Himself as the Son of God, the Saviour of the world, your personal friend, and your elder brother; He embodies in Himself every tender relationship of which we can conceive; and He asks, He claims as His right, that you should love Him.

If love were a sealed fountain, if you had never learned to love, you would be less to blame for neglecting to love Christ. But among the things taught earliest is love; among the things most experienced in life, is love; and among the things remembered latest, is love. When the child comes into life, almost the first thing he does is to send out his heart in trust and confidence and love; and though the objects of his primal affection are limited and imperfect, they are sufficient to excite in him the dormant spark of love. But when it is the infinite Creator; when it is the glorious God; when it is He that for you has laid down His own life; when it is He, rather, that has taken it up again, and lives to intercede for you; when it is He that sends you, day by day, fresh glories, and that, night after night, surrounds you with mercies; when it is He that through all the periods of your life watches over you with most tender solicitude and scrupulous fidelity; when it is He that outvies all other affections, and showers His own upon you more copiously than clouds ever rained drops, or seasons ever gave forth fruit; when it is He that comes to you, and says, " My son, give me thine heart," — what will you do with this Jesus that yearns for your love? Will you love Him?

DID you ever reflect that there is not, in the whole

New Testament, one caution or guard against our over-trusting and over-exalting Christ? You never would send a child to a person under circumstances such as those under which we are sent to Christ, if we are not to trust in Him, and exalt Him. You never would dream of sending a child into the presence of one in every way calculated to win its affections and confidence, unless it was right and proper that it should cherish affection for, and repose confidence in, that person. Suppose that children were to be placed under the charge of a teacher by whom would be presented to them all that was admirable in character, all that was winning in affection, all that was stimulating and glittering in imagination, that which drew about itself every one of the tendrils of sprouting life in them, when it was known that this was only professional, and that they were in the end to be wrenched and torn from the object to which their hearts had become so firmly bound, as the husk is wrenched and torn from the corn. What would be thought of such a course in the case of a teacher and his pupils?

Now behold Christ. What being can be conceived of that would be more likely to arouse aspiration, to catch the longing heart, to win the affection and the confidence? Consider what must be the result if we are brought under the influence of such a being. And if it is wrong, if it is idolatrous for us to love Christ, and depend upon Him, how cruel it is that we should be placed in such relations to Him that we are drawn to Him and led to throw ourselves upon Him, and obliged to say, "Our life is hid with Christ in God. Without Him, we are nothing. In Him, we are all things. He is our way, our hope, our light, our bright and morning star," and receive not one word of caution, not one monitory remark, not one hint

10

or admonition that it is not worth our while to trust in
Him, or that it is wicked to worship Him; not even so
much as this: Be careful that you do not put the **crown**
on His head, lest you cheat the eternal Father! And **if**
it is not right for us to love Him, and trust Him, and
worship Him, then, instead of a Saviour, we have a rav-
ening, destroying being in the Christ of the New Testament. If I may put my being on Him; if I may feel
that He has suffered for my sins, that He has borne my
sorrows, and that my life is **grafted into** Him; and if **I**
may pour out everything in me of thought, and zeal, and
worship toward Him, — then blessed be God for Him;
but if it is wicked for me to do these things, then I cannot thank God for Him. God should not have added to
the misery of our condition by giving us such a being,
and then making it wicked for **us to worship Him.**

But I am **not** afraid to worship **Christ.** I will trust
myself to worship Him. I will **trust those dearest to me**
to worship Him. In the arms of Christ's love nothing
shall hurt you. **Love** on, trust on, worship on. Let go
your most ardent devotions toward Him. There is no
Divine Jealousy. The anxieties that afflict the sons of
earth in their ideas of God, never exist in heaven. Christ
is the soul's bread, — eat ye that hunger. He is the
water of life, — drink ye that thirst. He is the soul's end,
— **aim at Him.** He is the soul's supreme glory, — yield
to every outgush of joy and enthusiasm of worship that
springs up in **your heart** toward Him. Those that are
in heaven bow down **before Him, and** ascribe blessing,
and honor, and glory, and power, to Him that sitteth upon
the throne, and to the Lamb, forever and ever. Let us
not, then, fear to worship Christ.

Your honors here may serve you for a time, as it were for an hour, but they will be of no use to you beyond this world. Nobody will have heard a word of your honors in the other life. Your glory, your shame, your ambitions, and all the treasures for which you push hard and sacrifice much will be like wreaths of smoke. For these things, which you mostly seek, and for which you spend your life, only tarry with you while you are on this side of the flood.

———

When a man, standing before a magnificent work of art, or some wonderful phenomenon of nature, — some rugged mountain, some thunderous fall, like that of Niagara, or some beautiful landscape valley, — finds his taste so waked up that he loses command of himself, and breaks forth into an ecstasy of admiration, his sensations are transcendent.

But when we stand, not before unspeaking canvas, or inert mountains, or senseless water, but in the presence of some hero, some man that has stood among men nobler than the noblest, and truer than the truest, and has carried the fate of a nation in his hand without betraying it, how grand a thing is a true man, that carries in his life and conduct something of God! And who is there that is so unfortunate as not to know what a glorious thing it is to go out in admiration, almost in worship, toward such a man?

But what, then, ought our feelings to be when we stand, not before a man, nor before a mere spark, but before the everlasting God; when we stand before that Being who created the innumerable orbs of which this earth is but a specimen; when we stand before that Being whose ways generations and ages have sought in vain to find out; when we stand before that Being of whose love all the affections of father, and mother, and husband, and wife, and child, and brother, and sister, and friend, and lover, are but faint intimations, and of whose attributes the divine qualities of men are but the slightest hints? And when he comes as our maker and preserver, and the author of the eternal inheritance of bliss prepared for us, and asks that we experience this rapture of admiration for Him, how reasonable is His request, and how blessed to us ought to be the prerogative and privilege of making Him the object of our highest worship!

To me it seems, and has always seemed, very strange that there should be a kind of hesitation at worshipping Christ by those who believe that their ideas of the Father are derived from Him. "No man hath seen God at any time; the only-begotten Son, who is in the bosom of the Father, hath declared Him." If you take a given number of qualities, and lift them up, and call them God, you worship, not the name, but the qualities; and if you take the same qualities, and lift them up, and call them Christ, you still ought to worship the qualities, and not the name. There are many persons who do not hesitate to lift up the qualities which they see in Christ, and call them "Father," and pray to them, and worship them, who have a superstition about praying to these same qualities and worshipping them when they are called "Christ." But they are the same, whether you call them "Father" or "Christ." All that you know of God, and all that you have in distinction from the heathen world, has come to you through the revelation of Jesus Christ. It is what you see in Him, and though you may worship it under the name of "Father," it is Christ that you worship.

Why not, then, worship Him under His own name? We need not consult our fear, we may consult our longing, as to whether we shall lean upon the Saviour.

———

CHRIST says that in every burdened hour He is your staff; that in every peril He is your rescuer; that in every temptation He is the gate through which you are to escape; that in every sickness He is your physician. Yea, He stands in the portal of the grave itself, and declares that He has power over death. "Because I live, ye shall live also." He takes the very keys of the other life, and opens the door thereof, and stands the universal Saviour, and with a voice like that of one born to command, and clothed with the supremacy of Divine power, He says, "Lo, I am with you alway, even unto the end of the world."

Consider what scope there is in these representations of Christ. All our wants for time and for eternity are made to point toward and centre in Him, as their everlasting supply. Suppose, then, instead of hunting texts, and attempting to prove by force of logic that He is absolute God, we should take that other process, which consists in every day attempting to employ Him as He is presented to be employed in the New Testament; suppose our life should settle this matter; suppose we should find in our personal experience evidence of His divinity, — what would be the effect? If He feeds you, if He quenches your thirst, if He wakes your imagination, if He inspires your sweetest thoughts and feelings, if He sustains you, if He is your vital breath and your strength here and your salvation hereafter, and you acknowledge what He does, and accept Him as what He is, then, I ask, can any worship be higher than that which you offer to

Him? Can you reserve anything better than you have given to Him?

THE angels sang, " Glory to **God in** the highest, **and** on earth peace "; but the angels were prophets. They saw through a long tube, and the peace which they saw was the bright crystal gate of the future. Christ at the **other end of** the tube, said, " I came not to send peace, but a sword." **He came to** send tumult, revolution, war. **And why?** Because He meant to have peace. That **is** just what He meant to have.

Suppose when a man goes to make a violin you follow him, saying, " He must, of course, have music at every step." When in the forest he cuts the timber, you hear the blows of the axe, and the crash of the falling tree, and you say, " **That is what you call a** musical instrument, is it ?" Yes, that is **the beginning of it.** And when the saw rips through the log, when the plane glides over the board, and when the file and rasp are brought **to bear** upon it, the sounds that greet your ear are harsh and un-musical. All the processes by which you make the sound-ing-board are accompanied with disagreeable noises. And even when it is finished, **it does** not produce pleasing sounds till it has been tuned. And have you ever heard anything more unearthly than the scream of a violin string when it is being screwed up? How it yells and yelps! But when the instrument is tuned, a Paganini or an Ole Bull **will take** it up, and upon it discourse the sweetest music.

Christ did come for peace, but the process of work-ing it out is like sawing timber, or like screwing up the string of a violin. It is not meant that there shall be peace till there is a consummation of **purity**; till an adjustment has taken place inside of every man; till the relations of men are adjusted to their outward life; till men are adjusted to their fellow-men, and the **vast** multitude are chorded for God's choral harmonies. Therefore you need not look for peace right away. Peace is not going to dawn very soon, if there is to be no peace till there is perfection in the individual.

In a man's head there is an **up** and a **down.** The upper and the lower faculties reside there. And every vote that is taken in the mind is carried by a majority of the ruling forces ; not by a majority of the faculties, but by a majority of the *ruling forces.* Just as long as a man is not in danger of changing from bad to good, of going from wrong to right, just so long is he allowed to think and meditate as much as he pleases about it. And therefore the higher faculties of a man's mind are like prisoners — good men — confined up stairs in a great castle. Veneration, an admirable fellow, walks **up** and **down the apartment, and talks about the beauty of worship; the sanctity of religion; the** nobleness of prostrating one's self before God. Imagination, hearing Veneration preach **in such a** beautiful manner, gets **up,** and begins to talk about the glories of the eternal sphere. Yea, it flies thither, and sees the very battlements of heaven, its pearly gates, and its walls of many precious stones ; and in ecstasy **of joy,** it comes back with seraphic intelligence from that blessed abode. Conscience, that always sits like a chief-justice on the bench, pronouncing judicial decisions, talks about duty, about right and wrong, and fills the other prisoners with excellent views of truth and rectitude. Each **one of** the higher faculties having spoken in a way to inspire a yearning for liberty,

they take a vote, and decide that they will break away
from their confinement. "Agreed," says Veneration,
"I'll go"; and Ideality says, "I'll go"; and Conscience says, "I'll go"; and Faith says, "I'll go";
and Love says, "I'll go"! Accordingly, they all start,
and the first thing they meet is the bull-dog, Temper.
He says, "No, you won't"; and Pride, the jailer, says,
"No, you won't"; and greedy Avarice, the sentinel,
standing and pushing in double bolts, says, "No you
won't." And by watch-dogs, and jailers, and sentinels,
they are ignominiously driven back to their cell, to look
out of the window, and think again!

How often does a man, on Sunday, sit in the upper-
rooms of his mind, and think of glorious things that he
means to do. Veneration is all right, Conscience is all
right, Hope is all right, Faith is all right; and they say,
" God, and divine purity, and true manhood, and nobleness, — we are for those things: let us try to-morrow
to live for them." To-morrow comes, and the first step
the man takes, " Bow wow," says bull-dog, Bargain, right
before him. The next step he takes he is confronted by
that old tyrant, Party. Then in succession he comes
upon Partnership, Social Pleasure, Custom, and Habit.
Old Adam, multiform, briarean, crosses his path at every
turn. And he does not get a vote till the top of the head
and the bottom of the head have both voted; and the
bottom carries it, usually.

NOT golden veins in mountains, not diamonds in the
sands, nor precious stones, not treasures which are heaped
up in cities, nor the things which minister to the senses or
to bodily ease or comfort, are best. They are second best.
They are useful if they serve; they are evil if they rule.

For the world is God's nursery. Here He brings up His children. And, as in our houses all things are good, — pictures, books, carpets, furniture, the table and the couch, — if they aid us to rear well our children, and are good but for that; as our children are themselves the chief treasures to us, and their character the chief part of themselves, so is it in God's great household-globe, **on which** we dwell. We are to despise nothing as if the being transient or physical were **a** reason for contempt. We are to treasure all things, — only we are to measure their value **by their relation to our** higher nature.

THE cradle empty blesses us more than the cradle filled. Therefore if **I** had had my **way, how** much leaner I should have been ; how much less I should have been built up in affection ; how much more deficient I should have been in faith ! But against wish, and against strong crying and bitter tears, God held on His way, and took one, and two, and many ; **and I bless** His name. I am not good, **but I am** better. And that which **I could not** see then, is very plain **to me now. For each of the tears** that dropped has become a sentence, and the literature which they form is as the interpretation of the wisdom of God in His administration in **earthly** things.

IF you go into the great manufactories at Lowell and Lawrence, that which **you** see is that which you never see elsewhere ; and **that** which you see elsewhere is what you almost never see there. You see there, not colors, but dirty dye-vats ; **wool** rather **than thread,** or thread rather than fabrics. Instead of seeing rolls of finished carpeting or cloth, you hear the rattling of looms, spinning-jennies, and other machinery. These things, which absorb your attention, you leave behind you, when you go out; whereas it is in New York, in London, in the great commercial mart, that you see the fabric which is produced by them.

Now, this world is a great rattling manufactory, and all these physical things are but the stationary engines and looms. These are the things that men never carry with them from this world. And yet, how important they are! Our life, as it were, is placed in a loom, and woven by these things. It rolls up, and is hidden as fast as it is woven; and it is to be taken out of the loom only when we leave this world. We shall see the pattern of it only when we abandon the things which act upon us here.

I PREACH the Gospel just as my Master gave it to me. He told me that it should be a sword, and I am bound that it shall be. He said it should be fire, and it does set men on fire. You cannot find anything in the Gospel that makes for peace when men are wicked. As long as lies are told, so long every word of Christian truth is an executioner of lies, that ferrets them out and visits summary punishment on them. As long as dishonesties are rife, so long every honesty of God's Word is God's sheriff sent out to arrest them. As long as there is cruelty, so long every humanity of the Gospel is God's angel sent like Gabriel abroad to defend the right and smite the wrong. As long as men are corrupt, so long the Gospel is God's firebrand to burn out of them the dross, leaving but the pure gold.

IN all the abysses of God's nature, in all the infinite out-stretchings of His being, in all that wondrous personality that fills heaven and eternity, in all that incomprehensible magnitude that we call God, what extraordinary capacity there must be of loving! How strange must be the conception of an infinite God, higher than the heavens, and broader than the earth, upon every one of whose attributes, upon every one of whose affections, we put the term "infinite," — a term expressing that which is boundless, limitless, exhaustless!

DID you ever see men made in this world? They had no great wisdom; they had no great honor; they had no great heroism; they had no great patience; they had no great meekness; they had no great wealth of love. But they had a certain muck-wisdom; they knew how to thrust their hand in where dirt was to be moulded; they knew how to amass property; they knew how to construct ships and houses; they had a kind of ferreting eye, a sort of weasel sagacity; they were keen and sharp; they were said to be prosperous, thriving men; they were being built up according to the estimation of men. Give a man a thousand pounds, and you have laid the foundation on which to build him, — you have got his feet built; give him five thousand, and you have built him up to the knees; give him ten thousand, and you have built him to the loins; give him twenty thousand, and you have built him above the heart; give him fifty thousand, and he is made all over. Fifty thousand pounds will build a man in this world. One hundred thousand makes a splendid fellow, as the world goes. The great trouble, however, is, that although the materials may not be very costly as God looks upon them, men find it difficult to build themselves in this way. Besides they are very easily unbuilt. Where a man is merely what he owns, it does not take long to annihilate him. There are thousands and thousands of men of whom if you take away their houses, and ships, and lands, and fiscal skill, and such other qualities belonging to them as they will not want in heaven, and cannot carry to heaven, there will not be enough left to represent them there, of righteousness, and godliness, and faith, and love, and patience, and meekness, and such like qualities. They have used all these qualities up for fuel for their machine. It has been their **business in** life to sacrifice probity that they might be rich ; that they might gain power and influence ; that they might make their hold on this world broader and stronger. And if they cannot carry forth these things, which have been the objects to the attainment of which they have devoted all their energies, what is left for **them** to go out of life with ? You see not only single specimens, but whole **ranks of** these dwarfed, insect class of men, patting each **other on the** shoulder, registering each other, weighing each other, and speaking **of** each other as " our first men," " our largest men," " our influential men," " our strong men" ; and yet, if you were to take away from them that of which the grave will divest them, you could not find them, even with a microscope !

EVIL is eternal in the sight **of God,** unless **it be** checked and cured. Sin, like a poisonous weed, **resows** itself, and becomes eternal **by** reproduction. Now God looks **upon the** human race in the light of these truths. And tell me what **other** attribute of God, what other inflexion of His **character, is** so noble **and** sublime as this, — His gentleness ? How wonderful has been its duration; how deep its nature ; how exquisite its touches ; how rich its fruit ! What assurance does it bring to our hope ! How boundless **is** the scope **it** opens to our eye !

How wonderful is the combination of traits in His disposition! It was because the lion and the lamb first lay down together in the heart of God, that the prophet declared that they should yet do it on earth!

HE who unites himself to any great idea or truth which God has established, may be sure that he will go forth from conquering to conquer; not by reason of any might or skill in himself, but because he is united to God, and is a laborer together with Him. The man that adopts any divinely-appointed truth, no matter what the world thinks of it, rides in God's chariot, and has God for his charioteer. No man rides so high, and in such good company, as the man that allies himself to a truth that God loves and men hate. Where a thing is true, and just, and pure, and noble, and right, let law say what it pleases, let institutions say what they please, let men say what they please, let the world say what it pleases, do you cast yourself into that thing without heed, without calculation, without fear, and you will be in the hollow of the hand of God Almighty, and will be on the sure road to victory, since He himself is the all-victorious One.

I THINK the most piteous thing in this world is never written. I have read many a poem, and novel, and tale, that made me cry, — and whether they were true or not, it was all the same; but of all affecting poems and novels and tales, I think life itself is the most affecting, — common life, just as it turns out in the world. And when I go out to measure men, I say to myself, as one after another they pass before me, "Suppose that man should drop out of life, what would become of him?" It pains me to see how worthless men are, — to see how **men** stand in life, and what they are. I am sometimes called to perform the burial-service over men of whom I could not say a word, and of whom, if I had expressed what I felt, I should have said, "I bless God that he is gone. The world is better off for his having been taken out of it." Look at human life, break through all the sentimental ways of society, weigh men as you weigh gold, unmixed with dirt or quartz or any other substance, take men up and see how much there is of them that really answers the end of the life to come, and how many there are that, dying, would not be missed. How few there **are that, dying,** would make the community feel poor! **How few** there are that, being dead, would yet speak!

WITHOUT fault of their own, persons of other countries, **being** driven from their homes by revolutions, flee to Britain or America. They were educated to be gentlemen, in their own lands; and being born noblemen, they had some seeming right to be educated as gentlemen, — that is, to live a lazy life, and have others support them. But driven forth from their seeming fate, how can they subsist? They cannot teach, for they cannot speak the language. They cannot **work, for they have** learned no **trade. They** have only learned to open their mouth and **take the food** ready to drop into it. Of all miserable men, I think they are the most miserable who have been educated intellectually, and who have fine tastes and strong emotive powers, but who have no sort of ability **to** get along when they **are thrown out** of the circumstances in which they were educated, and are obliged, under new circumstances, to shift for themselves. I have **seen very** many such men, — men built exquisitely for mortification and suffering, and apparently for nothing else. But how dreadful, compared with the misadjustment of these men, is that of those who, having striven to make themselves something in this life, die and go into the other life to find that they do not know its business; that they cannot speak its language; that they have no faculties educated which have respect to their relations there; that those faculties which they have educated have no function there; and that those which they need to use there, have not been trained! Such men will stand fools and foolish forever! The life that is substantial they have thrown away. Their education, instead of being for the other life, has been for this life alone.

God will never receive us upon any invoice sent from this world. Every man is to be reappraised, unpacked, examined, mostly thrown away; and that which is least esteemed here is to be measured most and judged most, and the reverse; so that the last shall be first, and the first shall be last. The ten thousand who go without a procession to the grave, whom no man knows to have died and no man misses, have their procession on the other side, and armies in triumph shout them home; while men who are followed to the grave by a long procession, who are buried with much state, and who fill the world for a time with the sound of their fall, are received on the other side silently and without procession. And happy is it for them if they do not rise to shame and everlasting contempt.

If a man is righteous and godly, if a man's life consists in soul-treasure, no matter what may befall him, his nature cannot be touched; it will ever shine on. If he is deprived of his worldly surroundings, it is all the more affecting and influential. When a truly great man has these things taken away from him, it is as when a cocoa-nut has the rind taken off; it is as when a grain has the husk taken off. Take a man who is good and noble and true, and remove from him everything through which he has stood and glowed and radiated, and men will bow down to him, and say, "That is virtue! That is godliness! That is God in the soul!" And the man will be more known, more felt, more revered, when standing merely in his own intrinsic wealth, than when clothed with the trappings of this world.

THE whole globe, it seems to me, is a sacrament; and time is full of the most solemn lessons and the most momentous truths. And yet we let day after day and year after year pass over our head, and our constant thought is, — what? That the winter is severe; that the day is inclement; that the rain incommodes our party, or mars our pleasure. We sit and judge of the various events of the seasons with reference to our selfish convenience. We fret, and fume, and complain of God's phenomena, judging them by our wishes, and without thanksgiving, or admiration, or gratitude, or reverence, but full of spite and peevishness and ill-feeling.

MEN are seeking for only this life. A short life it is, and exceedingly imperfect and rudimentary, at best. It is like a road, which is good for travelling, but poor for sleeping. This world is magnificent for strangers and pilgrims, but miserable for residents. The very moment a man carries himself as though this were his home, and begins to build as though he would live here, that moment the world is not a fit place for a temporary residence for him. It is only when a man considers this world as a school-house, and not a dwelling, that it will serve the purpose it was intended to serve. The academy is not a place to live in. We go into it that in due time we may come out prepared for a higher sphere. What the anvil and the blacksmith-shop are to the sword of the warrior, that this world and its instrumentalities are to us. We are forged here to be used hereafter. We are to receive our perfected selves, and to come to the fruition of ourselves, only when God shall open the door of this world, and let us out. We are like a ship that, being built, lies high and dry, and whose sea-going qualities cannot be known till she is launched upon the ocean. We do not know our own powers. When at death we are launched upon the sea of eternal life, then we shall know what we are.

Do you not know that the Devil never makes a rout in a man's heart so long as he bears undisputed sway there? It is only when it is attempted to throw him out, that he shows the man how strong a hold he has upon him. He lets him talk, and say, "I can rid myself of this habit whenever I please," and such like things. It rather pleases him to have him talk so. But when he undertakes to rid himself of the habit, he lets him know that he cannot do it so easily as he supposed.

" Who have fled for refuge to lay hold upon the hope set before us, which hope we have as an anchor." These figures do not succeed each other, but they intermingle. It may be a violation of rhetorical rules, but it is the fulfilment of a rich imagination thus to commingle figures ;

for no one who is apt to see things in symbols and by pictures, but knows that for the same thought there will often arise several distinct figures striving to represent it, and that the mind will, in its more fervid moods, take both figures or many of them in part. A fervid imagination uses figures just as freely as words, and as we often change words or inflect a sentence from the very overflow of feeling as the progress of thought develops in our mind, so is it with figures and illustrations. In this case I think there is a sublime unity in these figures that is not often seen. It is as if the apostle had seen the soul beset with great troubles like storms. Doubts and temptations fill the air black; the poor driven soul flies for shelter, the very wind drives it; the peril of the elements and their terrible threat speed it to some covert, and so it makes for the refuge. And then, in the universality of his imagination, the apostle sees the storm not alone upon the land, but upon the sea; the mariners are swept with the wind and dashed with the overwhelming waves, and for his peril the anchor is the refuge. The storm is common to both figures: the refuge is for the land, the anchor for the sea; and both of them mean one thing, — security. For what a strong house is in the one sphere, that a sure and steadfast anchor is in the other.

WHAT strange creatures men are! They bow down and bend under God's mysterious dealings; and when they find their hands empty, their hearts full, their plans frustrated, their wishes crossed, and their life burdensome, they go mourning and wondering why it should be so; and then they go back to the household and pursue upon their sons and daughters the same policy that has been . pursued upon them, and marvel that the little child cannot understand that it is for its good that it is denied things that it desires, and that it has put upon it things that it dislikes; and why it cannot understand that life is a unit, and that its welfare in the future depends upon its right management in the present! They reproduce in their dealings with their children God's dealings with them, and are yet forever wondering why God deals with them as He does, and why their children do not understand that their administration over them is beneficial and wise!

———

The nature of a seed is such that when it is thrown into the ground it unfolds itself without culture, without any exterior influence beyond the light and air and soil, to be just that thing which it was meant to be. Every flower comes to its own nature; and although culture may make it larger and finer, yet it expresses the radical idea involved in the seed. It is so with every insect, and every animal. But man is not a creature that, according to this analogy, being born into the world opens and develops himself to that which God meant manhood to be. When left in the most favorable conditions, man does not, and will not, so develop himself; for that which is required to make manhood is not in him. There were elements left out of the nature of man without which that nature never can come to its perfection. For, as in fruits sugar comes from the sun, so in man grace comes from the Sun of righteousness, working in us, and elaborating the things that we need. But they are never wrought out by any process that takes place by the natural faculties in the soul.

———

As in a piano two chords are united to make one sound,

and they both respond to one stroke of the hammer, so in Christ His own will and the will of His Father were united to make one parallel motive, and they both responded to the action of one nature. There was no distinction between them. To please, to honor, to expound and declare, to serve, to love His Father, was that which gave Him rest and comfort. Without this meat of doing the will of the Father, His life would have been empty, and His soul forever hungry.

It is a noble view, this, to take of Christ's life, — namely, that it was spontaneous; that it had calm zeal and the willingness of enthusiasm. It was not borne as a load; it was performed as a joy. "Who for the joy that was set before him endured the cross, despising the shame." I know that Christ is predicted as a man of sorrows, and acquainted with grief; yet it is the very wonder and mystery, that up through every sorrow His heart sent such a flame of love and joy that affliction became the very fuel of gladness. I think that our views of the Saviour are perfectly destructive to all respect even. I think the painters' ideas of Christ, as represented in material suffering, are simply vulgar and infernal; and if I had the power I would take every one of those disgracing canvases and rip them and burn them, that make such a masquerade of the divinity of Christ in His suffering state. For do we not know that there are in our own houses children who, for their father's sake, will bear suffering, and not shed a tear? and are they more than Christ? Are there not parents and companions that will carry troubles vehement, for the sake of those round about them, and make them so luminous that none shall see them? And is it not woman's peculiar office to walk a martyr, and yet wear a face of joy and hope and radiancy, so much does her affection overcome and quite subdue material suffering and lower forms of disappointment? And how many men carry a world of trouble for the sake of their country and their fellow-men, and yet stand prophets of peace and joy themselves! How many confessors and martyrs have borne inexpressible torments for the sake of truth, singing while the flame itself was scorching their flesh, their soul beating down the nerve and overcoming the body, and making them triumphant over physical and mental suffering by the power of higher feelings which quite adumbrated and put out the lower ones! And must we conceive of Christ as one who crouched under suffering? Was He the only one that did not know how to make clouds carry colors; or all of whose clouds were lead-color or black? Was He one who bore suffering with weakness? Was He one that was overcome and cast down by suffering? No, the glory of Christ was this: that He accepted His mission with such cheerfulness and gladness and enthusiasm; that He did the will of God with such alacrity; that though He was pre-eminently, and above all that ever lived, a man of suffering, yet He counted it a joy to suffer; that He was an overmastering sufferer.

THAT Christ loved, longed for the personal presence of His disciples, was very patient with their rudeness, ran to their help with more love, when they fell into sin, than before, pitied and excused their infirmities; that Christ mourned over those whom He condemned, and sadly denounced Jerusalem, amid tears; that He loved birds, flowers, children; that He loved to sit at twilight under the olive-trees on the mountain over against Jerusalem,

and commune with His followers of the day's experience;
that He loved the solitude of the mountain, and prayed
through the night; that He would gently steal **upon the**
evening walk to Emmaus, and talk like a stranger to
those whom He entirely knew, and hesitate at the door,
to draw forth a more earnest welcome, — in short, if these
ten thousand shades of thought, and feeling, and conduct,
that give individuality and personality to Christ, also interpret the disposition of God, how near do they bring
Him to our tastes, our affections, our imaginations, and
our reason! I love to carry every act of Christ right
home to Him as very God; and to say, This tells me
how God feels, and what He is, for it is God himself!

THERE are two ways in which the word *nature* unfor-
tunately is employed. One represents the characteristic
use which we make of ourselves. That we call nature;
but only when the word is used in its perverted sense.
A man's nature is spoiled in that sense. But there is a
higher and prior use of the word, — namely, that which
represents the soul and the faculties as God created them,
and meant that they should be. Now, I hold that the
original nature of man was to love God and serve Him;
that that is the secret of harmony in the soul; that any
other theory by which you attempt to reconcile man to
himself on earth will fail; and that the only way for a
man to have the full possession of the powers and forces
of life, is that in which he is most addicted to love and
trust in God.

THE faculty of veneration is itself to be educated into
. Christ, and every one of its offices is to be made Christian. For, according to the law of Nature, fear and

dread are the handmaids of worship. Worship should be festive; but ever since the ascetic element entered it, it has been the darkest and most dreaded thing possible. Men have symbolized it in their churches. Stone above, stone below, and stone on either hand! Darkness in the roof, and darkness in the window! Churches have been crypts. It would seem as though men had drawn their conceptions of the sanctuary from the places of worship of the earlier Christians who were forced to worship under ground. Cathedrals and churches have been dimly lighted; and the little light that has come into them has come through paint and ground glass, in a way that has misinterpreted God's sunlight. And men have entered them shuddering, and on tiptoe, as if the presence of God was to be dreaded; have bowed down as if to worship Him was the most terrible thing in the world; have risen up scarcely daring to whisper; and have hurried out as if they had been disembodied spirits, rather than warm-hearted men of flesh and blood. The conception of worship has been sombre and dark. It has been heathen; for the conception of worship in Christ's time was as light as the canopy of heaven. A most noble doctrine of Christian life was that which the Saviour taught when He declared that whatever proceeded from any heart Godward, was true worship; and that not in Jerusalem, nor in the mountain of Samaria, nor in any one place, but wherever a heart went out to God, was acceptable worship. In that great teaching Christ showed us that worship is to be Christianized. We are in the bondage of old superstition, and the worship of nine hundred and ninety-nine churches in a thousand is yet tinged with the sombreness illustrative of the heathen element of fear. The lightness, the gayety, the cheer of true wor-

ship, is but little known among men. What the hilarity
of children is, breaking away from masters and schools,
and romping home to overpower the household with joy,
such is to be the worship of God's children. The name
of *Father* ought not to make any man tremble that is a
child.

SOMETIMES, in dark caves, men have gone to the edge
of unspeaking precipices, and, wondering what was the
depth, have cast down fragments of rock, and listened for
the report of their fall, that they might judge how deep
that blackness was; and listening!—still listening!—
no sound returns! no sullen splash, no clinking stroke as
of rock against rock,—nothing but silence, utter silence!
And so I stand upon the precipice of life. I sound the
depths of the other world with curious inquiries. But
from it comes no echo, and no answer to my questions.
No analogies can grapple and bring up from the depths
of the darkness of the lost world the probable truths.
No philosophy has line and plummet long enough to
sound the depths. There remains for us only the few
authoritative and solemn words of God. These declare
that the bliss of the righteous is everlasting; and with
equal directness and simplicity they declare that the
doom of the wicked is everlasting.

The incorrigibly wicked, the deliberately impenitent,
have nothing to hope in the future, if they set aside the
light and the glory that shines in the face of Jesus Christ.
And therefore it is that I make haste, with an inconceiv-
able ardor, to persuade you to be reconciled to your God.
I hold up before you that God who loves the sinners and
abhors sin; who loves goodness with infinite fervor, and
breathes it upon those who put their trust in Him; who

makes all the elements His ministering servants; who sends years, and weeks, and days, and hours, all radiant with benefaction, and, if we would but hear their voice, all pleading the goodness of God as an argument of **re**pentance and of obedience. And remember that it is **this God** who **yet** declares that He will **at** last by no means **clear** the guilty.

WE must not confound devotion with piety. The one **is** the means: the other is the result. The one is **the** fire: the **other is** the food which it cooks. Devotion **is merely a method by** which you attempt to enkindle in yourselves spiritual life. It is not piety; it is the instrument of it. A man may read his Bible, the Prayer-book, and devout treatises, and give much time and attention to religious services, and yet be far from piety; just as a man may whirl a millstone and have no grain, no flour. And there are many persons that run the mill of piety, who grind nothing but bran, who certainly grind very little flour for the bread of life. There is a hundred times more devotion **than piety in the world. Many men pray not so much for** the sake **of** being better, as to furnish a substitute for not being better. They are not honest, they are not truthful, they are not noble, they are not loving, **they are not** disinterested, they are not ingenuous, and **they** know it, and they pray hoping that their prayers will be put against their deficiencies. They are conscious of doing wrong, and they have an idea that they can make amends for it by praying. They seem to think that if they praise God a good deal, and tell Him what they think of Him and of His government **a good** deal, and all that, He will accept their devotion as an equivalent for right conduct. Now, the only earthly object of devotion

11   **r**

is that it may afford means, instrumentalities, fuel, to en-
enkindle in men a true spiritual life. The life is something separate from the cause that produces it.

It is no virtue to be patient down hill; but to be
patient up hill is some virtue. In being patient with an
angel, in being patient with **a** saint, in being patient with
a model nature,—in that, there is no credit; but in being
patient with a man that is hard, and arrogant, and con-
temptuous, and that carries himself loftily, so that his
very look **and gesture** are an insult to you, there is some
credit.

Why to tell a nurse that she must be patient with her
sick ones, and yet excuse her from being patient with
those that have the dropsy; with those that have fevers;
with those that **are** delirious; with those that are weak,
and cannot help themselves, — that would be like giving
a direction to be patient with people in general, but
nobody in particular. But to be patient with *men*, is **to**
be patient with the whole sum of human infirmities, —
with all weaknesses, with all wants; and with all wickednesses, as well.

It is a period of the world when men should take
courage and be glad. I thank God every morning and
every night, and ten thousand times a day, that He permitted me to be born in such an age as this. Now a man
lives a year in a day. Now men are **not** living in January, in mid-winter, in a frozen ground where the roots
can suck no juice, where no leaves are playing in the
wind! We are living in the month of May, when winter
is gone, when the snows no longer cover deeply the earth,
and when birds are singing in the air. There are storms,

to be sure, but, after every thunder-storm, the leaves play, the roots grow, and ten thousand influences are operating to bring summer. Let us, then, be patient. Let us be hopeful. Let us have faith in God. He is very near to us: we know it by the wrath of the Devil; we know it by the way evil men cry out, saying, " Art thou come to torment us before our time?" we know it because some are cast down and are made to wallow, that the Devil may be driven out of them. Let him go; but let them arise, clothed, and in their right mind, and be found sitting at the feet of Jesus.

SOME men think of religion as if it were, on the whole, simply a title to heaven. They love the hymn, " When I can read my title clear." They understand deeds, and titles, and conveyances. Their heavenly title seems to them, in the earlier part of their religious experience, to be disputed. It is as if the Devil were some sneaking man seeking to invalidate their title to their property. They go into court, invalidate the claim of their adversary, and establish their own. That is to say, they are awakened, convicted, and converted. And now they say, " I have a title to heaven." It is as if a man had a large estate which he was carrying on in a certain way, and for which there had risen up a claimant, and he went before the tribunals, and there contested his right, and got a verdict in his favor, and then returned home, and lived on the estate as before, without repairing the fences, without better tilling it, without building new mansions upon it, but allowing it to remain the same old thistle-grown estate that it was before; the only change being that his title to it is confirmed, so that he can say, " I own it." There are a great many men to whom religion seems to

be simply the authentication of their title to heaven.
When they think they have obtained it, they say to themselves, "Now, whatever may befall the world, — while
they have a heritage, perhaps, of brimstone and fire, —
I am called, elected, sealed, and adopted. I am going to
heaven!" But their life remains the same as before.
They are no better, no more honorable, no more truthful,
no more spiritual, no more devout, no more holy.

WHEN, after a long, frigid, barren winter, the spring
comes and loves the earth a little while, how wondrous is
the change that takes place! When the month of May
comes and sits upon the North as a bird upon her nest,
there come forth from under its feathers sounds of new
life; the forest echoes with the voices of joyous songsters;
the roots start; the grass grows; the air smells sweet;
all things are full of richness and beauty. Just so it is
when spring comes to the soul; when the heart is touched
with the fructifying power of love. How instantly, under
such circumstances, does there grow up beauty, and fitness, and satisfaction! When it is human heart that
touches human heart, what a wondrous spring it brings!
what flowers and promises of fruit! But O, when it is
the heart of God that brings spring to our hearts; when
it is the heart of God that sets every root, and every bud,
and every leaf in us a-growing, how wondrous is the
beauty that is evoked! how wondrous is the promise of
fruit that is held out! And when we have once loved
Christ with all our heart, and soul, and mind, and strength,
and are able to say, "To do Thy will is my meat and my
drink," we have achieved the victory; we have overcome
all adversaries; we have found the way that is cast up,
on which the ransomed of the Lord are to return and

walk, with songs and everlasting joy upon their heads.
When we serve God reluctantly, fitfully, by turns, partially, we are living a hard life, a starved life, a wretched
life; but when we are so brought to Christ that we can
say, "Thy will be done," we are living an easy, a fed, a
happy life. The heart that every day can say " Father ";
that every day can say, "I love Thee"; that every day
can say, " Not my will, but Thine"; that every day can
say, " Lord, what wilt Thou have me to do?" that, in
short, can say, " My life is hid with Christ in God," —
the heart that can say that is able to pronounce the words
of consummation, the words of victory. There is little
more in life for him to do except to go on as an exemplar
and laborer for God, waiting till the Divine call summons
him to his glorification in heaven.

CHRISTIAN brethren, we are advancing nearer and
nearer, every year, to the consummation of our life-work.
We are coming, every year, nearer and nearer to that
final disclosure when God shall reveal to us what we are.
I have sometimes fancied what would be the cause of
most surprise and joy in the other life. In some hours,
when higher moral feelings predominate, it seems to me
that the first thing that will fill the heart of men will be
the vision of God, — the vision of the Redeemer. In
other hours, when craving affections are strongest, it
seems to me that whatever may be the glory of the presence of God, the first things the heart will recognize will
be its lost ones. At other times, when high and heroic
purposes of life are in the ascendency, it seems to me that
the sanctified spirits of the noble men that have dwelt upon
the earth — the great assembly of the just made perfect
— will first astonish and rejoice the heart. But I think,

after all, that scarcely less **than** before God himself, we shall stand in utter surprise and wonder before ourselves, when what **we** are is brought out; **when what life** has made us begins to be disclosed; when, standing in **the** Divine presence, the soul seems, even in that comparison, so noble **and** so full of glory that it is able to say, "I am satisfied." The glory that is to be ours doth not yet appear, but there are glimpses of it.

THE life of every Christian **on earth** has much **in it** that is mysterious; for it is aiming at an awful grandeur, which has never yet been unveiled. God carries in His bosom the full ideal. We know it not. We go moaning after music. We rudely grope for beauty. We are sick **men leaning on a** staff, and walking slowly for convalescence. **We do not know the things toward which we are** tending; **but** God **knows them.** There **are** few that suppose their moanings or yearnings mean anything, but God. The apostle says, "The Spirit helpeth our infirmities; for we know not what we should pray for as we ought; but the Spirit itself maketh intercession for us with groanings which cannot be uttered."

We see, then, the meaning of those strange longings and aspirations which so many have. They are the foreworkings in us of that which is to appear in the heavenly estate. **They** are not a mere vagrant restlessness. They are the yearning of the soul for itself. They are **the** homesickness of the heart for its future home. They are the attempt of the child to say "Father." We see, too, the meaning of those glimpses and visions which so many have. John says, "It doth not yet appear what we shall be." We are the sons of God, we know; but **what** that means, we do not know.

How unhappy must be a community bred to the inevitable meanness of slavery. **Men** that have such a load to carry may well stagger. Society built upon a foundation of injustice cannot bring forth just men. Slavery **does not eat** the slave half as much as it does the master. **It is a** scorpion-whip, deadly to **the hand that wields it, as well** as to the back that receives **its lash**.

A MAN that makes **cloth cannot eat** cloth. A man **that** makes porcelain, off **which men eat, cannot eat** porcelain. **That which is to hold men's food cannot** satisfy **their appetites. It is not your** worldly avocations, nor the immediate results **of your** worldly avocations, that can **satisfy you.** There **is a** great mistake made in this regard. Men suppose that if they rise early, and sit up late, and give themselves to right callings in right ways, they ought to be happy. No! your calling never was meant to be food. You must have something better than that **to feed upon.** Suppose a man does rise early, **and sit up late, and drive** a profitable **trade, and suppose that to do it he extin-**guishes taste, takes no pains to contemplate Nature, refuses to walk where **God speaks** through His works, cares for the family only in a small way of duty, and neglects to develop his higher affections, is it to be expected that he can be happy? He means, he says, to succeed in business; and when he has come to be fifty or sixty years of age, and has succeeded in business, he wonders that he does not enjoy what he has made. But it is not that that can satisfy him. I think that when men are stranded on wealth, and left to wander on its desolate shores, where nothing can grow, they are among the most pitiable of all men in the world, — and not the less so because they have made the mistake of supposing that a man's worldly avocation will feed his soul.

MIRTH is God's medicine. Everybody ought to bathe in it. Grim care, moroseness, anxiety, — all this rust of life ought to be scoured off by the oil of mirth. It is better than emery. Every man ought to rub himself with it. A man without mirth is like a wagon without springs, in which one is caused disagreeably to jolt by every pebble over which it runs. A man with mirth is like a chariot with springs, in which one can ride over the roughest road, and scarcely feel anything but a pleasant rocking motion.

THERE is no isolated thing known to us in creation. Everything is a part of something else. Nothing lives except by depending on some other thing. The bird eats the insect; the insect ate the leaf; the leaf fed upon the sap; the sap came from the ground; the ground drank at the cloud's lips; and so you may push all things back, and find that one stands on another. In this arrangement of creation, we need food for every part of the body. The body was not built so that it should stay built, but so that it must be rebuilt, in part at least, every single day. The bone needs one food, the hair another, the nerve another, and the muscle another. And, in analogy with this, the mind, just as much, demands stimulus and occupation that shall give to it the nourishment and vitality which food gives to the body. The child feeds upon the mother and the father. The parents' affections wake up the child's, and then feed them. The child's thoughts, too, are waked up by those of the parent, and fed by them. The mind-influence of the parent stimulates the child's mind, and gives it fulness and satisfaction. The soul will not have solitariness. That is hunger. It loves to dwell with those congenial to it. In the ordi-

nary and casual relations of life this is true. Men love
to travel in companies, and to work in companies, simply
because, it is said, they are social. But what do you
mean by that, but this: that there is a yearning thought
which goes out to the life by which one is built.

And it is to be remarked that the lower down upon
the scale a nature stands, the less it is developed, the less
it is civilized, the more it seeks food for the body and
from matter; while, on the other hand, the higher we
rise upon the scale, the more our nature is educated, the
more characteristically we become men, the more we
reach toward and touch the divine idea in our creation,
the more do we find that our life and our life-food are
in commerce with other natures. Now, all the while, this
nature is developing, and life is educating it, that it may
find its true nature in feeding upon God. What we are
doing every day is tending toward that which we are to
do when we come to the fulness of our being, and take
hold of the soul's real end and final supply — God. This
is the final end of every man. Plants do not express
themselves as soon as they come up. They *grow* to what
they mean, in the vegetable kingdom. So do men. They
are growing to their final forms. But everything in life
is in analogy. Everything is tending upon each lower
to develop the next higher, — upon matter, passion;
upon this, affection; upon this, sentiment; and upon this,
Divine love.

The Lord Jesus Christ declares Himself to be, and has
by thrice ten thousand believing ones been found to be,
the soul's true food. That is, there is not one single
thing in a man's nature which, if brought into commerce
with the Lord Jesus Christ, will not find its development
and satisfaction. There is not one element of a man's

11 *

being that cannot be so brought into connection with
the Lord Jesus Christ that intellectually he shall be both
developed and fed.

Do you suppose Paganini, who can play on one string
of the violin, could play on one key of an organ, which is
capable of giving forth but one sound? Even under the
hand of Paganini, one string can be made to discourse
only but poor music. But here are men whose being is
provided with forty strings, who have left thirty-nine,
and go about fiddling on one and wondering why they
do not succeed in playing high harmonies with orchestral
lives. They neglect all but one of the many instruments
the use of all of which is necessary to the attainment of
happiness, and wonder why they are not happy.

It is supposed that a man ought to preach what is
called *practical truth.* I think so myself. But then
some truths are practical just as a whip is which has no
lash, and with which you can touch only a near horse.
Other truths are practical as is the whip of a stage-driver
when driving a team of four or six horses, — a whip with
a long lash. He has to take a long stroke behind, and a
long throw forward, in order to get the crack; but when
he has got it, it is a good one. Some truths are without
lashes, and are only good to whip with close by, and others are long-lashed, and have to be carried through long
circuits before they can be made to produce their legitimate effects. That is the distinction I make between
preaching practical ethics and doctrine.

I believe, therefore, in doctrinal preaching. Doctrinal
preaching that has no feet, and does not know, when it
has taken flight, how to get down to the ground again;

doctrinal preaching that never touches life : all that gaseous stuff called doctrinal preaching, — this I heartily disbelieve in. But that doctrinal preaching which is like the moisture that rises from the ocean, the lakes, the rivers, and the damp places, **and** fills the upper sky, and, collecting in clouds, descends **in** the form of rain, to give **seed to the** sower, and bread to the eater, I most firmly believe in. I care not how broad you make the foundations of it, I care not how voluminous you make **the** principles of it, **I** care not how exact you make the intellectual processes of it, so that **it** is juicy, so that it is bud-bearing, so that **it** yields fruit, so that it aims at this **thing** — the building **up of** men in human life.

I HOLD that a world without a Sabbath would be like **a man** without a smile, like a summer without flowers, and like a homestead without a garden. It is the joyous day of the whole week. Men, however, feel, " Why, I thought the Sabbath-day **was** holy. I was taught **that it was** wicked to laugh or whistle till after sundown. **But now** I perceive that I was wrongly instructed, and **that I can** do what I please without committing **any** crime."

You may not break Sunday, but **you may** do great mischief. **You** have no right **to take a** liberty without thinking that there **are** children around **you, and** considering **what effect your** example is going to have on them. You are to hold this liberty of the Sabbath-day — if you choose to take it — subject to this law of edification. And I, for **one,** cannot conceive how any Christian man can **make the** Sabbath-day **a** day of **secular** pleasure, instead **of a** day of religious improvement.

" FOR my thoughts are not your thoughts, neither are

your ways my ways, saith the **Lord**. For as the heavens are higher than the earth, so are my ways higher than your ways, and my thoughts than your thoughts."

What is the teaching here? It is this: that God does not sit at the North Pole in cold, iceberg glory, saying, " Come here, and I will save you." He sits in the very bosom of tropical summer, and says to every one that wants to repent, "Come toward daylight; come toward growth; come toward blossoms; come toward fruit, — come; for with royal power I will draw you, and with royal power I will forgive you. **Do not** think that I am like other potentates: do not think that I am like a vengeful king that will lay some severe penalty upon his subjects, and then, perhaps, at last, accept their submission. My thoughts of generosity and of magnanimity are as much higher than those of the noblest man, as the heavens are higher than the earth. Therefore, forsake your way only, and return to me, and you shall live."

" AND I saw thrones, and they sat on them, and judgment was given unto them; and I saw the souls of them that were beheaded for the witness of Jesus, and for the word of God, and which had not worshipped the beast, neither his image, neither had received his mark upon their foreheads or on their hands, and they lived and reigned with Christ a thousand years."

This is an account of the resurrection of the witnesses. I do not know what the commentators make of it, but I prefer to think that the resurrection of the witnesses is going on all the time. We are now beholding the resurrection of men that a thousand years ago laid down their lives for principle. Nobody was capable then of appreciating the act or giving it publicity. The Devil had swept his pall over the whole world; but when these men had slept a thousand years they were to have resurrection in this world. Old Cromwell, — why, they trod him into the dust, and despised his grave. Even down to our day, they would **not let a** statue of him stand in **the House of** Parliament, — and he has been made more memorable **by its** not being there than he could **have** been by its being there. It would have been a disgrace to the memory of this heroic Christian to have placed his monument in the midst of those base men who treated with contempt his noble example. But he has had a resurrection in old England. To-day the spirit of **Crom**well is felt there. He is judging in that country. It is Cromwell, and Cranmer, and Latimer, **and** Ridley, and Rogers, and Wickliffe, and the other great men of England that died gladly for truth, and justice, and equity, and humanity, who are the enthroned sovereigns that sit now crowned in that nation. No man shall eject them; **no revolution shall throw them out of** their sovereignty. **Who rules in Florence to-day? Old Savonarola. They hung him, and quartered him,** and trampled **him into the** dust. But God hid him, and in these latter days God **has said** to him at last, "Come forth, **my son, and witness; now** thou shalt **live and** reign a thousand years"; **and he is** coming forth to live and reign. Old Huss was **burned in** Bohemia. He is not alive yet. He is only beginning to shake off the cerements of the grave. But he is yet to come forth and witness for the right, and live and reign a thousand years. **All** true men away back **to** the days when Noah built the ark, when patriarchs believed **in God,** when Daniel, rather than sacrifice his convictions, **went to** the lion's den; all the old prophets and **confessors, with Christ at** their head; all the disciples and apostles; every martyr all the way down to the present day that has been slain for the sake of principle, — these are royally to live again. It takes a great while **for** such seed to come up, because when it is up it is not going to die. The longer anything is to endure, the longer it is in being organized.

THE Christian truly accepts God as a father; not as a father in the sense of exterior fatherhood, but as a father of the soul. **And the** Christian is united to Him, as a child is to a parent, more by affection than by mere external ties. For my father is not father to me merely 'because he is blood-kindred, but a great deal more because he **is** soul-kindred, to me. And this is the case **with** the fatherhood of God to the Christian. It is not in **a** figurative sense that he accepts God as his Father, but in a real, literal spiritual sense.

O, THE insignificance of most **of our** lives! **Very** few men are permitted to be poets; very few men **are** permitted to be wise; very few men are permitted to be eloquent; very few men are qualified to be statesmen.

A woman that seemed to be endowed with everything that was noble, and that was calculated to fit one for the **most** eminent service, was called, in God's providence, to **marry a** man **that was** not her equal. She was placed in an obscure position. She was eclipsed in the household. She could not **walk the** saloon. She did not move in the midst of a circle of admirers. Her duties were to stay at home, to nourish the little sickly child, and to serve her stupid husband. While she might have been listening to the chime of the spheres, while she might have been communing, one would suppose, with the very Eternal, she was occupied with rocking the cradle, darning, knitting, sewing, washing, and cooking. She worked out her life in these little insignificant things; and sometimes, perhaps, she thought to herself, "Woe is me! To what end am I living?" Her child developed under her care, and learned to call her mother; and when it said, "Mother," she thought God spoke, so sweet was its voice to her. Now she began to walk up the golden path of love. In that child, born of her sufferings, and reared by her hand; in that child, for whom she had been a vicarious sufferer and saviour, freely giving her inward life, as first she gave her outward life; in that child, summoned to go forth as a messenger of truth, appointed to do some great work of love, — in that child, she expected more than a thousand times to reap her reward for all that she had done and suffered. But her hopes in him were blasted. Just as, after having passed through the glorious period of boyhood, he was touching manhood, in a moment the wave closed over him, and he was gone forever; and the labor of her life was ended, and she was stranded on the shores of despair; and she cried out, "Why was I born? and to what end have I lived?"

A hundred had marked her fidelity, and she had been schoolmaster to every one of them. A hundred had witnessed her patience, and all the sermons they had ever heard had not preached such a lesson to them as her silent example. Multitudes that had learned of her, in turn became teachers of others. Her influence spread wider than she dreamed. It was not until she had gone up to the end of life in obscurity, and God had caused the light of eternity to shine on her work, that she understood how glorious little things might be.

MANY men carry the promises of the Word of God as a miser carries bank bills, the face of which calls for countless treasures, but which he does not carry to the bank for presentation. An ignorant man takes a hundred-pound-note. He does not know what the stamp means, but he has been told that it means that the note is worth a hundred pounds sterling. It is worth nothing at all to him unless it will draw what it promises; and the way for him to ascertain whether it is worth anything or not, is to take it to the paying teller and see if it will draw the money. It is time to say that there is no money behind it, when, on its being presented, it is rejected.

I HAVE sometimes had the misfortune to sit in concerts where persons would chatter and giggle and laugh during the performance of the profoundest passages of the symphonies of the great artists; and I never fail to think, at such times, "I ask to know neither you, nor your father and mother, nor your name: I know what you *are*, by the way you conduct yourself here, — by the want of sympathy and appreciation which you evince respecting what is passing around you." We could hardly help striking a man who should stand looking upon Niagara Falls without exhibiting emotions of awe and admiration. If we were to see a man walk through galleries of genius, totally unimpressed by what he saw, we should say to ourselves, " Let us be rid of such an unsusceptible creature as that."

Now I ask you to pass upon yourselves the same judgment. What do you suppose angels, that have trembled and quivered with ecstatic joy in the presence of God, think, when they see how indifferent you are to the Divine love and goodness in which you are perpetually bathed, and by which you are blessed and sustained every moment of your lives ? How can **they** do otherwise than accuse you of monstrous ingratitude and moral insensibility which **betoken** guilt as well as danger?

THROUGHOUT the Bible it is declared that the things that we are permitted to see in this life are but intimations, glimpses, of what we shall see hereafter. " It doth not yet appear what we shall be." There are times when it seems as though our circumstances, our nature, all the processes of our being, conspired to make us joyful here ; yet the apostle says we now see through a glass darkly. What, then, must be the vision which we shall behold when we go to that abode where we shall see face to face ? What a land of glory **have** you sent your babes into! What a land of delight have you sent your children and companions into! What a land of blessedness are you yourselves coming to by **and by!** Men talk about dying as though it were going toward a desolate place. All the past in a man's life is down hill, and toward gloom ; and all the future in a man's life is up hill, and toward glorious sunrising. There is but one luminous point, and that is the home toward which we are tending, above all storms, above all sin and peril. Dying is glorious crowning; living is yet toiling. If God be yours, all things are yours. If Christ be yours, all heaven is yours. Live while you must, but yearn for the day of consummation, when the door shall be thrown open, and the bird may fly out of his netted cage, **and be** heard singing in higher spheres, and diviner realms.

GOD governs in the affairs of men, though we do not see Him. God watches the flow of daily life. He stands

in the market; He walks in the street; He beholds the
ways of business, the paths of temptation, the lanes of
pleasure, the sinks of evil, — in all places where men are
tasked, and tried, and made temptable, there stands God
looking, taking account; and not only beholding, but encouraging, cheering, and saying, if men would but hear
His voice, "It is always safe to be right; there is always
reward in virtue; there is always solid foundation in
righteousness." Everywhere the voice of God to men
is, "Seek first the kingdom of God, and His righteousness," — that is, seek, as the best and highest end of desire, my kingdom, and my righteousness, — and it shall
take nothing from, but shall add all things to you.

TRUE religion carries health and strength into the soul.
It regulates all things; it subordinates all things to their
just positions; it withdraws from men no faculty; it ties
up no power; it extinguishes no instinct; it imprisons no
part of the mind, — it directs and regulates. Religion is
only another word for the right use of a man's whole self,
instead of a wrong use of himself. It puts men into connection with God; it brings them into harmonious relations to their fellow-men; it gives them direction for the
achievement of duty; it opens to them the coming world,
and inspires them with ardent desires for it; it makes
them love whatever is good, and abhor whatever is bad;
it inspires reverence, obedience, and love toward God and
toward our superiors among men; it inculcates justice,
mercy, and benevolence toward our fellow-men; it indues
us with courage, with patience, with contentment; it commands industry, frugality, and hospitality; it enjoins honesty, truthfulness, uprightness, simplicity, and integrity.
And that men, in their ignorance and weakness, may feel

the importance of virtue and of the truest piety, Christ reveals the immortality of man's nature, the glory of the heavenly state, the sympathy of God with the struggles of human life, and, above all, sets before men, in a perfect pattern, the example of the life of Christ, who was tempted in all points like as we are in this earthly strife, and yet without sin, teaching us both by precept and his victorious career.

No man knows half the fulness of his own being until inspired to a Christian life. If you will walk with me in January over the fertile places in the fields, and through the forests, you will see what man is in his natural state. The earth is full of roots, not one of which knows how to live. The trees are full of buds, every one of which is closed and bandaged so that it cannot expand. All things are populous, but all things are curdled, congealed, restrained. Although, in his natural state, man is full of high, godlike powers, yet they are in a condition of bondage, and inactivity; and the coming of religion to him is like the coming of spring to the soil and the forests, when all things begin to grow. When a man attains some degree of ripeness in his spiritual nature, he may be likened to the fields and the forests in midsummer; and when he has passed through life under the stimulating influences of religion, he may be likened to plants and trees in autumn, when they yield their fruit in exceeding abundance, and in a state of perfect ripeness.

It is not what a man gets, but what a man is, that he should think of. He should first think of his character, and then of his condition. He that has character need have no fears about his condition. Character will draw after it condition. Circumstances obey principles.

Our Master said, " Strive to enter in at the strait gate, for many will seek to enter in, and shall not be able." For it was taken for granted that no man could **afford to** be damned. No man can afford to lose immortality **in** heaven. No man can afford to be condemned to shame, and swept out from the presence of God with the off-scouring of the earth.

There are times, I suppose, in which the most zealous would, if it were God's will, be glad to die, — to retire from the battle of life, — because they think it will make no difference whether they live or die. They have such a consciousness of imperfection, of inferiority, of unfitness in themselves, that they feel that it could scarcely be worse, and that it might be much better, if they were out of the world, and their places were filled by others.

What is a drop of water of itself? What can be more harmless? **What is weaker? What is less** potent for any effect? **It is** mist, invisible. **It rises** through **the** imperceptible paths of the air, and hangs unseen in the heavens, till the cold strikes it, and it congeals into clouds, and falls in the form of rain, perhaps on the mountain's top, and is sucked up by the greedy earth. Still sinking through the earth, it reaches the line of the rocks, from whose sides it oozes out and trickles down, when, finding other drops as weak as itself, they unite their forces ; **and** the sum of the weakness of all these drops goes **to make** the rill ; which flows on, making music as it flows, until it meets counter streams. These, combined, form the river ; the river forms the estuary ; **and** the estuary the ocean itself. And now, when God has marshalled the sum of the weakness of myriad drops together, they lift the mightiest ship **as if** it were but a feather, and play with the winds as if they were mere instruments of sport. And yet, that very drop, which a man could bear upon the end of his finger, is there, and has its part and lot in the **might** of the whole vast, unbounded **sea.**

We in our singleness, in our individuality, in our own selves, are **weaker than a** drop of water, and more unstable ; but as **gathered** together **in the great** ocean **of life, as** kept together by the mighty currents which God's providences make, we attain, working together with Him, under the inspiration of His Spirit, **to** a might that makes life not ignoble, but sublime. **It** is most worthy **of** remark that the things that have called forth the most strength and endeavor of life have been things that we have most utterly failed in doing ; while the things that seem to draw about themselves only the endeavors of weakness, have been the things that God has established **most.**

I THINK **that if you will look back upon the** history of scholarship **for two thousand** years, **you** will find that **those things to which** the pride of human **intellect** has **addressed** itself, those things which were expected to be monuments of triumphs of thought by the men that put **them forth,** have achieved next to nothing. As it is with **webs that are destroyed as fast as** spun, and that are respun as fast as destroyed, **so it** has been with the scholasticism of two thousand years. If you look **at** the efforts **of the most** learned statesmen, if you **look at the most** laborious plans and the wisest endeavors **of the chief men of** almost every nation, you will find that **they have** toiled and labored to build up things that stood only while they had their hand upon them, — and hardly as long as that.

Laws have been overthrown almost before the face of men that thought they had done most curious and wonderful things in the scale of legislation. Administrations have ceased almost before the last vote had rung upon them in their structure. The things that men have done in their own strength have been things that have scarcely outlived their makers.

IDEAS are cosmopolitan. They have the liberty of the world. You have no right to take your swords and cross the bounds of other nations to enforce upon them laws or institutions which they are unwilling to receive. But there is no limit to the sphere of a man's ideas. Your thoughts and feelings, — the whole world lies open to them. Every right-thinking man has a right to send abroad his thoughts into any latitude, and to give them sweep around and around the earth. He has a right to do it, but of course, like all other rights, it must be regulated with prudence. It would be difficult for a man to propagate his thoughts in some lands ; but his right to do it exists, nevertheless. I have a right to preach Christ wherever my heart will. It may be that the crescent, the scimitar glittering under it, may say to me, " At the peril of your life ! " but that does not affect my right. I have a right before idols, before Juggernaut, everywhere on the whole earth, to preach not only Christ, but the ethics of Christ ; and not only the ethics of Christ, but the civility that is drawn from essential Christianity, and that must flow from it. I have a right to carry all the ideas developed in consequence of Christianity, in their ideal forms, to the mind of every living human being.

A CHRISTIAN accepts, first, the Divine idea of his own

development of character, and labors to produce in himself those things which God seeks. It makes no difference that the results are imperfect. The artist that seeks to make a portrait, seeks it just as much when by unskill he makes no resemblance to the subject, as when by skill he makes a perfect representation of the subject. He seeks to make the portrait, whether he succeeds or not. And a Christian perceives what is the Divine idea in human life and character, and aims at it; and though every day he comes short, or overacts, though his results are filled with manifold imperfections, and the whole work, to him even is a blur, instead of a true picture of the joy and righteousness which he meant to paint, nevertheless, he has aimed at it. For what we set out to do is not to be measured by our success in it. The bankrupt aimed at wealth as much as the millionnaire. The man that was defeated aimed at victory as much as he that wore the laurel. And the Christian, though from weakness and temptation he may stumble, if he accepts the Divine idea of what human life and character should be, and seeks it with all his heart, works together with God.

THERE are two kinds of heroes in the world, one of which we stand outside of to admire, and the other of which we take inside of us. The former are men indifferent in morals, but of great intellect, great genius, great executive force. Peter the Great, Napoleon, and many others, were men of such singular power that we cannot but admire them. But there have been some men in the history of the world whom we not merely admire, but whom we desire to take into our souls, and into whose care and keeping we desire to yield up our life. Men that are willing to stand up for the truth against all

comers; men that never equivocate; men that are always
full of truth, — those are the men that the soul elects to
be its heroes. It is a glorious thing indeed for a man to
be able so to carry himself that every one who sees him
shall say, "He is transparent in all that he says and
does: his *yea* is *yea*, and his *nay* is *nay*." If only such
are heroes, we are not in danger of being surfeited.

In those ages of the world when God more apparently
guided the courses of man personally, promises were
made to individual men. For the most part the men of
old believed with the simplicity of childhood. It was
counted to Abraham for righteousness that he believed
God against the evidence of his own senses. With them
a promise of God put an end to all controversy and
doubt.

In so far as we are concerned, it may be said that
God's promises respect conduct and character, rather
than personality. We are to make them personal by
coming into certain states of character, or into certain
conditions of life. And in this way God's promises become applicable to the whole human family.

Thus, the Word of God is filled with assurances of
blessings. No book was ever so characterized by the
element of promise. There are threats not a few, but
I think promises greatly outnumber them, as if it were
the Divine wish to draw us by hope, rather than drive
us by fear. Promises cover the whole period of human
life. They meet us at our birth; they cluster about our
childhood; they overhang our youth; they go in companies into manhood with us; they divide themselves
into bands and stand at the door of every possible experience. You cannot bring yourselves into a condition

for which I cannot find in God's Word some promise. Therefore, there are promises of God to the ignorant; to the poor; to the neglected; to the burdened; to the oppressed; to the discouraged; to the solitary; to the imprisoned; to the sick; to the heart-broken; to the remorseful; to the weak; to the strong; to the timid; to the brave; to every affection; to every one of its exigencies; to every sphere of duty; to all perils; to every temptation that waylays good men in their journey. There are promises for joy; for sorrow; for victory; for defeat; for adversity; for prosperity; for those that run; for those that walk; for those who can only stand still. Old age has its garlands as full and fragrant as youth. The sick, the dying, all men, everywhere, and always, have their promises of God.

GOD's promises are fresh with everlasting youth. The stars never wear out; they are just as good to-day as when Abram saw them directing the Oriental people by night. The sun is not weary from the number of years: there are no wrinkles on its brow. The urns of God are replenished by outpouring, and they increase their fulness by that which they yield. And so God's promises are of the nature of laws. The heaven and the earth shall pass away, but they shall not change in one jot or tittle, nor pass away.

THE music of this world has been for the most part in a minor key. This choral globe has groaned and travailed in pain until now. God knew the fallen condition of the race, and His promises were made explicitly to sinful men. And when He wrote to you, do you suppose He thought you an angel? He knew well that you were

12

not. He knew that the world was full of men tempted and temptable. He knew that men were in a world of sin, themselves sinners. **And He sent His Son to you** because you were in peril, and because unless there was Divine rescue there would be universal ruin. And shall a man say, "I cannot plead the promises of God, because I am sinful?" Therefore plead them, because you are sinful; therefore plead them, because you are wicked; therefore trust them, because though you are bad God is good, **and** the nature of goodness is to relieve want, even though that want be founded on sin.

. OFTEN and often Christ comes walking to the disciples on the stormy sea and in the night, and it is necessary that there should be some power of faith, some cogent influence, that shall make a Christian man willing to follow rectitude, duty, honor, truth, no matter where they seem to lead. And therefore it is that God has put all the bows, all the coruscations of his Word around about the issues and ends of essential truth, honor, duty, and rectitude, and that He says to us, "If you would save your life, lose it. Do not be afraid." You are oftentimes brought into trials when it seems as though everything would be wrecked, and the world says, "Prudence"; experience says, "Draw back"; policy says, "Change a little"; and expediency — not the noble expediency of Divine wisdom, but the lower and baser expediency of human calculation — says, "Commute, compromise"; but the Word of God stands saying, "If you would save yourself, be willing to throw everything away; if you would be safe, risk everything, and stand by that which is essentially right and true and noble." The Word of God that stands sure and steadfast, and is yea and amen, says, " He that will lose his life for a right principle, shall save it." And in the end, when you come to count the wrecks along the shore, you will find that those men who would save their lives by losing their principles are the men that have lost their lives; while those men who braved the storm, those men who followed the superior light that shone in their hearts, those men who said, " **Come what** will, there is but one way for me, and that is the way that **God has** marked out," are the men that have saved themselves.

MEN know where **they are going** when they follow a principle; because principles are like rays of light. If **you** trace a ray of light in all its reflections, you will find that it runs back to the central sun; and every great line of truth, every great line of heroism, every great line of honesty, every great **line of** honor, runs back toward the centre of **God.** And the man that follows these things **knows that he is steering** right Godward. But the man that follows policies, and worldly maxims, does **not know** where he is steering, except that in general he is steering toward the Devil.

" **CAN** the Ethiopian change his skin, or the leopard his spots? Then **may ye also do** good that are accustomed to evil."

This is not the language of exact physical science. **It is said** simply to signify how terribly difficult it is to break off from a bad habit. Ten thousand witnesses testify, **too,** that there are sins which carry such branches, **such roots,** such amazing vitality, that they **fever** the whole soul and body, where **one is** subject to them, till it is almost like giving up life itself to be freed from them.

THE Jew thought that God was the God of the Jews, that the Jew had a right to be saved, and that no other man could be saved without becoming a Jew, or yielding obedience to the requirements of the Jewish religion; but the apostles declared that Christ might be preached to the Gentiles as well as to the Jews, and that the benefits of Christ's blood were for the whole world. And Paul here goes into this reasoning: " God has a right to do as He pleases; He has a right to save men that do not belong to the Jews, nor fulfil the demands of their religious system; He has a right to call people unto Himself wherever and whenever He pleases, for the sake of making known His own excellent glory, the beneficence of His nature, and the richness of His grace; and who art thou that thou shouldst question His wisdom?" That is to say, here is a question of Divine mercy which involves the whole schedule of government, and which, therefore, you cannot understand. You cannot understand what God ought to have done, and what would have been the wisest thing, in matters of creation and administration. You are obliged, respecting such things, to take facts as they come to you, and not attempt to go behind the facts, as though you had greater wisdom than God.

IT is folly for a man to question the Divine wisdom in respect to mere matters of administration about which he is of necessity most ignorant; whose elements are beyond his reach; whose conditions involve complexities incalculable; and into which enters a principle of time that is infinite. Thus, for example, suppose a man should say to God, " Why did you make the world as you did? Why did you make men as they are made? Why did you establish the law of hereditary descent, by which the qualities of the parent go to the children, and through the children to many generations? Why was the world made so **that** the abstraction of heat should produce ice?" Such questions as these addressed to God are supremely foolish, and the man that addresses them to God **is a fool.**

But suppose that God has, with infinite pains, instructed us as to what is the difference between selfishness and benevolence, between sympathy and love, between indifference and self-seeking and seeking another's welfare, until there is formed in us a clear and **correct** ideal of moral character, then it **is** not either **presumptuous or** blasphemous to apply **to** the Divine character that very criterion of moral excellence which He himself has given to us. The difference, in other words, between applying a moral measure that has been given to us, and asking questions in respect to administrations and governments which are beyond our reach, is a world-wide difference.

God's Word is a great unopened treasure. **It seems** to me like some old baronial estate that has descended to a man who lives in a modern house, and thinks it scarcely **worth while to go and** look into the venerable mansion. **Year** after year passes away, and he pays no attention to **it,** since he has no suspicion of the valuable treasures it contains, till at last some man says to him, "Have you **been up in** the country to look at that estate?" **He makes** up his mind that he will take a look at it. **As he goes** through the porch he is surprised **to see** the skill that has been displayed in its construction, and he says, "Indeed, they had some ideas of architecture when this **house** was built." And he is more and more impressed as he goes through the halls.. He enters a large room, and is astonished as he beholds the wealth of pictures upon the walls, among which are portraits of many of his revered ancestors. He stands in amazement before them! There is a Titian, there is a Raphael, there is a Correggio, and there is a Giorgione! He says, "I never had any idea of these before." "Ah!" says the steward, "there is many another thing that you know nothing about in this castle "; and he takes him from room to room, and shows him carved plate and wonderful statues, and the man exclaims, "Here I have been for a score of years the owner of this estate, and have never before known what things were in it!"

But no architect ever conceived of such an estate as God's Word, and no artist or carver or sculptor ever conceived of such pictures and carved dishes and statues as adorn its apartments. Its halls and passages cannot be surpassed for beauty of architecture, and it contains treasures that silver and gold and precious stones are not to be mentioned in connection with.

If there are any that have made up their mind to know life, I say to them, Stop! you may pay too dear for your knowledge. Men have looked into the crater of a volcano to see what was there, and gone down to explore, without coming back to report progress. Many and many a man has gone to see what was in hell, that did see it. Many and many a man has looked to see what was in the cup, and found a viper coiled up therein. Many and many a man has gone into the house of lust, and found that the ends thereof were death, — bitter, rotten death. Many and many a man has sought to learn something of the evils of gambling, and learned it to his own ruin. And I say to every man, the more you know about these things, the more you ought to be ashamed of knowing; a knowledge of them is not necessary to education or manhood; and they ought to be avoided, because when a man has once fallen into them, the way out is so steep and hard. Many and many a man has begun to climb the giddy cliff of reformation; but, O, how few have succeeded in getting over its brow! Methinks I see men sweltering in passions, and swimming out to the base of the cliff, and attempting to climb up. Some are higher than others. One after another falls back, or is plucked down by some fiendish hand. Some are half way up the cliff, and struggling hard to reach the top. Some turn ghastly pale when they look down at the abyss below; and they are filled with despair when they look up at the height above them. And where one goes over and is saved, ninety-nine fall back and are lost.

EVERY praying man and every woman on the globe who lives in the intelligent knowledge of Christ, and employs the Spirit and truth of Christ intelligently, just as much as councils, and synods, and conventions, and churches, has the power of the keys. God gives it to every one that desires to have the living nature of Christ in him. Ah! do you not suppose there have been thousands of men who have gone down through life arrogating this claim that never opened the door of heaven to one single soul? There have been hundreds of popes, I suppose, who have opened the door of the future, — but it was the door of perdition, — who have not opened the door of heaven even for themselves, and much less for any that came after them, or went before them. And yet there have been hundreds of poor bedridden Christians whose key was bright with perpetual using, and who, by faith, and example, and testimony, did bind iniquity in the world, by the golden cords of truth, and did set loose, by the same truth, those that were bound, giving them power of spiritual insight, giving them emancipation, and bringing them into the large light and liberty of the children of God. Emancipators of the soul, they were, — humble, uncrowned, uncanonical, unordained, God-sanctified souls. They knew Christ, and loved Him, and poured out His spirit upon men.

There is a solemn sense in which they that are enlightened and converted by the truth should hold the keys to enlighten all those who are vicious and ignorant beneath them. By your superiority you are tempted to make yourself the monarch of those beneath you. But God ordains you to be the schoolmaster of all who are less enlightened than you are. Are you higher than men? It is not that you should sit enthroned in their praises, and demand their suffrages, and the tribute of their admiration. The higher you are, the more prompt you should be to go down to those that sit in the region and shadow of death. Has God given to your soul the knowledge of salvation by Jesus Christ? Are you linked with other brethren that are of the same blessed procession? Do you constitute a class? Do you rear your own children in the light and knowledge of these truths? Where are those that are below you? Where are the vicious? Where are the criminals? Where are the unlettered and ignorant wanderers in the street? Where are the great mass that have subsided to the bottom of society? Somebody must be their illuminator. Somebody must point their way to the city. Somebody must open its flashing gates to them. Every one that has the mind and will of Christ, and abides in His Spirit, stands in the relation to those below him of the holder of the keys. Woe be to him that in time of famine has bread and lets men starve because he will not part with it! Woe be to him that in time of plague has medicine, and lets men die untended! Double woe be to him that has been enlightened of God, and lets men perish because he will not take, by the authority of God, the light that he has received and carry it to them. Are there not within the touch of the hem of your garment; are there not in your business places; are there not in your daily travels; are there not in the thoroughfares of the city, scores and hundreds into whose darkened minds never pierced the light of God's truth, to whom you never came with a lantern? Here you stand unconcerned, — you whose soul is luminous, you that by the power of the Holy Ghost have been ordained to be a teacher, a leader, and a dispenser of spiritual things, — and men are wasting and dying in darkness all round about you! God has given you the keys, and He will hold you to a responsibility for the right use of them.

It has been said with a fatal carelessness, that God lives for Himself, — that is, for His own glory.

I do not deny that all the way through the Scriptures this monarchic idea is maintained, which represents God as creating and ministering for His own glory, and that He may be said in a certain sense to live for His own glory; but He does not create and minister and live for such a glory as it has been represented that He does. We are not to dwell upon one class of texts, and form our ideas of God's nature and government from them.

We are to take all the representations of the Bible in respect to God, and our conception of His nature and government is to be the resultant of them all. And in interpreting even those texts which seem to make God's glory the end and aim of His existence, we must beware of employing the analogies which come from the weak side of human nature. We are obliged to interpret God from ourselves; and our danger is that we shall interpret Him from the baser side of human experience, and not from the nobler. If we interpret the Divine government from human monarchy, we must take the ideal monarchy, and not the real; we must take those conceptions of monarchy which have carried in them the most gladness and generosity and royalty for others, and not those which have produced the impression of an iron nature, and a sceptre clenched for the sake of oppression and wrong. But a man that is a natural-born governor; a man whose self-esteem and firmness are large, and whose benevolence and social faculties are small, in interpreting monarchy, and applying it to God's government, will think and feel that a being that possesses supreme power has a right to govern as he pleases. But such a view perverts the analogue from which we form our conception of the Divine nature.

THE true glory of God must be interpreted in Christ Jesus; and when you understand what it is that God makes to be His glory; when you understand that the glory of God is not self-laudation, nor enriching His own power, nor multiplying His own treasures, but that it is supremely to make others happy; when you understand that the glory of God means loving other people and not Himself, mercy and not selfishness, the distribution of His bounty and not the hoarding it up; when you understand that God sits with all the infinite stores of redemptive love only to shed them abroad upon men forever and forever, then **you** form a different conception of what it is **for God to** reign for His **own** glory. If love is His glory; if generosity is His glory; **if** giving is His glory; if think-**ing** of the poor is His glory; if strengthening the weak **is** His glory; if standing as the defender of the wronged is His glory; if loving and watching over every being that **He** has created forever and forever, is His glory, then, blessed be that teaching which represents that God **does** reign for His own glory. That **is a** glory which is worthy **of the** Divine **regality.** It will bring out blossoms of joy **and** gladness in heaven and on earth.

———

WE measure things by the point wherein their superiority lies. The swine we estimate for fatness; oxen for strength and flesh; dogs for scent and sagacity; horses for speed and endurance.

Now, man is to be measured by that which makes **him** MAN, in distinction from everything else; and that is not foot, nor hand nor body, **nor** appetites, nor passions, nor **economic** or commercial power. These **are** not the things that make **him** man. It **is** that which has been stamped on him — God's image — that makes him man. That part of his nature which introduces the moral element, **right and** wrong; the spiritual element, invisible reali-ties; and the benevolent element, the very **divinity** of love. Here **man** must be measured; for here, and only here, he becomes man, among the creatures of the world. And our substantial judgment of what we are, what our character **is,** and what we are worth as men, is to be formed upon this high moral development, — You **are** worth *just how good you are!*

IT is one of the rarest things in the world to find a man who, when he looks upon a fellow-man, sees him as God sees him, — as a spiritual being. Men foremost in the church, fluent in prayer, and great at exhortation, when they go forth, do not see God in man. Such men have devotion as a sentiment, as an ecstatic emotion; they have temporary Christian feelings; but they are wanting in deep-seated piety. To make moral character the standard by which to judge of a man, and to look at him in the immortality, is a thing which is not done by one out of ten thousand. I think no more revolutionary thing could occur than for an angel to descend from heaven, and operate upon the mind of every man, so that he would of necessity look on every other man as God sees him; so that whenever you looked upon your child, it would stand to you as the babe Jesus stands to our admiration, — as a child of God; so that, whenever you looked upon your neighbors, you would not see what their bodies represent them to be, but as angel eyes see them, when their moral nature flames up invisibly before eyes that can see the invisible! O, if every day, when you went to your business, and executed your law of selfishness, you saw men just exactly as they are, how different would be your feelings on beholding them! If when men raise the lash above the head of the helpless, or lay the grinding hand upon the weak, they were instantly, by some mysterious change, made to see that it was God's angel they were holding in the dust, how would they start back amazed, and say, "I thought it was a man, and behold I was wrestling with an angel!" If men were to see their fellow-men as God's angels in embryo, and were to judge of them, not by their spheres in life, not by their physical relations, but by their relations to the eternal state, and were to feel that every man was a child of God, **and** an heir of immortality, what a revolution there **would be** in the structure **of** society !

___

I THINK that a man struggling against Christianity when under conviction, is like a fractious child struggling against a dear mother, when she reproves and punishes it until, overcome by discipline, it rushes into her arms, and kisses her with a paroxysm of tears, and sobs even when it sleeps. I have seen men who, under conviction, fought terribly against God till Christ was manifested to them, when they yielded themselves up to Him, saying, " My Lord and my God ! " and with sweet peace fell into His arms, and were carried by Him the rest of their lives. Is not Christ precious in such hours ?

___

CHRISTIANS are like freight-engines at night. They carry a powerful lamp in front, which casts a light far ahead, but in no other direction, leaving the everlasting snake-train which they drag behind them enveloped in darkness. This light corresponds to the Christian's hope, which casts its rays heavenward, but leaves the long train of bodily appetites and necessities which go with him through life unilluminated. Men regard their worldly business and their family duties as distinct from their religion. They carry the light of hope on their brow, and that is what they call their religion ; whereas, I understand religion to be this : the right carriage of body and soul, all together. I understand that no man is living a Christian life who is not a Christian in the world, in the family, in the church, in his mind, in his soul, in the emotions and appetites of his nature, in his hand, in

his foot, in his head, — who **is** not a Christian everywhere, and in everything in him.   To take every faculty
or power God has given you and bring it under Divine
influences, **and** make it **act** right, — that is being **a**
Christian; and all partialisms, **by just so** much as they
are partialisms, are, therefore, misunderstandings or mis-
appropriations of Christian truth.

———

DOES the Bible tell you the truth about your nature
and your condition?   Does it tell you how to make
yourself better?   Is it a book which reveals the grandeur
of immortality?   Above all, does it lift upon the crude
imaginations of men in every age, upon the imperfect
picturings which men have made of the Godhead, the
clear and sublime **light** of certainty?   Does it collect
from our higher experiences **and our nobler** feelings,
those **elements which** do **truly represent** God; and
magnifying them, passing **upon** them the proportions
of infinity, and lifting them **up** above all obstruction,
impurity, and unworthiness, does it hold forth to **the**
enraptured sight a God at once in sympathy with human
nature, yet transcendently greater than it : comprehensi-
ble **in kind** and nature, though, **by** virtue of infinity,
utterly unsearchable in degree and magnitude?   Does
it present a God standing upon Truth, and upon **Justice,**
but blazing upward into Love, which, like an atmosphere,
fills the infinite round of eternity; glorious **in** holiness ;
fearful in **praises** ; but sublime, above all **other** things,
for Love?   Is **it a** book which, **evoking from the** far
and impalpable heavens the **ideal** conception **of** God,
causes Him to walk in human form, interpreted thus
into human conditions; and in the life, the teachings, the
unexplainable sufferings, the sublime death, the sepulchre

hiding, the resurrection, the ascension, the glorification of Jesus Christ, presents a Saviour suited to a man's wants, weaknesses, and sins ; — taking hold of us by all that is tender and generous, touching whatever in us there is of honor, of gratitude, of pity, of love ; — transforming us both by the power of our own understandings, lifted up upon the mightiest truths, and by the co-operative greater power of the Holy Ghost, shed abroad upon the heart ? Does it present such a Saviour as every man feels that he needs, so soon as his moral life is thoroughly awakened ; so soon as he begins to measure himself by a law higher than any which the world gives ? Is it a book from which men without number have drawn motives of sublime life ? Is there any other heroism recorded on earth so sublime as that which has sprung from faith in Christ ? Without a revelation, now and then, rare and great souls there have been, capable of endurance, of self-denial, and the loftiest heroism. It is the New Testament that has taught the poor, the ignorant, the common people, to live heroic lives. And since men began to believe in it, and to form their lives from its inspiration, heroism has become cheap. Yea, it is oftener found in the cottage, now, than on the battle-field. And when the last great day shall reveal the unknown things of time, the heroes of the cradle-side ; the heroes of the sick-chamber ; the heroes of poverty ; the heroes of the dungeon ; the heroes of labor ; the despised heroes, that grow, thick as grass, in the low places of the earth, and, like the grass, are trodden down, often, under the hoofs of men ; these — that great army of the last that are destined to be first, this illustrious host that shall flame upward from the bottom to the very top and summit of glory — shall tell of the divinity of the New Testament what it does, declare what it is. Its power upon men measures the power of God in it. That which can bring men *to* God must itself have come *from* God.

IT is Christ that I would make personal to you. He is not a Being that dwells in the inner recesses of the eternal world, inaccessible, incomprehensible. He is not the stern king, unbending, upon a throne of justice, lifted up above the reach of sighs and sinful wants. He is not as one fortified behind the bulwarks of law, so that one must cannonade, and breach the walls with prayers, and then rush in to take Him captive. Men never find Christ, but are always found of Him. He goes forth to seek and to save the lost. It is not the outreaching of our thought, it is not the attraction of our heart, it is not the strong drawing of our sympathy and yearning, that brings Him to us. It is the abounding love of His heart that draws us up toward Him. His love precedes ours. "We love Him because He first loved us." We kindle our hearts at His. As the sun is up before the sluggard, so the twilight and dawn of His love is upon the hills when we wake; and when we sleep, even, His thoughts burn above us as the stars burn through the night!

It is this willing, winning, pleading Christ, who wields all the grandeur of justice and all the authority of universal empire with such rare and sweet gentleness, that in all the earth there is none like unto Him, that I set before you as your personal friend! He knows each of you better than your mother knew you! He has called you by name! In your households you are not so familiar to your most cherished friend as you are to the thought of Christ! Not so indelibly is your name recorded in your father's memory, or in the baptismal register of the sanctuary, or in the family Bible, where the tabular leaf for births holds your infant name, as upon the ever-remembering heart of the Lord Jesus Christ!

BE not discouraged because you are sinful. It is the very office of Christ's love to heal your sin. Not, then, when you have overcome them yourself, is He prepared to receive you; it is His delight to give you help while wrestling with your sins. He is your pilot to lead you out of trouble. No pilot would he be that only then would take my ship when I had gone through the narrows, and could see the city, and was quite free of all danger. Who would need a physician if he might not come to his bedside until after he was healed? What use of a schoolmaster if one may not go to school till his education be complete? What hope of salvation if God would give us no help till the whole work of subduing the natural heart were completed? And our Saviour is one who begins and completes in us the work of grace. He is the author of our faith, and the finisher of it. It is His power that works in us to will and to do of His good pleasure. He comes to you when you are dead, and by His touch brings you to life. When you are weak, He inspires you with strength. When you are tempted, He opens the door of escape. When you are vanquished, He appears to lift you up and binds your wounds. Yea, bending under all our burdens, and loaded down with our own sins, behold that Christ of whom it is said, " He was wounded for our transgressions, he was bruised for our iniquities; the chastisement of our peace was upon Him; and by his stripes we have healing,"

WATCH unto prayer! Many have supposed that it

was impossible for a man to be in this state of watchfulness, and yet be a buoyant, singing Christian. Just as though a man could not whistle while acting as a sentinel! Just as though he could not think of home, of his lady-love, and of a thousand things beside, while faithfully watching at his post.

———

A MAN is said in the Bible to be more precious than the gold of Ophir; and of a woman it is said, " Her price is far above rubies." These were common comparisons. There is something in the glow of precious stones that peculiarly fits them to serve for such spiritual figures. There is about them a subtle light — a brilliancy — that burns without fire; that consumes nothing, and requires no supply; that forever shines without oil; that is ever living, unwasting, unchanged by any of the natural elements. A diamond that glows in the sunlight flashes yet more beautifully in the night. No mould can get root upon it; no rust can tarnish it; no decay can waste it. The jewels that were buried two thousand years ago, if now dug up from royal and priestly tombs, would come forth as fair and fresh as they were when the proud wearer first carried them in his diadem. Such stones seemed to the ancients, and are, fit emblems by which to represent spiritual qualities, and the beauty and imperishableness of Christian virtue. And a company of holy men, resting upon the Lord Jesus Christ, may well be compared to a palace built upon broad foundations, and sparkling to the very summit with living stones, which throw back to the sun a differing flash through every hour of his rise or fall through the long day.

———

IT is one thing to be a believer in God's government;

it is another thing to hold company with God, — to behold Him, to love Him, and to commune with Him, to twine your life about Him.

Sometimes a child is removed from its mother's care, and put out to nurse to a foster-mother. Through all its earlier years it is, as it were, the child of this new-found mother. For some reasons the parents may not choose, for a time, to own their child. They may secretly go where it is, and look upon it as it sleeps. It shall hear about them, and shall know that all its wants are supplied by them. It may even yearn for mother and father, and wonder what those words must mean at last. And yet the child never sees its parents. But, by and by, they send for their child, and it is brought home. Now, little by little, it grows acquainted with them. It rides with them; it eats with them; it talks with them; it loves them; it begins to *live* with them. And is there no difference between depending on parents whom you do not know, and a conscious communion with them when you are united to them? Is there no difference between the relation of a child to its parents when it is a foster-child, kept aloof, supported by the parents through others, and its relation to them afterwards, when it is brought home, embraced, embosomed, and made hourly conscious of their presence and personal love? Now, there is such a thing as our being put out to nurse in this world. There is, also, such a thing as our being brought home to God, as our Father; and in the light of this illustration it is easy to perceive that there is a world-wide difference between a conscious *dependence* upon God and a conscious *communion* with Him.

You may ask, "What will become of those men who

are so good, but whom you do not class among Christians?" I do not know. Thank God, I am not God! Every man hears the drum-beat of the eternal world. Every man must stand for himself, and every man must answer for himself there. It is enough for me to bring myself and my own charge to God, without stopping to answer questions which belong to the future. One thing I know, and that is, that there is no other name but the name of Christ given under heaven, that we know anything about, whereby we can be saved. One thing I know, and that is, that he who trusts in the Lord Jesus Christ shall never be moved. One thing I know, that there is a power in Christ to translate a man above his sins, and almost above temptations, in this world. I believe there is a power in Christ to disfranchise a man, and take away from him the livery of hell; and to enfranchise a man, and give him the livery of heaven. I believe there is a power in the faith of Christ Jesus to transform a man from evil to good, and from good to saintship, and bring him to the haven, to the home above. If there is any other way for a man to be saved except through this faith, I do not know what it is. But one thing I know, and that is, that the joy which I derive from faith in Christ is ten thousand times greater than any of the other joys which greet my heart in this world. I know no other light; I will steer for that. I feel no other influence; I will be drawn by that. I have no other faith; I will trust in that. For he who lives and dies believing in Christ, shall not perish, but have everlasting life.

———

HIGHER than morality, higher than philanthropy, higher than worship, comes the love of God. That is the chiefest thing. When we have that, we reach the very thing for which the New Testament scheme was administered. Love! it is that which brings forth out of obscurity the hidden God which we seek. Send forth all the powers of the soul to search for God, and there is not one of them which, making inquisition according to its own nature, can find Him out and reveal Him, except this divine spirit of love! Put wings of imagination upon Conscience, and let it fly forth. Say to it, "Go, and find thy God!" Flying through night and through day; above and beneath; among clouds and thunder; through darkness and through light; it would return at length, wing-tired, only to say, "I have found marks of God, in law, in pain, and penalty; I have seen the traces of thunder, and the path of lightning, and the foundations of eternal power; but nowhere have I found the full God."

Give the wings of faith to Reason, and send it, in turn, forth from east to west, around the earth, and through the heavens, to see if by searching it can find out God; and it shall say, "I have seen the curious work of His hand, and have marked the treasures that He hath heaped up. The whole earth is full of His glory, and the heavens are unsearchable by us. What God hath done I have felt, but God himself is hidden from my sight."

Let Fear, equipped with faith, pursue the same errand. It would not even know which way to fly, and, turning downward, groping or flying directly amidst infernal things, it would rehearse a catalogue of terrors, of gloomy fears, or brooding superstitions; but the bright sun-clad God it could not see.

Let Reverence go forth. But what there is in Reverence can never interpret what there is in God. This feeling can touch the **divine** orb but **in a single** point. And the Heavens would say to Reverence, "Such an one as you seek is not in **me**"; and Hell would say, " He is not in me"; and Earth and Time would repeat, " He is not in us !"

It is only Love that can find out God without searching. Upon its eyes God **dawns.** Wherever it looks, and whatever it sees, — that **is** God; for God **is** love. Love is that **regent** quality which **was** meant to reveal the Divine to **us.** It carries **its own** light, and, by **its** own secret nature, is drawn instantly toward God, **and** reflects the knowledge of Him back upon us.

I KNOW that my Redeemer liveth. I have stood near the grave, and then I knew that my Redeemer lived, **and** that because He lived I should. I have gazed through that most powerful glass of all, through which God reveals the invisible, — the fresh-opened graves of my children ! — and there, in the tumults and revolutions of grief, I knew that my Redeemer lived, and that He was with me to comfort me. I have seen trials and troubles of various kinds in my life; and I bear witness that there was never a time when I needed help that He was not by my side to help me. And I have no sort of doubt that Christ will stand by me to the end, and conduct me through the gate of death to eternal life. And no man shall move me from my faith in Him !

TELL me that it is an impossible thing for a **man to** love the Lord Jesus Christ, who is invisible ! You might as well, if I were now to go forth beneath the glorious sun, and its rays were to fall down through the air **upon me** and about me on every side, tell me there was no sun! Councils of owls and bats may come to me, under the **name** of philosophers, and say, " Do you not think that all these which you are talking about — rays of the sun, flowers, singing-birds, curling smoke, **and** the like — are a delusion? We have lived almost as long as you **have,** and we have consulted the oldest owls **and** bats, and we do not believe in them." Let owls and bats take their experience from dens and caves, but let men take their knowledge from the open heavens. I know, — whatever men may say, in the low places and the high places of life, — I know that there is such a thing as loving Jesus Christ **as a** friend, **as a** brother; and that there **is no** other love that **is so sweet,** so deep, **so** lasting, so wondrous, as that which the soul can bear toward Him.

WOULD you think that man fit for a hero who should occupy the leisure of peace in telling what hard commissions he had during the last campaign, how tired he **was** on the march, and how painful it was to wear his armor? Would you think that man fit for a hero who should **thus** rehearse **all the** petty annoyances that he experienced in **the camp and on the** battle-field? What idea **would** you **have** of a general or **a** soldier **who** should be more thoughtful of such contemptible personalities than of those things that pertain to the interests of the cause in which he is engaged? You that are called from darkness to light, and made to know the eternal obligation **of your** own souls; you into whose hands are put **jewels** more precious and glowing than stars in **the heavens;** you who are made God's instruments for redeeming men, you ought **to be ashamed to talk** about your cares and responsibilities, as if they were onerous things. The **permission for laboring** for God's cause is undeserved,

and granted by His free grace, and yet you are moaning
and repining about your sufferings! Either die, or else
work and hold your peace about your sufferings!

I HAVE seen the vision of Christ a thousand times as I
wanted to see Him. I have seen the vision of Christ
bend over me with tenderness. I have seen the vision
of Christ instruct me with divine wisdom and radiant
knowledge. I have seen the vision of Christ standing
up as the advocate of the poor, and the defender of the
wronged. I have seen the vision of Christ clothed with
clouds; and I have seen those clouds changed to gorgeous colors of glory. I have seen ten thousand visions
pictured of Christ Jesus; but I have never yet seen *Him!*
There is a day coming when I shall see Him as He is;
not as I feign Him to be; not as my heart paints Him;
not as my wants interpret Him; but *as He is!* In that
illustrious day I shall have no fear. Chief among ten
thousand, He shall then be precious to me, and forever
and forever my heart's treasure and my soul's delight.
Even so, come, Lord Jesus, — come quickly!

HAD you a mother that was a woman of God? and
was faithful? Do you scarcely dare to look back and
think of the instructions which, upon her knee, you received? I have hope for you; not because you are
good, — you are base and most unworthy; but, O, the
power of a mother with God, — it is great! And I
believe that for the children that are consecrated in the
lap and bosom of maternal love, there is hope until
they pass away, and the whole scene closes. The whole
world may seem to thwart her counsels, rising up against
them; but I think there is a golden thread, which a

mother's love spins, that will not be broken. Tossed about like a gossamer, it may be tangled, and apparently broken and gone; but by and by, when storms come, and the sea roars, and the heavens are black, something is seen beginning to hold the drifting human heart. And then it shall appear that, stronger than hempen cable or iron chain, a mother's teachings and love hold fast the imperilled heart, and it rides out the swelling gale, and is found, even if crippled and damaged, yet safe anchored at length on a tranquil sea. Great is the promise and great the hope.

THERE are some **persons** who seem so constituted that their religious feelings almost never flow so readily as when they act for other people. They are persons of great constitutional benevolence. They make benevolence their conscience. When they go forth into life, benevolence is their guiding principle. Such persons oftentimes say, " I never can have deep religious feelings by ordinary means; but when such a man was in trouble, and told me of **the wants of** his family, — **his** wife and **children,** — and I took my **hat** and **went** home with **him,** and mingled my tears with theirs, it did seem as if I was **not a** handbreadth from heaven. **I** never had such a **sense of** the goodness of God as I had then." Probably you were never so near like God as you were then. No wonder you felt near Him. You are not far from Him when you get so near Him as to give your time and energies for the good of His needy creatures.

DID you ever, in a summer's day, when you had drawn from the bottom of the well the cooling draught to slake your thirst, stand and dream, and gaze at a drop, orbed and hanging from the bucket's edge, reflecting the light of the sun? What the rounded form and size of that drop is in comparison with the whole earth itself, that **the** round earth itself is in comparison with God's majesty of being or degree of magnitude! And that such an One, living in such a wise, — so far above the earth, so far above its inhabitants, so far above the noblest spirit that stands in the unlost purity of heaven, — that such an One should deal with His erring creature with a gentleness and patience, such as characterizes the administration of God toward man, is sublime and wonderful!

THE Bible says that God is past finding out. But it does not mean that His physical power is past finding out. It is His disposition, His moral nature, that are beyond research and measurement. The unsearchableness of the love of **God** in Christ Jesus; **the** greatness, the grandeur, and the glory of the Heart that, hating iniquity with an intense hatred, can love the doer of it, **and** that, abhorring sin with an infinite abhorrence, can give itself to save the sinner, — these are the things that are past finding out. The marvel of meekness, and sweetness, and love in the arch-Thunderer of eternity, — this **it is** that is past finding out!

THERE are a great many persons who think, " I must take care of my religion." They have got something that they call religion, which **they** conceive needs to be guarded. Just as **if I** should **say**, " I must take care of my health," and should yet neglect my body, so that my nerves were out of order, and my heart was out of right beat, thinking that I had something distinct from the body, which was health; whereas health means a body

acting right in every one of its parts! And religion is to
the soul what health is to the body, — it is the right ordering of all the faculties. Many persons think it is confined to certain faculties, which must be set buzzing **at**
particular times. They treat it very much as a boy
would a caged bird. They keep their religion at home
all the week, and on Sunday they go and slip it into the
cage, and let it sing; but its voice is hushed the moment
they take it out. They say that you must not act outside of the church in a way that is inconsistent with your
religion, or violate it, but that you are not to mind right
living. Their religion is a **certain** spiritual partialism.
They skin off and set aside a part of their nature, and
regard that as the element of religion. How many times
do men carry this thing to such an excess, that it becomes
a glaring absurdity before the world!

There is this damnable heresy, that religion is a tech-
nical element, which you can separate from a man's throb-
bing life! Why, whatever you do at twelve at night, or
at twelve in the daytime; whatever you do at **six in the**
morning, or at six in the evening; whatever **you** do on
the Sabbath, or on any week-day; whatever you do in the
ship, or in the blacksmith's shop; whatever you do in
the house, or in the street; whatever you do in the sanc-
tuary, or at the concert; whatever you do at any time, or
in any place, you are to do to the glory of God. By as
much as you come short of doing this, by so much is your
religion deficient.

CLOSET meditations and devotions which used to char-
acterize piety, are far less common than they were. In
old times, when men were persecuted for their religion,
they had nothing to do but to read the Bible, and pray,

and be burned, and what not. And in our own day, in
our childhood, the Bible was the principal part of the
library that we cared to read. Since that time there has
been created an enormous literature ; and no man is too
poor to have it in his house. It carries with it great
blessings. To be enfranchised from ignorance is, of itself, no small blessing. But with all the collateral blessings of this literature upon the world, there are some
side dangers to be guarded against. The mind may be
diluted. Men are covered over with papers, novels, and
books, as fences are covered with vines and weeds. The
time consumed is not the chief evil ; but the perversion
of taste, the destruction of a hearty relish for the sober
certainties and solemnities of God's Word. We have
fallen off immensely on the side of religious culture, —
earnest, prolonged, habitual, domestic, religious culture,
conducted by the reading of God's Word and by prayer
and its family influences. And this tendency is still further augmented by the increase of religious books, of
tracts, of biographies and histories, of commentaries,
which tend to envelop and hide the Word of God from
our minds. In other words, these things which are called
" helps " have been increased to such a degree, and have
come to occupy so much of our attention, that when we
have read our helps, we have no time left to read the
thing to be helped ; and the Bible is covered down and
lost under its " helps." Far be it from me to say that
we are worse off with all the books in our libraries than
we would be without them ; but while we are to have the
benefits of these, we are to mark the tendency to which
I allude.

O, now many different ways there are by which God

comes into the soul! The great God, so prolific of
thought, so endless in diversity of function, has a million
ways by which to express Himself. He, in His power,
works on the soul not through one thing alone, — not
alone through steeple, nor meeting-house, nor lecture-
room, nor closet, though often and much through these;
but through all things, — through the heavenly bodies,
and animals, and insects, and worms, and clouds, and
mountains, and oceans, and rivers, and the productions
of the earth; and not by these only, but by everything
that affects man's comfort and happiness in this life, — by
store and anvil, and plane and saw, **and** hospital and poor-
house, and music and forms **of** beauty, and sweet feelings
and trials, and sufferings and victories over temptation,
and light and darkness, and joy and sorrow, and ten thousand unnamable subtle influences that touch the human
soul; by all these God reveals His greatness and goodness to us, that He may win us to Himself, and make us
heirs of immortality; and, blessed be His name, not **to us**
alone, but to every one, everywhere!

THERE is a strange law of vicarious suffering wrought
into the very structure of human life. The child does not
come singing like a cherub from the hand of God. The
mother cries, and the child cries, and men say, "A man
is born." It is suffering that gives life, and then it is
suffering that is worn as a robe for life. For every one
that has been ministered unto; for every one that **has**
been educated; for every one that has been **advanced by**
development through the stages of animalism up to the
social element and the moral sentiments, — for every such
one there have been some to suffer. Our thrift and advancement in moral things are the result of the sufferings

of others. To say that we are morally developed is synonymous with saying that we have reaped what some one has suffered for us. There is no friend that does not suffer for friend. It may almost be said that we measure friendship, not by excess of joy, but by joyfulness of suffering one for another. There is no good accomplished that is not accomplished through the medium of somebody's suffering. No great thought was ever born that was not born through suffering. No great principle was ever wrought out except by toil and trouble and suffering. No great truth was ever applied to the cause of morals in this world that was not accompanied by suffering proportionate to the good that it effected. God measures the magnitude of blessings by the sufferings that men **are** willing to bear for the sake of attaining them.

When in the peace **and serene** joy of the tranquil household children sit round about the encircled table, how little do they know that all their delight and **all** their sweet peace has been purchased by midnight vigils, by maternal tears, by parental strivings with God! We that buy our joy and peace by trouble sow seeds. Tears are God's seeds. They come up joys. It might almost be said that groans are the key-notes of joy on earth. Weakness is the beginning of strength; humility, of exaltation; shame, of glory; toil, of ease.

Men seem to set themselves against the monstrous injustice, **as** they call it, of Christ's bearing the sins of the world. They seem to revolt at the idea of the just suffering for the unjust. They seem to think that this is a thing that cannot be either illustrated or proved by the moral sentiment of men. But I declare that there is in social life an illustration of the principle of vicarious suffering. As Christ suffered for the world, so one man suffers for another man. And in our joy we reap the fruit of what others suffer. The example of Christ is but a symbol and magnificent type of that which we in our several spheres find out in the details of life.

WHERE, in all the round of human experience, worthy men suffer, not from an accident, not under penalty, but for the sake of emancipating themselves or others from an evil; where they suffer for the sake of advancing a truth or establishing a nobler principle in their own life or in the lives of others, every tear, every watching, every weariness, every groan, every sorrow, every exclusion, every self-denial, every pain, is known, is registered, and will ever be remembered and honored. Our sufferings seem barren here, but when we see them blossom in heaven we shall not know them. Here they are like sharp thorns; there they will be like flowers waving in the garden. We see the seed-form, the sprout-form, of our troubles, we see our troubles without comeliness or beauty; but when God shall have developed their full growth and symmetry in heaven, how different they will seem to us!

A GREAT many persons deny themselves with the most superfluous self-denial. They seek for things of which they can deny themselves. But you need not do that. Let your opportunities for self-denial come to you; but when they do come, do not flinch. God will send you occasions enough for denying yourself. There is wood enough in every man's forest to build all the cares he will need to carry. You need not withhold yourself from any proper joy; but when for the sake of honesty, or benevolence, or love, or purity, or truth, it is needed that you should suffer, step boldly forward, even if to do so is to go into fire. The form of Christ will be by your side, and the smell of the fire shall not be on your garments.

————

ONE would suppose that there had never been a printed Bible in some men's houses. Some men do not appear to have any conception of the sufferings of their Lord and Master. There are parents that seem to think that their life is well worn out and worthily bestowed, if they spend it in accumulating a fortune. And for what? To save their children from the toil that they have endured. But what made the parents? What made your arm stalwart, and your head clear and discriminating? What was it that made your life patient and enduring? What **was** it that made you a force among men, accomplishing and achieving? **What was it but that very necessity** from which you wish to hide your children? Ah! your trouble was your armor, as well as your arms, and yet you would send your children down into the battle of life naked, with nothing to cover them! There are a great many whose thought, by **day and by** night, is, "How **shall we** put our children in a position of honor and ease **and** comfort?" The wish of Christian parents, oftentimes, is, not that their children shall be less than virtuous, but that, being virtuous and pious, they shall be where no hardships shall be able to come to them. O, if the cherished **ones** of their bosom could be placed beyond contention and hidden from strife; if they could be lifted above the necessity of going forth to toil and conflict, the great desire of their life would be realized!

What God-blighted children such children must be! What a baptism of desire is that which you put on your children, — you that wish to shield them from trials and cares! You are like the mother of the sons of Zebedee, who went to the Saviour, and said, "Grant that these my two sons may sit, the one on thy right hand, and the other on the left in thy kingdom." Not understanding that solemn response, "Are ye able to drink of the cup that I shall drink of, and to be baptized with the baptism that I am baptized with?" you want honor and distinction for your children, but you do not want that they should be exposed to that strife out of which these things must inevitably come.

THERE are a great many persons who think themselves equipped to do good, but who can find no proper place wherein to exercise the eminent gifts which it has pleased the bounty of Providence to confer upon them. They are so elegant, so refined, that it is a pity that they should go among the vulgar! They are so large in their experience and reading, that it is a pity that they should go into societies where people have circumscribed ideas! They have such gentility on their side, that **it is a** pity that they should go into **a place** where folks are not gen-**teel**! And so these martyrs, these reformers, these would-be ministers of God's Word to this lost world, are unable to find a place suitable for them to labor in!

Have you never seen, at sunset, a hen walking around a tree irresolute as to the bough which she would take, stooping for one, and then quitting that and stooping **for** another, and then quitting that and stooping for another? Just like such a hen are some ministers that I have seen running about for a settlement, stooping for one, and then, thinking that it was not quite good enough, quitting it and stooping for another, thus frittering away their time

13 *

and energies to no purpose. Let such men turn away at once from the camp of God, and go to the camp of the world. There they belong. They are not ministers of God whose prime thought is as to how they shall serve God without incommoding themselves, and how they shall redeem men without suffering in anywise for them.

WHEN men have befriended us, suffered for us, perilled themselves for us, the whole of every noble feeling within us rises up and pours out like a flood from the temple of the soul, and we go to them with beneficences and benefactions. So it is with men, — men that yet are selfish, that are proud, that are circumscribed in all good.

What, then, must be the nature of the same feeling when it issues out of the heart of the infinite God, and manifests itself in the immensity of His generosity, and the glory of His magnanimity?

How wonderful is it, in the first place, that God should be pleased to accept as suffering for Him, the things which we suffer in the warfare of our dispositions in life! How wonderful is that grace that watches the whole earth, that sees all the innumerable sufferings of men, however hidden, obscure, or out-of-the-way they may be, and marks every tear and every heart-throb, and with wonderful magnanimity says, "These sufferings are for me!" How wonderful is that grace by which God identifies Himself with the poor, with striving and struggling sinful men who are seeking emancipation, taking as benefactions offered to Himself all things that we do or risk for ourselves or for our fellow-men! And what, think you, will be the wonder of God's heart when He pours forth from it tides of gratitude?

When God wished to express His thoughts of taste, He filled the heaven, the earth, and the sea with beauties varied and innumerable. When God wished to speak His ideas of skill, He covered the globe with wonderful and exquisite structures of animals and birds and insects. When God wished to display His wisdom, He created the universe, in all its various parts, and with its multitudinous relations. And if God writes such a handwriting as that, if such are the ways in which He is wont to express Himself in this world, what will be the sweep of His soul when with honor and glory He remunerates those who have suffered for Him?

I AM ashamed when I think how we find dissatisfaction where we should find satisfaction; how we extract bitterness where we should find sweetness; how we create stench where we should find perfume; how we strive to make ourselves unhappy in the very relations where God meant that we should be blissful. I am ashamed to think how we find argument for sullenness, for complaint, and **even for charge against God, who has rounded out the world in mercy,** fed us with His bounty, and clothed us personally in kindness. When I think how God has borne in upon our spiritual life the promises of help, and fulfilled those promises from day to day, from week to week, from month to month, and from year to year, and **how** we have met the acts of His goodness toward us with selfishness, and pride, and complaints, I am ashamed of myself and of my kind. God has not deserved such treatment at our hands.

You never know, till you try to reach them, how accessible men are; and if, with an earnest desire to promote their eternal welfare, you seek to bring them to a knowledge of the truth, you shall find that outside of churches, and outside of ordinary influences, by the mystery of providence, as well as by the mystery of grace, God is working in the hearts of men, and preparing them to be gathered by us into His fold.

It is said that at the battle of Solferino, what with the fear of being crushed, what with the mortal fear of the barbarity of the French soldiers, of which they had heard, hundreds of wounded men crept out of the fields into ravines, and coppices, and thickets; that after three days had been passed in searching for them, many were still lying unfound. Many were found so far spent that they died ere they could be taken to the hospital.

There are hundreds of men hiding themselves in ravines, and coppices, and thickets, on the battle-field of life, who need medicament, healing, care, and consolation; and if you were to go out searching for them, you should every day find men, here and there, crying out in their distress, and asking for sympathy and help.

THERE is an army of memorable sufferers who suffer inwardly, and not outwardly. The world's battle-fields have been in the heart chiefly. More heroism has there been displayed in the household and in the closet, I think, than on the most memorable military battle-fields of history.

One of Kaulbach's most remarkable paintings is founded on a legend, that on a certain anniversary spirits were in the habit of assembling and fighting in the air. However that may be, the battles of the spirits and the battles of the air, in the Christian conflict, are much more memorable than any of the declared battles of sense and of the body. And although these spiritual and airy battles seem to be without trumpet, and without record, and without a witness; although there are no poets that chant the praise of the closet; although there are no historians that chronicle the conflicts of a man with his own spirit, with pernicious habits, with evil inclinations, with violent temptations; although the eye of a man cannot see these things, yet they are not unwatched. Angel eyes see what our eyes are too gross to see. God, over all, takes notice of everything that concerns us. We are His children, and He hangs over us in love as a mother over the cradle. He sees our sufferings, and will remember them.

IT is a great thing to have been put into this life through a right gate. If it be a golden gate, covered all over with glorious inscriptions and legends and memories of past goodness, no man can thank God enough. Did your mother travail in faith and prayer? Were you born amid supplications? Were songs, not of angels, but of one scarcely less than angelic, round about your advent? Were you baptized in your cradle before priestly hands made aspersion of water? Did you come forth into life from out of a household of faith? It is no small thing that God nested you thus, and that He gave you such a parentage and such a beginning in life. Have you ever made it an object of thought?

AMONG the Alps, when the day is done, and twilight and darkness are creeping over fold and hamlet in the valleys below, Mont Rosa and Mont Blanc rise up far above the darkness, catching from the retreating sun something of his light, flushed with rose-color, exquisite beyond all words or pencil or paint, glowing like the gate of heaven.

And so past favors and kindnesses lift themselves up in the memory of noble natures, and long after the lower parts of life are darkened by neglect, or selfishness, or anger, former loves, high up above all clouds, glow with divine radiance, and seem to forbid the advance of night any further.

IF your God is made out of conceptions derived from the great and heartless round of the natural world; if you have a great crystalline God, such as philosophy deduces from the material globe, you can conceive of no such thing as His detracting from His dignity by coming down to *burrow*, as you call it, in this lower sphere. If you have a God whom mountains represent, or if you have a vast marble God, that sits as the central idol of the universe, it is to you contemptible to think of His bowing down and coming among men !

But if you have a God fashioned from the elements revealed in the human soul, if you understand that greatness in the Divine Being does not mean muscular greatness, nor physical greatness, but purity, and depth, and scope of all the feelings of the heart, then the greater your God is, the more exquisite will be the things He will do in detail, the more possibility will there be of His descending and coming among men, and the more certainly will He be expected to be found among His family. As the mother is found where her child cries, and as the father is found where his son stumbles, so we should expect that, if God is a being whom we may know from the analogies of our own nature, He would be found living where men are tempted, and where they sin, and suffer, and die.

This is the whole New Testament view of Christ. It

springs naturally and inevitably from a God who is Father. It cannot be grafted on any other view.

If you measure any religious proceeding according to the highest standard of the mind, there is nothing this side of Calvary that can be looked upon with complacency. The whole reformatory work of mankind goes on, and ever has gone on, imperfectly. The world is full of imperfection. And no person should measure things by strict propriety. Religious courses should not be measured by it. Such courses are scoffed at by men because they are so full of imperfections. They *are* full of imperfections, — as full as summer woods are of flies ; as full as the harvest-field is of worms ; as full as the corn-field is of mildewed ears ; as full as nature is of rudenesses. The tropics bear, the temperate zones bear, the extreme zones bear beautiful flowers and delicious fruits, and the earth is full of evidences of God's goodness ; although there is bark, although there are poison insects and noisome things, although there are cutting edges of rocks, although there are morasses, and although there is miasma.

Carrion-crows and turkey-buzzards are the only things that like carrion, and hunt for it. And where I see men going round and watching for faults and imperfections, and seeing nothing **good,** I mark those men, "Turkey-buzzards and carrion-crows." For the dove shall fly through that sunlit air that reveals naught but loathsome corruption to the crow and the buzzard, and shall see no carrion, and only blossoming growths and sweet fields. What you see, depends upon the eye with which you look. If your **eye is** gangrene, you will see only putrefying sores. And if a man wants to see evil things, he can see enough of them, — in ministers; in churches; in sects, new or old; in professed Christians that do not hold out; or in professed Christians that do hold out, O, how queerly! For men are crazy and sick. The whole world is an hospital. The best men walk like men just trying to walk. And what would you think of a man that should stand at the door of an hospital, and laugh till he could not hold to the door-post at the men that had been cured and discharged? There comes a man with one leg; there comes another staggering from the effects of a wound that has made him a cripple for life; there comes another whose face was burnt and scarred by the powder-flash in battle, because he was so close to the enemy, before whom he would not retreat; and what would you think of a man who should stand and look at them, and laugh, and say, "Cured! cured! That is the beauty of health, is it?"

Now, the world is full of invalids. All men are sick. Everybody is imperfect, and will be till God gives us final perfection. And what do you think of those men that stand looking at revivals of religion, the results of God's influence in the world, and only see the scars, and the staggering, bloated, dropsical forms of the men that emerge from them? It is pitiful for the men who are the subjects of them, but it is a thousand times worse for those who are critics of these.

I SEE in many churches, and among many Christians and devout ministers, what seems to me to be uninstructed wisdom, or rather great folly. A man supposes that he is converted. They say, "If he is converted, his conversion is a work of God; and if it is a work of God, it will stand. If he holds out, we will receive him: and if not, he will go back to the world!"

Suppose I had lain where all night I had heard the discharge of minute guns; suppose as the morning dawned I saw here and there parts of a ship that had sunk; suppose among the fragments I saw a man that had survived **the** wreck, and who, clinging to a plank, was working his **way** to shallow water; suppose that as he got off and staggered toward the shore a wave took him and swept him out again; and suppose that, as he gathered his remaining strength and got upon his feet once more, and made a desperate struggle to save himself from a watery grave, I sat and said to myself, " I think that fellow may escape : I will watch him, and if he succeeds in getting **to** the shore and out of the water, I will take care of him"? I would deserve to be drowned myself! If you see a fellow-creature in a perilous situation like that it is your business to rush down and seize him, and give your strength to his weakness, and bear him so that the refluent waves shall not carry him back.

Here is a man that has been gambling. In some affliction he goes to this or that church, that perhaps is a godsend church to him; and he says, " Would to God that I **could live a better** life!" Men seeing him there, say, " I wonder what he is here for!" as if a gambler had not a soul, and **had** no business in a church! He weeps; and they say, " As sure as I live, I saw the fellow cry!" **And** it is whispered about that he is under conviction; and these good people say, " God's grace is very powerful, and even this man *may* be saved: we will watch him, and if he holds out let us receive him, and be kind **to** him!" But in the beginning when ten thousand fiery fiends are round about him; when his evil associates are plucking at him; when the channels are yet deep in which his **life** has run; when hundreds of malign influences are crying out to him, "Return! return! return!" and when God's call comes faint to his ears, so that he is in doubt as to whether it is God that calls, — then is the time to run down to him, and, if he is not quite sincere, make him so by kindness and sympathy.

LET me tell you that those hours when you feel a strange drawing toward that which is pure and true and right, are hours of God's visitation. Your soul is not far from its Maker in such hours. Be grateful for those periods of peculiar yearning away from evil and toward good. Take them. They are open doors to your prison-house. Are there any bad habits, any evil courses to which you have been addicted, about which you have pondered, and of which you have said, "O that I could be set free from them"? Now there will come hours, probably before a week passes, in which God will say to you, "Awake, thou that sleepest, and arise from the dead, and Christ shall give thee light." Venture; break away from your wicked ways; do not wait till your impulses are stronger; do not wait till the spark becomes a flame; take a little, and go to that toward which it points. You know it was a star that led the wise men to the place where Jesus lay. When but a single star shines from that which is right and pure and true, follow it, and it will lead you to the place where the young child Jesus lies. Are there not many in our midst that are borne down by perplexities of business, cares of the family, and trouble of various kinds, who feel themselves solemnly called of God to reformation of life, reformation of morals? Are there not men that are pursuing secret courses of undetected wrong, who have aspirations to lift themselves above their entanglements and besetting sins? Are there not times that come to some in which they reflect upon their wrong conduct, and desire to do right? These are times of salvation to you: I do not mean to men in general, but to you, dishonest man; to you, insincere man; to you, impure man; to you, drinking man; to you, sinful, worldly nature. These times when God calls, and you cannot but hear, are your set times of salvation, in which God has come with all-helpful power.

It matters little to me what school of theology rises, or what falls, so only that Christ may rise and appear in all His Father's glory, full-orbed, upon the darkness of this world! It matters little to me what church comes forth strong, or what becomes weak, so only that the poor, the sinful, the neglected, the lost among men, may have presented to them, in the church, a Saviour accessible, reached easily by the human understanding, and available in every hour of temptation, of remorse, or of want!

If a man lives for his own selfish enjoyment, it makes no difference that he wrongs no one. It is wicked for a man who is blessed of God with great intellectual power, and who is born to a station in which he can command his support without labor, to shut himself up in a library, **and be** a student, and devour books for eighty years, even though he may never injure a fellow-creature. To gormandize books is as wicked as to gormandize food. You have no more right to be a literary epicure than to be a physical epicure. And if a man makes **his** only aim in life scholarship, and lives **merely for his** own mental gratification, he is a criminal. If a man follows art simply for his own pleasure, he cannot justify himself by saying,

" I never injured a fly." That is not the question. Did you ever benefit a fly? With all your powers and opportunities, what have you done for the good of others? You should give as well as receive. We are divinely taught that it is more blessed to give than to receive; and we should hold a man accursed in this world just in proportion as he has capacities and opportunities for usefulness, if he appropriates those capacities and opportunities merely for his own private enjoyment. For if there be one truth taught in the New Testament more emphatically than another, it is, that moral indifference to another man's welfare is a sin and a crime. It is not enough to say, " I have not imbrued my hand in blood; I have not stricken down anybody; I have wronged nobody." Moral indifference is culpable. The fact that we are stronger and better than our fellow-men does not justify it. That fact makes it more guilty. **We have** no right to live entirely for our own sake, and not at all for the sake of others. " Freely ye have received, freely give," said the Master to the disciples. He made the benefactions of which they were the recipients, the endowments which had been conferred upon them, to be the measure of that which they were to bestow upon others. Paul said, " I am a debtor to the Gentiles." Why was he a debtor to the Gentiles? What did he owe them? Well, it pleased God to give him such abundant revelations in spiritual truth and life, that he knew more than the wisest philosophers and priests of the Gentiles, and he felt himself to be their debtor in the measure of his superiority to them.

————

THE heart of God is the world's hospital; and men that have been striving to get well by medicating themselves, becoming no better, but rather growing worse, at last gain this conception of God as one whose nature it is to accept man, not on account of any arrangement or plan that He has made, but for the purpose of healing him. When a man lays his case at the feet of his Master and says, " Lord, I am a sinner come to be healed of sin," with grace and benignity his Lord and Master says, "Thee I accept. Thou art my child, I forgive the sins thou hast committed in the past, and accept thee for guidance, and education, and salvation in the future." The point of adhesion between the human heart and the Saviour is just the same as that between the patient and the physician, which is the incompetence of the patient to take care of himself and heal himself. It is his inability to take care of and heal himself that leads the patient to go to the physician, that he may be taken care of and healed. It is of this that Christ speaks when He says, " They that are whole need not a physician, but they that are sick." " I am not come to call the righteous, but sinners to repentance."

WHEN a sinner can go to Christ and say, " I have committed my soul to Thee; Thou hast accepted it; Thou wert not deceived when Thou didst accept it; Thou knewest what was the strength of my pride and vanity; Thou knewest the whole gulf-stream of selfishness that was in me; Thou knewest the force of my inordinate affections; Thou knewest all the imperfections of my nature; there is nothing in me that Thou didst not know; Thou didst undertake my case with a knowledge of all my weaknesses and wickednesses; and I am no worse now than when Thou didst take me. Thou art my physician; Thou art my schoolmaster; Thou art my guide;

and in the end Thou shalt be my exceeding great reward, — and this not because I am good, but because Thou art good." That is enough. It will meet every case. **In** every exigency of life, Christian brethren, this is your refuge ; not your own works of righteousness, not your own power to do good, but O, the exhaustless bounty and power of Him that has loved you for His own name's sake.

————

HAVE you never seen how when they were finishing the interior of buildings they kept the scaffolding up? The old Pope, when he had Michael Angelo employed in decorating the interior of that magnificent structure, the Sistine Chapel, demanded that the scaffolding should be taken down so that he could see the glowing colors that with matchless skill were being laid on. Patiently and assiduously did that noble artist labor, toiling by day, and almost by night, bringing out his prophets and sibyls, and pictures wondrous for their beauty and significance, until the work was done. The day before it was done, if you had gone into that chapel and looked up, what would you have seen? Posts, planks, ropes, lime, mortar, slop, dirt. But when all was finished the workmen came, and the scaffolding was removed. And then, although the floor was yet covered with rubbish and litter, when you looked **up it was as if** heaven itself had been opened, and you looked into the courts of God and angels.

Now, the scaffolding is kept around men long after the fresco is commenced to be painted ; and wondrous disclosures will be made when God shall take down this scaffolding body, and reveal what you have been doing. By sorrow and by joy; by joys which are but bright colors, and by sorrows which are but shadows of bright colors; by prayer; by the influences of the sanctuary; by your pleasures; by your business; by reverses; by successes and by failures; by what strengthened your confidence, and by what broke it down; by the things that you rejoiced in, and by the things that you mourned over, — by all that God is working in you. And you are to be perfected not according to the things that you plan, but according to the Divine pattern. Your portrait and mine are being painted, and God by wondrous strokes and influences is working us up to His own ideal. Over and above what you are doing for yourself, God is working to make you like Him. And the wondrous declaration is, that when you stand before God and see what has been done for you, you shall be " satisfied." O, word that has been wandering solitary and without a habitation ever since the world began, and the morning stars sang together for joy! Has there ever been a human creature that could stand on earth while clothed in the flesh, and say, " I am satisfied "? What is the meaning of the word? Sufficiently filled; filled full; filled up in every part. And when God's work is complete, we shall stand before Him, and, with the bright ideal and glorified conception of heavenly aspiration upon us, looking up to God, and back **on ourselves, we shall** say, "I am satisfied"; **for we shall be like Him.** Amen. Why should we not be satisfied?

———

THE work of securing your salvation is a real business. Not by dreaming; not by sweet sentimentalities; **not by** going into a congregation and chanting **hymns that** bless God, and weeping at **prayers that touch the** fountains of susceptibility, and thinking airy thoughts of the past and **rosy thoughts of the** future, — not by these things can you be saved. Be born again. Turn round and say, — and you might as well say it, — "The day in which I begin to try to live for God is my birthday."

O, blessed promise! O, wondrous economy of grace! by which a man, after having lived forty or fifty years in sin, can start again, God saying to him, "I will cancel the past; we will let that go for nothing; you may set up business again, and begin as if you had never stumbled and done wrong." Is there grace to help in such a time of need? Yes. There is a descending Spirit of God, there is an inspiration of God, there is a Divine power, which, when you are willing to be helped, will help you in every time of need. God will help a man that will help himself. Try it. Put God to proof, and see if these words be not true.

————

When we shall come to Zion, and stand before God, it will then plainly appear that of all the myriads whose radiant faces shine like stars in the firmament there, not one from earth has come up except by the mediation, the patient instruction, and the forgiving love of the Redeemer; and we shall turn and say, "Not unto us, but unto thy name, be the praise of our salvation, forever and forever!"

INDEX.

Cambridge : Stereotyped **and Printed** by Welch, Bigelow, & Co.